KING'S COUNSEL

KING'S COUNSEL

A MEMOIR OF WAR,

ESPIONAGE, AND

DIPLOMACY

IN THE MIDDLE EAST

JACK O'CONNELL

with Vernon Loeb

W. W. Norton & Company

NEW YORK · LONDON

For information about permission to reproduce selections from this book,
write to Permissions, W. W. Norton & Company, Inc.,
500 Fifth Avenue, New York, NY 10110

For information about special discounts for bulk purchases, please contact
W. W. Norton Special Sales at specialsales@wwnorton.com or 800-233-4830

Manufacturing by Courier Westford
Book design by Chris Welch
Production manager: Anna Oler

Library of Congress Cataloging-in-Publication Data

O'Connell, Jack, 1921–2010.
King's counsel : a memoir of war, espionage, and diplomacy
in the Middle East / Jack O'Connell with Vernon Loeb. — 1st ed.
p. cm.
Includes index.
ISBN 978-0-393-06334-9 (hardcover)
1. O'Connell, Jack, 1921–2010. 2. Hussein, King of Jordan, 1935–1999—Friends
and associates. 3. Political consultants—Jordan—Biography. 4. Political consultants—
United States—Biography. 5. Lawyers—Washington (D.C.)—Biography. 6. United
States. Central Intelligence Agency—Officials and employees—Biography.
7. Israel–Arab War, 1967. 8. Jordan—Foreign relations—United States. 9. United
States—Foreign relations—Jordan. 10. Middle East—Politics and government—1945–
I. Title.
DS154.52.O26A3 2011
956.04—dc22

2011003263

W. W. Norton & Company, Inc.
500 Fifth Avenue, New York, N.Y. 10110
www.wwnorton.com

W. W. Norton & Company Ltd.
Castle House, 75/76 Wells Street, London W1T 3QT

1 2 3 4 5 6 7 8 9 0

To the people of the Middle East, who deserve peace,
to King Hussein, who wanted the truth written,
and to my family, who supported me throughout.

CONTENTS

Introduction   ix

Chapter 1   SUMMER IN AMMAN, 1958   1

Chapter 2   A SHOTGUN IN THE CLOSET   15

Chapter 3   CALM BEFORE THE STORM   31

Chapter 4   THE PRELUDE TO WAR   43

Chapter 5   THE SIX DAY WAR   51

Chapter 6   MAKING THINGS UP AS WE WENT ALONG   60

Chapter 7   "CAN I TRUST THIS LITTLE KING
OF YOURS?"   68

Chapter 8   JOUSTING WITH THE SOVIETS, TALKING
TO THE ISRAELIS   77

Chapter 9   SEPTEMBER 1970   95

Chapter 10   BACK TO WASHINGTON, BACK TO WAR   110

Chapter 11   FROM WASHINGTON TO CAMP DAVID   130

Chapter 12   GIVING UP THE WEST BANK   144

Chapter 13   SADDAM HUSSEIN: FRIEND OR FOE?   156

Chapter 14   A WAR THAT NEED NOT HAVE BEEN WAGED   171

Chapter 15   COLD PEACE   180

Chapter 16   MISSED OPPORTUNITIES, MISCALCULATIONS,
              AND MISTAKES   192

Chapter 17   "A PLACE BEYOND OURSELVES"   205

Chapter 18   MOST OF OUR ENEMIES, WE MADE   214

Chapter 19   MANY DRUMS TO POUND   228

Chapter 20   IRREPRESSIBLE OPTIMISM   237

Acknowledgments   249

Index   251

INTRODUCTION

I joined CIA by default. A friendly senator referred me to the agency's legal department. He assumed it dealt with international law issues, for which I was well educated. I had earned, by the early 1950s, a bachelor's degree in foreign service, a law degree from Georgetown, and a master's in Islamic law at the Punjab University in Lahore, Pakistan, as a two-year Fulbright Fellow. I later added a Georgetown PhD in international law. But when I went for my CIA interview, the agency's general counsel didn't think I would enjoy writing leases and purchasing contracts, which he claimed was all the legal division did. He was right. He sent me down to the Operations Directorate, for which he thought I was well qualified. There, I met with a couple of young and idealistic spies who gave me their "change the world" pitch. I didn't think I could change the world, but I thought I could spend a few years seeing it, before returning to the law.

After high school graduation in Sioux Falls, South Dakota, in 1938, our family moved to Washington, D.C. My father was dying and wanted his two sons to base their future in Washington, where his mother and favorite brother resided, and more opportunities existed. A high school teacher helped me obtain a clerk's job at the Federal Deposit Insurance Corporation (FDIC) through her brother, who was the deputy director. I then pursued my childhood dream of attending Notre Dame and playing football. One year of work would provide enough savings for a year of school, which was unbelievable, only $750 board, room, and tuition per year. I saved $1,000. More exciting to me was that I received a football scholarship in the form of a job in the university library. An automobile accident resulting in a severe concussion and fractured skull ended whatever football dreams I had. I returned to my FDIC job and entered Georgetown Foreign Service School for my sophomore year and the beginning of my international law program, having satisfied, at least partially, a childhood dream.

Studies at the Georgetown undergraduate level were interrupted by the war: V-12 school at Villanova College for four months, Midshipman School at Northwestern University for ninety days, becoming an ensign and minesweeping officer on a 180-foot minesweeper (one hundred men and ten officers) in the Pacific for over a year. Our ship was assigned six months of postwar sweeping of Japan, Formosa (Taiwan), Korea, and the Yellow Sea of China. There were two highlights. First, an unauthorized visit by ship and crew to the smoldering ruins of Nagasaki a few days after it was bombed. This awesome experience was the basis for my doctoral dissertation: *The Right of Self-Preservation Under International Law*. I found the atom bomb illegal, per se. Second, due to the postwar minesweeping, our ship received a presidential citation for sweeping more mines than any other minesweeper in the Pacific theatre.

Influenced by my overseas experiences during the war, I already knew by 1946 what I wanted to do with my life—or thought I did. My association with Dr. Carroll Quigley, the outstanding Harvard graduate who taught history at the Georgetown Foreign Service School, and my uncle's exciting local trial law practice, combined to inspire me to teach international law at the graduate or law school level. Quigley affected many students that way. Wishing to emulate him, President Bill Clinton, a Georgetown alum, credited Quigley in his acceptance speech at the 1992 Democratic Convention for teaching him about personal moral responsibility. I not only knew what I wanted to do, but what I needed to do to get there, upon the advice of other international lawyers. To be fully qualified I needed a law degree for credibility and an international specialty for distinction. So, as soon as I obtained my Foreign Service degree from Georgetown, I enrolled in the law school for morning classes and the graduate school for a PhD in the evening. It was against school rules to be enrolled in two schools at the same time, so I did not attend my law school graduation, which was held in conjunction with the other schools at Georgetown. I feared professors in the graduate school might recognize me and that I was in violation of school rules, with dire penalties.

With a law degree and my academic credibility in my back pocket, the next jobs were to continue my work for a PhD in international law and a legal specialty. The specialty was easier to decide than would be expected, mainly because of my acquaintance with Dr. James Heyworth-Dunne at the Georgetown Institute of Languages and Linguistics. He was an Oxford don—an exchange professor from England—and a renowned Islamic lawyer and scholar. He was married to a wealthy lady from an aristocratic family from India. They lived in a mansion and were part of high society in Washington. They included my wife and me in some of their parties. Dunne said he joined MI6 during World War II and was stationed in Cairo. One of his closest friends in Washington was Kim Philby, MI6 station chief in the British Embassy. I ran into Philby on a number of occasions at social events and visits to the Heyworth home. The meetings were uneventful. I did not know then that he was a Soviet mole. But our paths would cross again, eventfully, in Beirut during the period before he escaped to the USSR.

Professor Heyworth-Dunne not only helped seal my decision to follow his lead by specializing in Islamic law, but helped me obtain a two-year Fulbright Fellowship at the Punjab University in Lahore, Pakistan, to earn a master's degree in the subject. As he pointed out, there were many Islamic lawyers in Europe, but the United States was virgin ground. We finally picked Pakistan over Egypt for the studies because no one had applied for a fellowship to Pakistan. I was the first candidate, so the Fulbright program pushed me to choose Pakistan rather than Egypt. That's why I received a two-year fellowship, while only one year is normal—it takes two years to earn a master's degree.

Pakistan and my Islamic studies were extremely important to my subsequent government career. I learned a Middle Eastern language and the Arabic script. More important, I learned through the Quran and other Arabic writings the basic beliefs of Islam, which is more than a religion, or the law, it is a way of life. I traveled a lot, so met a great cross section of people. The Middle East, including Afghanistan and the Northwest Provinces of Pakistan, is tribal, not nationalist. The natives are very hospitable, and if treated respectfully, as equals, they will be your friends. If not they can be your enemy. Because of my American law background, the head of the Islamic Department at the university requested I write my master's thesis on whether it was possible for an Islamic country to be a democratic state. Basing my writings on the premise that the essence of a democracy is elections and a bill of fundamental rights, I concluded that there was nothing in Islam that would prevent this.

Pakistan was in the process of writing its own constitution during this period (1950–52) and the Constitutional Committee was located in Lahore, where I was studying. The head of the department arranged for me to present my paper to the committee. I never knew whether it made any impression. It was one of two highlights of my Pakistan venture. The other was being selected for the 1952 Pakistan

Olympic Basketball team. For lack of funds, the team never went to Helsinki. The only souvenir is a picture of the team.

Even though spying is illegal, I did not consider it immoral. Spying against friendly states, with few exceptions, is a waste of time. Spying against enemies is a legitimate act of self-defense. And what is treason against an illegal or enemy regime is often a patriotic act.

Recruiting foreigners as spies can be reduced to formulas. You can write a script that a CIA officer can follow to recruit agents. I spent a lot of my time with a few close colleagues doing that—figuring out how to recruit people. You can develop a checkoff list which will pretty well tell you whether someone is recruitable. It fascinated me. In the Arab world, where I was assigned, recruitment is facilitated by the social structure, including the recruitment of terrorists. Why? The most important ties in the Arab world are family ties. It's a tribal system. You will find in the same family the prime minister and the head of the opposition. Families are large and complex. If you know a family with members who are terrorists, you can ask a brother who is not a terrorist: "Do you agree with what your brother is doing? What can we do to stop this? You think if his mother talked to him, or his uncle, or if the Mullah talked to him, we could convince him to stop what he's doing?" A terrorist is often not that tied to his cause. He's looking for alternatives, too. There are better alternatives, and you may be able to persuade him to choose one.

In the early 1950s I feared that one brief, deep cover visit to Egypt to meet a sensitive third country agent had ruined my career. I arrived at Cairo International Airport at 11 p.m. on a weeknight and went directly to my hotel. It was after midnight when I got there. There was no one in the lobby and one reception clerk on duty. I showed him my passport and he found my reservation. Then out of the blue he looked up from filling in my registration card and asked, "Did you come from CIA?" My mind went blank. I looked down at the front of my jacket to see if I'd put my agency badge on by mistake. Nothing. I thought of grabbing my only bag and running out of the hotel, but was literally too paralyzed to move or answer him. He just stood there looking at me quizzically. How did he know? Was he tipped off by the Egyptian Security Service? If so, where were they? As my mind raced in senseless circles, I heard him repeat the question: "Did you come from CIA?"

I paid no attention. My career was probably ruined before it had even begun. Should I finish the mission or get in touch with my emergency contact? Not if I was already a marked man. Obviously irritated that I did not respond to his question, the clerk repeated in a louder voice: "Mister, did you come from CIA—from Cairo International Airport?" I almost fainted from the shock—and relief—as I blurted out, "Of course! How else could I have gotten here?"

He finished filling out my form, gave me a key, and rang for a bellboy. After regaining the use of my legs, I followed him. I spent the next hour wondering if the clerk figured out why it took me so long to answer his question. It was a midnight example of the "double think" that is a constant part of the intelligence game. The only antidote is experience.

I first met King Hussein in the summer of 1958. I was working at the old CIA headquarters in Washington for the brilliant Frenchman Roger Goiran, who had aided the OSS during World War II and became an American citizen. He was chief of the Middle East Division. When CIA found out about a nascent coup plot aimed at the young monarch in Amman, off I went. By summer's end, I was able to hand King Hussein twenty-two signed confessions from Jordanian military officers—without harming a hair on their heads. There's an object lesson there for the CIA today as it regroups under President Obama. I was thirty-six at the time, and the king was twenty-two. He'd already survived an earlier coup attempt by Arab nationalist officers and watched his friend and cousin, King Faisal of Iraq, murdered in a successful coup that ended the Hashemite dynasty in Iraq that same summer.

Few in Washington would have bet much money on King Hussein's long-term prospects as a moderate Arab leader caught between Israel, the Syrians, the Egyptians, and the PLO. Indeed, it was always an open question in Washington: Should the United States support King Hussein? Is he worth supporting? Is he going to be around? What's the cost of supporting him? In the end, Hussein proved to be a deft ruler. He knew where his strength lay, and he spent his whole life making sure that the army and the Bedouin tribes were behind him. They were his insurance policy, and those around him knew it. Without it, his support from Washington would have dissolved.

From the start, my relationship with King Hussein was an unlikely one. I was the son of a small-town banker in South Dakota. I'd grown up with a statuette of Knute Rockne on my bedside table and wanted nothing more than to play football for Notre Dame. He'd grown up a king, an absolute monarch by the age of seventeen, heir to the Hashemite Kingdom, and a direct descendant of the Prophet Muhammad. Even at twenty-two, he had a presence. He was almost ageless. He radiated personal charm, but never overdid it. He always maintained his dignity. Avi Shlaim, the Oxford historian, wrote this of my relationship with the king in his book *Lion of Jordan*: "Jack O'Connell had a closer relationship with King Hussein than any other American official before or after, one that was based on mutual respect and absolute trust." I don't want to sound immodest, but I do think that was the case.

I realized from the very start that nobody around the king was going to appreciate me. I was an outsider, and they naturally resented me and any influence I had on him. They never knew what I was telling the king. So I purposefully downplayed my association. I also never had a close relationship with any of the king's wives, because I think they naturally resented me, too. Being ultra-discreet was part of my life. I have lots of pictures of King Hussein from various circumstances over forty-something years. But I don't have a single one with both of us together. I never tried to get in the picture with the king. I'd always stand back. And I didn't push him. I figured—and it was the wisest thing I ever did—if he wanted to tell me something, he would tell me in his own time and in his own way. He didn't like to be pushed.

I am not going to write about the king without painting as full a portrait as I can. As much as I admired him, I thought he occasionally made mistakes in some of the people he appointed to high office. He had favorites, and gave people the benefit of the doubt sometimes to a fault. But overall, I'd say his judgment in people was excellent, and he was well served. He always listened to me, but it was frustrating at times because he often wouldn't react. I'd raise something with him and never hear about it again. Other times, a couple of weeks later, almost apropos of nothing, he would return to a matter we had discussed and say, "Let's do it." He always had the ability, with me and everybody else, to keep us at arm's length. You were never buddy-buddy with him. George Shultz was amazed, when he was secretary of state, at how the king never gave up. And the people around the king marveled at how he maintained his composure, despite the critical challenges he constantly faced.

I realized early on that I could have been an embarrassment to him and left those around him with the impression that he was somehow beholden to the agency, and/or to the Americans. He used the agency as his channel to the president. I think he thought it was more efficient and secure than working through the State Department, and it probably was. Dick Helms was very receptive on his end—the king was a close friend of Helms, who was about as facile and confident as a CIA director could be. I didn't want the king to look like a CIA man, because he wasn't. We didn't tell him what to do or pretend to tell him what to do. He wouldn't necessarily do what we wanted, in any event. That would have been one of the first ways of cooling the relationship. Frankly, we didn't know what he should do much of the time. And if we wanted him to blindly follow U.S. policy, we'd probably have told him to do what the Israelis wanted, because that was almost always our policy—and that would have been a mistake.

My relationship with the king was close and trusting during my time in Amman as station chief, from 1963 to 1971. In 1967, I tipped him off a day in advance that the Israelis were going to attack Egypt. If only Nasser had listened. In 1970, I watched as the PLO nearly took over the country, murdering a colleague on his front porch and firebombing my house. Back in Washington in 1972, when I became Jordan's lawyer at the law firm of Connole & O'Connell, later O'Connell & Glock, I had a unique vantage point on the 1973 war, the Camp David Accords, the king's 1984 peace plan, his 1988 transfer of the West Bank to the PLO, the 1991 Gulf War and, ultimately, his own peace with Israel in 1994.

In the early 1990s, King Hussein commissioned me to engage a respected American author to tell the story that had become a preoccupation with him: his vain quest for peace in the Middle East. The Israelis were willing to give back the Sinai to Egypt, which was its main enemy. Israel even said it was willing to give back the Golan Heights to Syria. But the Israelis were not willing to make peace with Jordan on the same basis, because of the land. They wanted East Jerusalem and the West Bank, as the king suspected all along. And all of his efforts to convince them to relinquish that land and return to the borders that existed before the 1967 War went nowhere. The United States seemed to support him in making peace, agreed with him on everything, but never did anything. So he felt betrayed, continuously betrayed—by the United States, by Israel, by the Palestinians, by the Egyptians. And he was prepared to reveal all he knew, or have me do so. But his real motivation wasn't betrayal, it was peace. He wanted the book written to tell the world why peace had failed—and what people needed to do about it—and he wanted me to find an author. My first choice was Philip L. Geyelin, a veteran foreign correspondent and former editorial page editor of *The Washington Post*. Phil and I flew to Jordan to meet with the king, who told Phil that the purpose of the project was to set the record straight. He would make himself available to meet with Phil any time he desired, and I would be Phil's day-to-day contact. Phil was free to write what he wished, how he wished. But after a good start, Phil fell terminally ill, and progress slowed, then ended.

My next choice was Dick Helms, the best leader the CIA ever had. It was now the late 1990s, and Dick was writing his memoir. I thought he might be able to include many of the events the king had in mind, since several had occurred on his watch. Dick was amenable, so we met with the king at the Four Seasons Hotel in Washington to discuss the project. King Hussein repeated what he had told Phil, then turned to me and said I should tell Dick everything I knew.

"Everything?" I asked. "What about your secret meetings with the Israelis?"

"I said everything!" the king replied. "I am not ashamed of anything I did."

The meeting ended shortly thereafter; the king bid us adieu and left the room. Dick remarked that he had never seen him so "bullish." I said that the king was obsessed with the truth, even when it wasn't in his apparent interest. I began submitting papers on various subjects to Dick. But after many months, he confessed he was having difficulty incorporating the material with the rest of his memoir and said he did not think the arrangement would work. Shortly thereafter,

His Majesty fell ill. He died in February 1999. Then Dick fell ill and died in 2002. I can only presume the king passed away assuming I had arranged for his story to be included in Dick's memoir, which was published posthumously. It contained none of my contributions and only four pages on the Middle East. I would break a trust if the story is not written. The obligation is mine through default.

Despite contrary wisdom, the June 6 attack on Egypt by Israel, triggering the 1967 War, was not a surprise to the United States, Egypt, or Jordan. I believe President Lyndon Johnson approved the attack in advance. The U.S. Military Attaché's office in Israel, covertly or overtly, obtained advance knowledge of the timing and nature of the attack, which it sent to Washington and, surreptitiously, to an assistant in Amman, who immediately informed me. I told the ambassador and the king, who then warned President Nasser twice the same night.

Israel attacked on schedule. Nasser was dumbfounded; he didn't believe the king's warnings. Jordan was helpless and overrun. Syria's Golan Heights were captured as an afterthought. Israel proclaimed a litany of fabricated false defenses. The United States solemnly feigned surprise and neutrality.

I also believe Henry Kissinger instigated the 1973 war against Israel by the Egyptians so that the United States could negotiate a cease-fire and begin a process which would remove Egypt as an enemy of Israel. It ultimately led to the Camp David Accords and the Egypt-Israel peace treaty. I base this on conversations I had with Eugene Trone, CIA liaison officer in Cairo, after the 1967 War. So now the time has come to tell the truth about what happened in 1967, and in 1973, and beyond. So much of what's been done over the past fifty or sixty years in the Middle East has been based on falsehoods, continuing through our wars with Iraq. I'm certain, going back to my days as a young intelligence officer in Lebanon in the early 1960s, when CIA had first penetrated the Ba'ath Party, that the United States could have recruited and/or later made peace with Saddam Hussein on its terms, any time it wanted to. But nobody wanted to, particularly Israel, except Prime Minister Yitzhak Rabin—privately. Beginning with the 1967 War, this was an era of lies and betrayals by the United States, by Israel, by the Palestinians, and by the Arabs. Indeed, this whole period in the Middle East has been a charade. A peacemaker, even the most persistent one, such as King Hussein, did not have a chance.

This is a book I never intended to write. But it has become apparent that if I do not write the story, it will probably never be told. Not to tell the story would cheat history, break a trust with the king, and probably evade an ethical duty. Having listened to the king exhort Phil Geyelin and Dick Helms to tell "everything," I have assumed the same royal mandate in what I have written.

KING'S COUNSEL

Chapter 1

SUMMER IN AMMAN, 1958

I landed in Amman in early summer 1958 to help protect the Hashemite Kingdom of Jordan. I didn't know much about the young monarch or his country, but I was soon to find out. It felt surreal to be in this hot, sand-colored backwater capital, holding what could be the future of the monarchy in my pocket: a copy of a secret FBI tape recording. Instinctively, without authorization, I had pocketed a copy of the tape as I left headquarters for Amman. I wasn't an ideal choice for this assignment because of my lack of knowledge of Jordan and limited interrogation skills. However, the fates of many operations, careers, and history are decided by a turn of the Washington intelligence roulette wheel, without reference to much else. I was available. My number came up.

In May 1958, the Central Intelligence Agency received an audio-tape from the FBI containing several incriminating telephone conversations between the Egyptian military attaché and Major General Mahmud Rusan, the Jordanian military attaché, both assigned to their embassies in Washington. The tape implicated Rusan as the leader of a group of Jordanian Army officers in an Egyptian-supported plot to overthrow King Hussein, Jordan's third monarch since the British carved this nation out of the desert in the aftermath of World War I.

Rusan was scheduled to return to duty in Jordan in one month, after which the coup was to be executed.

Hussein had become king in 1953 on the eve of his eighteenth birthday, succeeding his father, Talal, whose mental problems had forced him to abdicate the throne after little more than a year. Hussein's ascension had been set in motion by the assassination two years earlier of his grandfather, King Abdullah, who had been in power for thirty years after joining forces with the British against the Turks in 1916. The young Hussein was at his side when a Palestinian nationalist emerged from the shadows in the entranceway of the al Aqsa Mosque in East Jerusalem and shot Abdullah in the head, killing him instantly. The moment had a searing impact on the teenager and helped frame the risks and responsibilities he would carry for the rest of his life.

The Hashemites were an aristocratic Arab family who hailed originally from Hijaz on the Arabian Peninsula. They were descendants of the Prophet Muhammad, and the family's name came from Hashem, the Prophet's great-grandfather. As Abdullah first laid claim to the barren expanse of desert between Palestine and Iraq after World War I, Winston Churchill promised the throne of Iraq to his brother, Faisal, who had fought the Turks with T. E. Lawrence. Now, in this most eventful of summers, their grandsons ruled what they saw as the Hashemite union: Hussein in Jordan and Hussein's cousin, Faisal, also twenty-two, in Iraq. Both were threatened by restive Arab nationalist officers opposed to the Hashemites' historic ties to Britain.

I met with the CIA's two-man station on arrival in Amman to decide on the division of labor and basic logistics. I was thirty-six at the time. I'd left my wife and our baby daughter back at our white brick split-level in Chevy Chase, a suburb of Washington, without any real idea when I would return. My first two assignments with the agency were on the Pakistan desk and the Near East Operations

Division staff. During this time I was under loose, non-sensitive cover. I was also a part-time instructor at the Georgetown Foreign Service School. I had no overt intelligence connections. This enabled me to engage in covert operations in the Middle East without traceable ties to CIA. For example, I attended an academic conference in Cairo in order to meet secretly with a sensitive foreign intelligence officer on the CIA payroll, under highly complicated circumstances. That opportunity ended when I was sent by CIA to Amman without cover.

In Jordan, I was to be in charge of operational matters, dealing with the king and whomever he designated. The station was to develop information from its files and sources on possible plotters. The station was undermanned in those days, consisting of only two officers, Nick Andronovich, the chief of station, who had been based in Jerusalem for CIA during the 1948 Arab-Israeli War, and Frederick W. Latrash, who was in liaison with the king on security matters. Both were under cover. To keep a low profile, since I had no cover and no ability to explain to anyone what I was doing in Amman, I stayed with Latrash and his wife at their home. Unbeknownst to me, Latrash had been stationed in Calcutta in 1950 when Tibetan border guards mistakenly shot Douglas MacKiernan, the first CIA officer to die in the line of duty. MacKiernan had been posted in China's Xinjiang Province to plant listening devices in Soviet territory to monitor the Soviets' atomic bomb tests. Latrash, who had been preparing from Calcutta to arm the Tibetans to resist the Chinese Communists, was sent to recover the body and meet survivors from MacKiernan's party. His body was never recovered.

The day after I arrived, Latrash—a stocky, dark-haired, rugged man and former naval officer during World War II—took me to the meet the king at his residence in Hummar, a suburb of Amman. Even at twenty-two, Hussein had a presence. During the past year he had endured more crises than most people encounter in a lifetime. You knew when you walked into a room that he was the most important person there. He was very affable and thanked me for coming. I briefed him on what we knew, without sourcing it. I suggested to the king that we not tip our hand to anyone before identifying the other plotters. I recommended that General Rusan be given a respectable, non-sensitive job when he returned, that we bug his office, and place him under surveillance.

I then asked if I could meet the head of his Intelligence Service to establish a working relationship.

"You are looking at him," the king said. "I'm the head of the Intelligence Service."

It was true; Jordan did not have an intelligence service, and the king was his own intelligence chief in fact, if not in name. He recruited and ran agents clandestinely on his own, mostly in the military, with funds from the palace purse. Two years earlier, the king had disclosed this fact to a young CIA officer, who preceded Latrash as the agency's liaison. In response, the agency offered to underwrite these expenses. The cost: 5,000 Jordanian dinars ($15,000) per month. Years later, the amount of these payments would be exaggerated and sensationalized, unfairly damaging the king's reputation.

In part to assert his own independence and authority, Hussein had dismissed General Sir John Bagot Glubb, the longtime British commander of the Arab Legion, in 1956. A year later, the United States assumed Britain's traditional role as Jordan's financial backer under the so-called Eisenhower Doctrine, which held that the United States would provide military and economic assistance to friendly Middle Eastern nations and direct military support to any of them threatened by a Communist-aligned state. In this context, the CIA's covert channel to the king made perfect sense as Washington came to see the staunchly anti-Communist Hussein as a strategic ally in the region.

Whether he would survive the turbulent rise of Arab nationalism was always an open question.

As the CIA first began cultivating its relationship with Hussein, a flamboyant CIA political operative, Wilbur Crane Eveland, met with the king in Lebanon in 1956 at a sports car rally. Many of my colleagues considered Eveland a con artist. Eveland proposed that he open a communications channel to the king whenever he visited Beirut. But Kermit Roosevelt, grandson of Teddy Roosevelt and chief of the Near East Division, thought the better of that. The Amman station already had the modest ($15,000 per month) arrangement with the king to help him pay intelligence agents, and Roosevelt did not want Eveland involved. So Roosevelt cut off Eveland's attempt before it got off the ground.

Lacking an intelligence service, the king introduced me to a young lawyer from the Army Judge Advocate General's office, Lieutenant Mohammed Rasul, who would work with me on a daily basis. Rasul was brilliant, conspiratorial by nature, indefatigable, and devoted to the king, which explains why he became the first chief of the Jordanian Intelligence Service when it was established a few years later. He looked like Rasputin and acted rather like him. He was a classic "mystery man" and worked tirelessly to create this illusion. Without any formal intelligence training, he excelled at intimidating and manipulating people. Much of our spare time was spent discussing intelligence-related questions, with Rasul always seeking new solutions, insights, and case histories. His appetite for detail was voracious. I remember telling him that foreign intelligence officers were most vulnerable when they arrived or left a station, when agents had to be turned over. Extra surveillance often identified the agents they were running. I was later the victim of my own advice.

His Majesty then introduced me to the head of the army, his strong-armed, strong-willed uncle, General Sharif Nasir, perhaps the toughest human being I have ever known. He would find the proper interim job for General Rusan, facilitate the bugging of Rusan's office, and provide his own home as the listening post. Soon enough, thanks to Rasul's detective work, the station's reports, the king's own intelligence, and Sharif Nasir's physical and technical surveillance of Rusan and others, we developed solid evidence on twenty-two military officers involved in the plot.

The king's input was impressive. He knew all twenty-two officers personally. He took one name off from an earlier list of twenty-three, saying, simply, he was not involved. I assumed he was one of the king's personal agents, which would explain why the king was so well informed on the orientation of the others, and so willing to accept CIA's allegation regarding Rusan.

Another officer who fell under suspicion was Hussein's military secretary, Colonel Radi Abdullah, who I found myself dealing with regularly on my treks back and forth from Raghadan Palace downtown. He was related to two officers suspected in the plot and, unbeknownst to me, was himself a suspect on Sharif Nasir's list of twenty-two. One evening, about 7 p.m., Radi telephoned, said he was working late, and asked me to come to his palace office for a brief talk. When I arrived, Radi was alone in the palace, except for the Royal Guards. He asked me to sit while he finished some paperwork. Fifteen minutes later, four military policemen, led by a colonel, burst into the office, handcuffed both of us, and hauled us off to Military Headquarters. I protested from the outset that I was an American guest of His Majesty, but to no avail. Finally, at headquarters, a senior officer took me seriously enough to telephone the king. His Majesty confirmed my innocence and sent a car to deliver me to his home, where he and Sharif Nasir were having a good laugh. Sharif Nasir had picked up Radi to give him a polygraph, or lie detector test, and I had simply been caught in the middle. But it was not a coincidence. Years later, when I returned to Jordan, Radi became a confidant and close friend. Only then did I learn that he had called me to his office as a test, knowing that he would be arrested. He figured, if I was involved in arresting him, I wouldn't have shown up. So I passed his test, and he passed the polygraph.

As we slowly gathered evidence and tried to piece together who was involved in the plot, the station received a FLASH cable from headquarters in late June with the text of a radio message from Syria to the Jordan conspirators, ordering them to proceed immediately with the coup. Since these were the days of the United Arab Republic (UAR), the union of Egypt and Syria, Syria seemed to be aware of the Egyptian plot—and involved in its execution. It was 10 p.m. when I passed the information to His Majesty at Raghadan Palace. He asked what we should do. I said, "No choice. Arrest the twenty-two suspects tonight and keep them apart." He agreed. Before dawn, all twenty-two were behind bars.

The next morning, the problems began. Most of the arrested officers were from prominent Jordanian families or tribes. Complaints and protests to the king and prime minister, Samir Rifai, began to pour in. The only Jordanians who were clued in on what had happened were the king, Sharif Nasir, and Rasul. Up to this point the king had not asked me for proof of the allegation I brought from Washington about Rusan. The evidence against all the others was circumstantial. After a few days the king said he would need proof to give the prime minister, and that without evidence he could not detain the prisoners indefinitely. I notified CIA headquarters: I needed authority to play the audiotape for the king, or the prisoners would be released.

Days passed. I wondered whether headquarters had forgotten about my request. But just as the political pressure to release the prisoners had reached its peak, I received permission to play the tape for the king. We were both relieved as he sat on the floor in his den at home with earphones, listening to the tape. I could tell from his expression and the nods of his head that he was satisfied with what he was hearing. He admitted as much when he took off the earphones.

What I did not know, but found out later, was why it took the agency so long to authorize release of the tape to the king. The FBI chief, John Edgar Hoover, refused to release the tape. He was unwilling to admit to anyone outside the U.S. intelligence community that the FBI tapped foreign embassy telephones. Allen Dulles, the CIA director, took the case to the White House, where national security adviser Gordon Grey, I was told, ruled in favor of Dulles: "Play the tape for the King." Hoover was furious. In retaliation, he stopped sending taped conversations to CIA. He sent written transcripts, instead, which didn't reveal how they were obtained.

Meanwhile, on July 10, the king received a surprise visit from General Rafiq A'rif, commander in chief of the Iraq Army. He had been sent on a special mission by his government to warn the king of Egyptian plots against him. A'rif had nothing specific to add to our information. The king took the opportunity to return the favor. He was concerned about the security of his first cousin, King Faisal, in Iraq. His Majesty warned, in particular, that an Iraqi military contingent, under the command of Brigadier Abdul Karim Kassim and Colonel Abd al-Salam Arif, was plotting against the Iraqi regime and should not be trusted. The king specifically told General A'rif the names of the Iraqis whom he suspected were Communists, or pro-Communist. They had been stationed in Jordan a year or two before, when they first aroused the suspicion of their Jordanian hosts. A'rif, in effect, said, we can take care of ourselves, we're worried about you.

Four days later, on July 14, 1958, Brigadier Abdul Karim Kassim staged a bloody coup d'état that toppled the Iraqi regime. Nationalist soldiers commanded by Colonel Arif, who ironically had been sent from their base east of Baghdad toward the Jordanian border to shore up King Hussein's threatened position, executed the coup as they moved through the Iraqi capital. They took control of a radio station and government ministries, declared the beginning of the Republic of Iraq, and sent troops to the Rihab Palace, residence of King Faisal and Crown Prince Abdul Ilah, King Faisal's forty-five-year-old uncle. Both were shot in the courtyard. Soldiers entered the palace and killed the rest of the royal family, men and women. Crown Prince Abdul Ilah was beheaded, his body dragged through the streets. King Hussein had lost his cousin and lifelong friend, and any hope for a Hashemite union between Jordan and Iraq.

Both the United States and Britain were determined to keep the insurrection from spreading. As we worked to contain the coup plotters in Amman, Washington sent 1,500 U.S. Marines to Lebanon the day after the Iraqi coup in response to a request from Lebanese president Camille Chamoun, whose government was threatened by UAR-supported opposition groups. Two days later, on July 17, Britain sent two battalions of paratroopers to Jordan to secure the airport in Amman and bolster King Hussein's regime. On July 19, the king held a solemn press conference at the palace. "I have now received confirmation of the murder of my cousin, brother and childhood playmate, King Faisal of Iraq, and all his royal family," Hussein said. "They are only the last in a caravan of martyrs."

I didn't pretend to know what was going on in Baghdad or how important it was, but I felt confident doing my job. However, we were facing a fascinating roadblock: the prisoners weren't talking. Rasul said they were all in denial. He did not foresee that any of them would break, and we had no leverage to force them to talk. They seemed to sense this. The coup in Iraq only emboldened them. But Rasul had an idea, and this was pure Rasul.

"Jack, we don't have any interrogators here in the country with any experience," he said. "Why don't we get a foreign interrogator, a law-yer, not an American, to come out and pretend that he has been hired by the King to ensure that these people get a fair trial?"

"Rasul," I said, "who the hell is going to believe that—the King is hiring a lawyer to come out here to be sure the people who were going to kill him get a fair trial?"

"You don't know our king," Rasul said. "That's exactly what he would do."

I didn't think it made sense. But I went to the king and said, this is Rasul's idea, and the king acted like—that's a pretty good idea! So I sent off a cable to headquarters as though it were central casting, putting in an order for a non-American lawyer skilled in the art of interrogation who just happened to be available for a secret mission to Jordan. Sometimes, I found during my career, CIA capabilities were everything they were cracked up to be. No sooner had I made the request than an interrogator arrived from Washington, straight out of the movies. We knew him only as "Peter." He was a Polish nobleman, who had sought asylum during World War II and was picked up by CIA. He was a lawyer by profession and an experienced interrogator. He was a tall, elegant man, with a commanding presence. His mind was a steel trap. I was still skeptical about Rasul's plan. But after we briefed Peter fully, he introduced himself to each of the prisoners, stating that he was the lawyer appointed by the king to ensure they received a fair hearing. He reported back that they had accepted his role, without any questions, but all asserted their innocence. Rasul was right: I didn't know their king.

Peter made the rounds daily. He showed sympathy for their griev-ances, but had little leverage. The only thing he could offer was the king's leniency if they told the truth, and his anger and their punish-ment if they did not. Peter had gained the prisoners' trust, but not their confessions. He needed a breakthrough. Headquarters provided one, just in time, notifying the station that a prominent Jordanian officer who had been stationed for a while in the United States and was now in jail among the coup plotters had fathered an illegitimate child. I still cannot divulge the officer's name, but it was clear to agency officers back in Washington that this information could give us the kind of leverage we needed to break him. I immediately passed this bombshell along to Peter at our daily meeting, where we would game the situation and plot our next moves. Peter said this was all he needed. He could take it from here. Headquarters gave no indication the mother of the officer's child intended to cause any trouble. But Peter had us cable headquarters to keep tabs on her. If there was any indication she planned to come to Jordan, they should intercept her and pay her not to come, on behalf of the king. Headquarters agreed.

The next day, Peter visited the imprisoned father and, in the course of the conversation, asked if he had heard from "Alice" lately. The man's jaw dropped.

"You know she just gave birth to your son," Peter said, "and she may be planning to bring him to Jordan." The man fell to his knees. Peter calmed him, with a bit of fiction:

"Don't worry, His Majesty found out about it and paid her off. She's not coming."

"His Majesty did that?" the officer said. "He saved my life. I cannot thank him enough. What can I do to repay him?"

"Tell the truth about your plans to overthrow him," Peter said.

The prisoner made a confession on the spot, which he later repeated in writing. Over the next few days, armed with the confession, Peter had enough implicating facts to induce written confessions from four other prisoners.

It was late August and headquarters was pressing hard for us to finalize the case. Secretary of State Dulles was preparing to deliver a speech at the opening of the UN session in September attacking

Egypt's President Nasser and wanted to include his efforts to overthrow King Hussein in the speech.

Peter was up to the challenge. He had an idea. He assembled all twenty-two prisoners in one large room—the first time they had seen each other since they had been arrested. He lined them up in four rows in the middle of the room. Surrounding the walls were twenty-two small desks with pads and pens. Peter stood before the group and said that His Majesty had lost patience. Time had run out. For those who were willing to tell the truth, he would be generous. For those who were not, he was prepared to impose the harshest penalties. Peter asked those who were willing to confess to take one step forward. By prearrangement, those who had already confessed, scattered among the group, took one step forward. When the rest of their group saw five of their co-conspirators step forward, they knew their fate was sealed. So they all stepped forward, and wrote their confessions. The next day, I made copies, took all twenty-two signed originals, and delivered them to the king. He accepted graciously, as if this was the outcome he was expecting from the beginning. But he clearly understood the importance of what we had done. Had the CIA not intervened, there almost certainly would have been a coup. Given the number of senior officers involved in the plot, it might have succeeded.

Ultimately, the twenty-two plotters were placed on trial. Five were acquitted; seventeen received lenient sentences of ten to fifteen years. I was told some were pardoned earlier and that the king personally drove some of them home from jail when they were released. All returned to society and led constructive, loyal lives. Some actually ended up in the security and intelligence services. General Rusan served a short sentence. He was later elected to Parliament, where he served, notably, for several years. The consensus in Washington was that the kingdom was in good hands and the United States should support it—at least for now.

Peter departed as soon as his work was finished, never to be seen again, but never to be forgotten. I prepared a written report for the secretary of state, said my goodbyes to Latrash, Andronovich, the king, Sharif Nasir, and Rasul, and flew to New York. I remember feeling as though I'd been involved in one hell of an effort. We'd uncovered a coup, put everybody in jail, extracted twenty-two confessions, and kept the king in power.

My CIA contact in New York was Bill Eveland, the political operator who had courted the king and wanted to be his go-between with the agency. Now, he was my go-between with the secretary of state. I knew him only by reputation, which was as a wheeler-dealer with high-level U.S. and foreign contacts, especially in the Middle East. He was from the Political Action side of the agency, whom the intelligence gatherers largely considered to be phony elitists.

I met him in a hotel suite, which must have been the largest in the hotel. He took the report that I had prepared for the secretary of state and said he would personally hand-deliver it. He suggested I stay over a couple of days in case the secretary had any questions. I registered in the same hotel. Eveland asked if I had any plans for the evening. I didn't. He said the secretary was hosting a reception at the Waldorf-Astoria for the world's foreign ministers to honor Charles Malik, the newly elected president of the General Assembly of the United Nations, who was the foreign minister of Lebanon, and his wife. He said he thought he would crash the party; did I want to join him? I was too intimidated and intrigued to say no. We reached the Waldorf ballroom late. Most of the guests had arrived, but the receiving line, headed by the secretary, was still in place. As Eveland approached the line, with me tailing, the secretary greeted him effusively. After several words, he moved down the line with something to say to each. All seemed to know him. I followed Bill down the line as fast as I could politely move, with perfunctory nods and hasty handshakes. I knew nobody.

The ballroom was filled with the world's leading diplomats. I recognized, among others, Andrei Gromyko and Selwyn Lloyd, the foreign ministers of the Soviet Union and the United Kingdom, respectively, but saw no one who knew me. Bill said he was going to look up some friends and took off. I wandered, attempting to be as inconspicuous as possible. It was impossible to explain who I was, or why I was there. It was a social nightmare. Just as I decided to duck out, Eveland appeared with the new General Assembly president on one arm, his wife on the other, and introduced me to them. He said he was taking them to dinner and literally pranced out of the ballroom amidst applause and waves from the world's top diplomats with a quick farewell from the secretary. He had not only crashed the party but absconded with the guest of honor. I followed in his wake. It was an unbelievable, prize-winning performance in bravado. I returned to Washington two days later. The secretary never asked to see me and he did not include anything from my report in his speech. What played in Jordan stayed in Jordan.

Chapter 2

A SHOTGUN IN THE CLOSET

The summer of 1960 was as calm as the Middle East had been for two years. Lebanon was perhaps the calmest of all and at the peak of its glory, a virtual paradise. One could ski in the morning, swim or boat in the Mediterranean in the afternoon, and in the evening enjoy gambling and entertainment at a casino that matched Monte Carlo. It was a playground for the Arabs and a financial center for business executives. Its hotels, restaurants, and shops were world class.

It was also a playground for spies. I arrived in the summer of 1960 as deputy chief of station. My wife Katherine and I moved with our two young children, Kelly and Sean, into an apartment in downtown Beirut. But we soon moved to a new complex of spacious flats in the Hazmieh section on the edge of the city, overlooking the Mediterranean. While I enjoyed embassy cover, I had been trained back in 1952 as a "non-official cover" officer, a so-called NOC. My NOC indoctrination made quite an impression on me as a young officer, and I never forgot it. NOCs must live by wits and guile. Without any official tie to the U.S. government, NOCs go to prison if they get arrested, or worse. There is no diplomatic immunity. So, in Beirut, I kept a loaded shotgun in my closet. That was the first thing I was taught: Keep a shotgun in your house, and make sure your servants all know that it's there. Anybody who's going to come into your house is going to pay off one of your servants to tell him whether you've got a gun. And everybody knows what a shotgun does. It blows a big hole in you, and you can't miss, even if you're a lousy shot.

I was also taught to establish relationships with the best doctor and the best lawyer in town, to take care of emergencies, medical or legal. To that end, I was taught as well to contrive some reason to meet and cultivate the chief of police, even if it meant hitting his official car in the parking lot of the police station and overpaying for the damages on the spot to keep it out of the records. Finally, I was taught to get a dog, a big dog, because people in that part of the world are afraid of dogs. In Beirut, the dog, a big, black, unshaven French poodle, found us. He wandered into our courtyard and wouldn't leave. Nobody seemed to own him, and he seemed to want to be our dog, so we kept him and named him Casey. A lot of people don't understand that French poodles are bred to be hunters, and not just ordinary hunters—they're bear hunters. Casey was a great dog, though on a few occasions he demonstrated the killer instinct he was born with.

I don't want to create a misimpression, though, because Beirut in the early 1960s was not a place where we necessarily worried about personal safety. Indeed, Beirut was one big temptation. The social side of life could take over. Still, I was able to work hard because that's what I'd done all my life. My father died when I was seventeen, and I'd been studying, or working, full time since then. A reasonable mix was the working formula for Beirut. The social and the clandestine often overlapped.

Sharing the espionage playground with the CIA station was a small contingent from the agency's Political Action (PA) staff, a swash-buckling remnant of OSS, which had been absorbed by CIA after OSS dissolved. It was distinct from the Operations Division in terms of organization, purpose, personnel, and conduct. The Operations

Division was devoted to the collection of information otherwise unavailable; it consisted of a trained cadre of officers operating under strict rules of discipline, based in CIA stations or under unofficial cover around the world. The PA operators worked on their own, usually under unofficial cover, with limited contact to official Americans in the field, devoted to the manipulation and overthrow of foreign governments, the infiltration of foreign political organizations, major paramilitary operations, and propaganda campaigns. PA personnel had unhindered access to the station for information and communication needs.

I spent three years as deputy chief of the Beirut station, and although I knew the identity of the PA people in Beirut, I had no true idea of what they were doing, what they were supposed to do, or what they accomplished. What I did know was that, in Beirut, they hung out at the Hotel St. George bar, a watering hole for international journalists, all of whom they knew; they socialized with the president, the prime minister, foreign minister, other top government officials and politicians; they carried exotic calling cards reading "The White House" and "The National Security Council"; and they had access to large sums of money. For the information collectors, who formed the bulk of agency officers, the PA officers were spoiled, undisciplined elitists, who were not qualified for their work and accomplished little. This may be, in part, because they looked down on the rest of us.

Actually, as I learned later from ex-director Dick Helms's memoir, *A Look Over My Shoulder*, the godfather of the Political Action staff and its charter was CIA director Allen Dulles. As he explained to Helms, covert political action was critical to the CIA because it added billions to its budget. "Let me make this clear," Helms quotes Dulles as saying. "We have to face the fact that because espionage is relatively cheap it will always seem inconsequential to some of our less-informed friends on The Hill—in both houses of Congress. They're accustomed to dealing in billions. What kind of impression can it make when I come along and ask for a few hundred thousand dollars and a bag of pennies? Believe me, I know the way they think up there. If there's no real money involved, it can't be important, and they just won't pay much attention to us."

When I arrived in Beirut in 1960, Miles Copeland headed the PA group of about four people, each with a different unofficial cover. Copeland frequently walked into the station, read the latest cable traffic, and left, without saying more than hello to anyone. It used to drive the chief of station crazy. But there was nothing he could to about it. He was under instructions from CIA headquarters to service Copeland's needs. Allen Dulles was not only the creator of the Political Action staff; he and his brother, Secretary of State John Foster Dulles, were its case officers. They directed many of the PA operations personally, bypassing ambassadors and chiefs of station.

Bill Eveland, of Waldorf-Astoria notoriety, preceded Copeland in Beirut. Eveland must have left Beirut about the time I arrived in 1960. Some claim he ran the country of Lebanon in the 1950s from President Camille Chamoun's living room and the Foreign Office from Charles Malik's porch. He was more important in Washington, with direct lines to the Dulles brothers, than the U.S. ambassador to Lebanon—and the Lebanese knew it—which made him the most important foreigner in Lebanon. But what was the master plan, the end goal?

Eveland took off enough time in 1957 to lay the groundwork for a coup, next door, in Syria, and my friend "Rocky" Stone was sent out as chief of station, to execute it. When Rocky pulled the cord, nothing happened. The arrangements were incomplete and Rocky was unceremoniously escorted under arms to the airport.

For PA operations, failure is not necessarily a deterrence. In fact, it can sometimes be finessed. The famous Ajax operation—the overthrow of the Mosaddeq government in 1953, and the return of the Shah of Iran to the throne—is one example. Rocky Stone was also involved in that operation—and told me this story. The agency had hired General Fazlollah Zahedi, a senior Iranian officer, to mount a military coup against the Mosaddeq government. Rocky was in Tehran and was the case officer for Zahedi, who was so nervous the day of the coup he could not button his uniform. Rocky buttoned it for him, while Rocky's wife held Mrs. Zahedi's hand. The operation was approved and supported by the State Department, the Joint Chiefs of Staff, the secretary of defense, and the White House. Representatives of all these institutions were gathered in a safe house in the Tehran suburbs along with the U.S. ambassador to Iran, Loy Henderson, and CIA Near East Division chief Kermit Roosevelt, armed with radios, to monitor the battle and await the outcome. After patting Zahedi on the back, Rocky joined them. The outcome was rapid and unexpected. After early advances, Zahedi was turned back and forced to retreat from Tehran. In short, the coup attempt had failed. The safe house exploded with expletives and pointed fingers assigning the blame. Before the place became violent, Roosevelt raised his hand, calmed the group, and quietly announced that he accepted the blame for the failure—to the appreciative applause of all.

Unbeknownst to those in the safe house, General Zahedi regrouped his troops on the outskirts of Tehran, devised a new battle plan, and attacked again. This time he succeeded. Roosevelt won the equivalent of a trifecta. The agency received credit for a success it didn't fully deserve and Political Action was no longer a dirty term. After accepting blame for the failure no one could deny, Roosevelt and the CIA got credit for the success.

I heard Kermit Roosevelt tell of his meeting with Winston Churchill on his way home from Iran. Churchill, who was in bed at 10 Downing Street with a cold, asked to see Roosevelt. Roosevelt was ushered into a dimly lit bedroom and seated beside the bed. Churchill wanted all the details. Roosevelt expounded. When he finished, Churchill said, "Sir, it would have been an honor to serve under you." Roosevelt said it was the most memorable moment of his life. I wondered which version of the coup he gave Churchill.

Before coming to Beirut, Copeland was the friendly, secret, back-door channel between Nasser of Egypt and the Dulles brothers in the United States—and, indirectly, the president of the United States. This began shortly after Nasser assumed office in 1952, and ended after Secretary Foster Dulles's rejection of U.S. financing of the Aswan Dam in 1956, an apparent act of self-destruction. Some claimed it was unavoidable, because, thanks to Israeli lobbying, Dulles did not have enough votes in Congress to garner the money necessary to fund the dam. Copeland also oversaw CIA contacts with the Iraqi regime of Abdul Karim Kassim and its internal opponents, including Saddam Hussein and others in the Ba'ath Party after King Faisal II was deposed in 1958. After Beirut, Copeland was involved in the coup against Kwame Nkruma, the elected president of Ghana.

However one looks at it, PA in the Middle East, where most of it was carried out, was a mixed bag. The agency did not have the talent or the resources to excel in such operations. And U.S. policymak-ers did not have the wisdom to reshape or reorder the world. CIA's attempt to overthrow the Castro regime in Cuba with ex-Cuban renegades, the Bay of Pigs fiasco, helped establish the reality. Over-throwing governments without attribution to the United States usu-ally requires military force. CIA does not have military equipment or personnel—the U.S. Army does. Thus, CIA does not have the resources to succeed; and the Army is not a covert institution. It can't deny its involvement. When the Army acts, it is war. Covert wars are a contradiction in terms.

Be that as it may. I came from the foreign intelligence side of the agency, as did Helms. We believed that the agency's mission was to provide intelligence, which was defined as information that nobody else could get. And we had one advantage that nobody else had—we could pay for it. And that is our mission. We shouldn't be providing information that the State Department can get, or that journalists can get. That isn't our business. We didn't think we should be involved in overthrowing governments. We didn't think we had the capability for it, or that it was necessarily in our interest, or that we were overthrowing or installing the right governments, or that they'd stay overthrown. We felt collecting secrets and knowing the facts was a much more worthy mission.

My mentor at headquarters was Roger Goiran, a brilliant Frenchman who had worked for the OSS. After the war, he became an American citizen and joined the CIA. As station chief in Tehran in 1953, he adamantly opposed the CIA's planned overthrow of Muhammad Mosaddeq, arguing that it would forever link America to Anglo-French colonialism in the minds of ordinary Iranians. So vehement was his opposition that Dulles had no choice but to remove him from his post and bring him back to Washington. When I started working for him after I returned from Amman at the end of the summer of 1958, he was chief of the Near East Division. He was probably the best division chief we ever had—a perfectionist. When he toured stations in the area, he would take a junior officer as an aide. Once a year he would tour all the stations in the Middle East. For two years, I was one of those junior officers. In the process, I sat in on meetings about every sensitive operation in the Arab world. Several of us thought Goiran was the most brilliant intelligence officer in the agency. He was a genius in the way he would instruct operations officers how to go about recruiting foreign agents. He rivaled Socrates in his approach.

Shortly before I left headquarters for Beirut, James Critchfield replaced Goiran as chief of the Near East Division. Critchfield, who helped mine Nazi intelligence organizations for information on the Soviets in the aftermath of World War II, described many years later how Dulles had asked him to take the job and shift his focus from Europe to the Middle East because the Soviets were starting to focus on the region. At least during my years in Beirut, from 1960 to 1963, I do not remember the Soviets being an overarching target. For the Beirut station, Syria was our number one concern. We also paid attention to the Israelis, because they were active in Beirut. We didn't consider their intelligence service Mossad as friendly. I had an Israeli double agent—a Lebanese who was working for the Israelis, but also working for me. All intelligence services were considered an enemy.

Shortly after I arrived in Beirut, I recruited a top Lebanese news-paperman as a principal agent, a headhunter for spies. You recruit a principal agent because he knows everybody in the town. You tell him you're a spy, but you don't consider him a spy. You want him to be your partner in finding spies. You might match his salary, pay him $10,000 a year, or $1,000 a month—enough for his time and loyalty. You want to be able to say to him, "I'm going to go down a list of people, and I want you to tell me everything you know about them. How many do you think would work for an American? How many would work for a Russian?"

You had to polygraph principal agents, as well as all other agents. That was standard procedure. If nothing else, it's a threat—don't get involved if you're going to lie, because we're going to catch you. I did a lot of polygraphs, because I had a lot of agents over time. An important element of polygraphing is the operator. A good operator is the secret to success. But you have to have a lot of data on an agent or suspect so you can cross-check his information with the facts. You just can't wing it. Still, with a good operator and a good set of facts, the polygraph works, despite its many critics.

"The Newspaperman" and I became close friends, and he was very valuable. He was one of the top journalists in Beirut. He'd sit back and everybody would come to talk to him. We'd meet at the Excelsior Hotel, either in the lobby or the bar, which was never very busy. Nobody would question a journalist meeting an embassy officer. Early on in our relationship, he told me he knew a Syrian intelligence agent he thought I might like to meet.

The Syrian would come back and forth from Damascus. I first met him at one of the safe houses we had in different parts of the city. The thing that worried me about him was that he wanted to be recruited. One of the first things he told me was, "I've got some information that maybe the American Embassy would like to know." What was his purpose? Did he want to set me up for a misinformation coup? I didn't know. I gained a lot of credit for recruiting him. But I was never sure that I knew the whole story. He would tell me things about the Lebanese the Syrians had on their payroll, and what they were doing in terms of intelligence operations. He was definitely a senior Syrian intelligence officer and a steady source of information on the Syrian Security Service that we didn't know. Everything he told us that we could cross-check was positive. Our conclusion was that the agent was willing to serve the Americans in order to double his salary.

Thirty years later, practicing law in Washington, I attended a black-tie party at the Washington home of one of the wealthier Arabs who was part of Washington's social life. Ten Arab couples were in attendance. I knew eight of them. Two were clients. The ones I knew were certainly wealthy. The occasion was the graduation of one of each of their children from a Washington, D.C., university. The couple I didn't know turned out to be my old Syrian agent. He was a friend of everyone there. We were introduced as strangers. Everyone there knew I was ex-CIA, so we had to pretend we'd never met and were very discreet. When we were able to speak privately for a moment, I discovered he knew from his friends my total situation. I garnered from him and queries to other attendees that he had hit it big and was one of Syria's leading businessmen, a multimillionaire. We agreed to meet again but never did. He seemed very pleased that we had met. I had the feeling he would still be willing to be helpful, but I would never really know. In the intelligence business, you carry secrets, and sometimes ponder mysteries, forever.

On another occasion in Beirut, the Newspaperman told me that one of his friends in journalism who worked for the French Intelligence Service was helping a Syrian intelligence officer defect to Paris.

"I'm a good friend of this guy. Do you want me to try and get him to cut you in on this deal with the Syrian?" the Newspaperman said in the Excelsior bar.

"Yes, if it can be done," I said.

"I don't know, exactly, but he's going to Paris tomorrow evening with the Syrian officer, under an assumed name," the Newspaperman said.

I gave him contact instructions to pass to his friend, whom I'd met before. We arranged to meet at a church in a quiet section of Paris. My pitch to both him and the Syrian defector was quite simple: Tell me what you've told the French, and double your money. The church was out of the way and should have been largely deserted at the hour I chose. But as I walked up to it, I saw an odd number of tourist types lolling on the steps, with cameras. There were too many people just hanging around. The French security people are on to this, I thought to myself. This guy must be enough of a Frenchman that he's not going to turn the Syrian over to me without getting French approval, and he doesn't owe me anything. We met inside the church, then left and walked down the street together. All those people hanging around outside the church got up and left, too, and some of them followed us.

"This thing is blown already," I told the Lebanese journalist. "We're not going to be able to go through with this here. You've already told them something, or else they've figured it out, and I don't think they've figured it out. They don't know me from Adam. So this thing is not going to work. If you think it is going to work, you can get to me alone someplace back in Beirut. There's something there if he wants it, and you, too. I'm going to turn off at the next corner, and I'll see you later." He never came back to see me in Beirut.

Probably the best agent I ran in Beirut was one I inherited. Even now, I can't say anything more about his nationality. But he was able to maintain close ties to those inside the Ba'ath Party, in both Syria and Iraq. We didn't think the Ba'athists were that radical, and they weren't Communist. We were working with them, and this agent helped facilitate a relationship the agency maintained right up until the first Gulf War in 1991, and beyond. I was one of his contacts with the outside world. He was so important and so sensitive that we never communicated with him in a way that might have been detected, uncovered, or intercepted.

As if all this wasn't intrigue enough, I was out walking one day on a busy street when I passed a man who probably ranked as the century's most damaging and deceitful traitor: Kim Philby. We both started to speak, thought the better of it, then just passed each other and never turned around. I'd first met the charming Soviet mole in 1949 at the home of my Georgetown professor, Heyworth-Dunne. I was a student at Georgetown's Institute of Languages and Linguistics, and Philby was MI6's representative in Washington. His best friend in the CIA was none other than James Jesus Angleton. Many people later attributed Angleton's obsessive paranoia as counterintelligence chief to the fact that he was so completely taken in by Philby.

Philby was forced to resign from MI6 in 1951 when suspicion first surfaced that he might be the infamous "Third Man" who had tipped off Guy Burgess and Donald Maclean, classmates at Cambridge, that they were about to be arrested as Soviet spies. Both defected before they were arrested. Philby was publicly cleared in 1955, but suspicions persisted. When I saw him on the street in Beirut, he was working as a foreign correspondent. New evidence had just surfaced that he was, in fact, a Soviet spy. The Beirut station certainly felt strongly that he was dirty. Robin W. Winks, in his book *Cloak and Gown*, says Angleton ordered two officers in the Beirut station to keep an eye on Philby. One of them, my friend Ed Applewhite, the station chief and Angleton's classmate at Yale, was ordered to take Philby into custody and bring him back to Angleton in Washington. To accomplish this we had rented the flat next to Philby's and were planting listening devices in the wall when he disappeared on January 23, 1963. He turned up in Moscow shortly thereafter. He vanished after Nicholas Elliott, Philby's friend from MI6, came out to Beirut, extracted a written confession, and offered Philby immunity if he provided a full damage assessment. Philby asked for a couple of days to think it over, and vanished. Much mystery surrounds Elliott's visit. Elliott insists he went to extract a written confession and did exactly that. But most of us in the Beirut station believed that his mission was to warn Philby and persuade him to defect and escape to the Soviet Union in order to avoid the spectacle of a show trial in London. In fact, a member of the MI6 station in Beirut, with whom I had a special relationship, confirmed to me that convincing Philby to escape to the USSR was Elliott's official mission.

Several months after Philby defected, I said my goodbyes in Beirut. I met the Newspaperman at the Excelsior bar for a fond farewell. Even though he had introduced me to a number of valuable agents, I didn't turn him over to a replacement. I figured he had provided all that he could, and enterprising CIA officers would have no trouble finding principal agents of their own in Beirut. The Syrian security officer was another matter. I met him one final time at a safe house and handed him over to a new officer who would run him. I had grown to like and admire him, and my reservations about him had been mostly resolved. We embraced, thanked each other, and said goodbye. At the time I was certain I'd never see him again. But I was obviously mistaken.

As my tour reached its end in the summer of 1963, headquarters asked my preferences for my next assignment. I listed only one: Chief of Station, Amman, Jordan. Headquarters approved, and began processing my cover in Amman.

Halfway through the process the State Department turned my assignment down; the ambassador in Jordan, Bill (Butts) Macomber had opposed it, because he did not want the CIA chief of station dealing officially with the king. I obviously could not accept the appointment under any other conditions, since the king knew I was CIA from my work on the 1958 coup attempt. It would have been absurd, and an insult, to spend a tour there as chief dealing with the king through a subordinate. Macomber was adamant. Headquarters was unwilling to confront the ambassador, but gave me permission to visit Amman from Beirut and plead my case with Macomber.

Macomber was a Republican political appointee from upstate New York, with impeccable credentials. He was an ex-staff aide to Secretary of State John Foster Dulles and was in a long-distance courtship with Mr. Dulles's secretary, for which he had the secretary's blessing. They married when he left Amman. Macomber was brusque and brash but likable. He relished his role with the king, and did not want to share it. Our meeting was cordial. His position was simple: the CIA chief of station should not deal directly and officially with the

king. That was the ambassador's job, and no one was going to over-
rule him. I told the ambassador of my experience in 1958 in Jordan,
and said because of that experience, I was probably the best qualified
to be chief of station. I explained that since the king was very vulnerable and had been his own chief of intelligence, there were important
operational reasons for CIA to work closely with him on security
matters. I added that these reasons did not interfere with the issues
the ambassador and king would be discussing; they actually would
complement them. I concluded that the only reason he could really
have for opposing my appointment was that he did not trust me to
limit my dealings with the king to security matters or to fully disclose
everything the king and I discussed.

"It's not a matter of trust," he said. "I don't even know you."

"That's why you can't trust me," I said. "Call your brother Bob if
you think I'm not trustworthy."

"Bob, what does he have to do with it?"

"We spent World War II together on a minesweeper, he was my
best friend, we did everything together. He talked a lot about you. I
don't think you realize how much he admires you. Give him a call. He
will tell you that you can trust me."

I explained to the ambassador that his brother and I had been
assigned to the USS *Nimble* AM (Auxiliary Minesweeper) 266, a 180-
foot vessel manned by one hundred men and ten officers, as it was
commissioned out of the Philadelphia Naval Yards. After a brief
training session in Florida, we went through the Panama Canal and
stopped over in Hawaii before steaming on to the Pacific War area.
We immediately began sweeping mines, opening up landing lanes
to the various islands. We ended up at the battle of Okinawa, after
which we went through the worst typhoon of the war, which was
much more threatening than the Japanese. When the war ended on
August 15, 1945, we were sweeping the southern coast of Japan, in

preparation for an invasion that would never occur. A few days later, we unwittingly witnessed the nuclear destruction of Nagasaki.

All the reservists went home and back to civilian life when the war ended—except for a few minesweepers, including the *Nimble*. There were too many ports and shipping lanes still mined to leave unattended and the U.S. Navy did not want to leave it to the locals. So, working with the locals' charts and support, we swept the ports of Sasebo (Japan), Formosa (Taiwan), Korea, and the Yellow River entrance to China. We visited each of the ports we swept and the surrounding countryside. Often we were the only foreigners present.

There were two highlights: the unauthorized visit to atom-bombed Nagasaki and the 1945–46 Christmas holidays in Shanghai. We had a day off, Nagasaki was only three hours up the coast, and the crew voted to visit. The brass agreed. Nagasaki was an eerie sight, nothing but rubble, small enough to be picked up, as far as the eye could see. Among the smoldering rubble were the indistinguishable remains of forty thousand inhabitants who had been instantly vaporized by the blast. Forty thousand more, who were on the periphery of the blast, died from radiation and injuries within the first four months. Many of those still surviving would have been better off dead, to quote knowledgeable medics. The only standing object in this vast panorama was a ten-foot Shinto shrine, which had been preserved either by its ceramic surface or a Shinto god. Two old women dressed in white, with white masks over their mouth and nose, scavenged the ruins, without apparent success. They were the only Japanese in sight.

The only other people present were a platoon of American soldiers tented near the dock site where we landed. They were doing nothing more than providing a presence, and were as unaware of the dangers of radiation as we were. It was an awesome and horrific scene. We were all happier to leave Nagasaki than we were to make the visit.

We returned home in February 1946. With an extra five months of minesweeping we won the distinction of sweeping more mines than any other minesweeper in the Pacific, for which we received a presidential citation.

As a reward for lengthening our tour in the Pacific by six months, the ship was granted a one-week leave in Shanghai over Christmas. Still under Nationalist control, but surrounded by the Communists and under curfew, Shanghai was a nightlife extravaganza. After-hour clubs rocked, bars burst, the streets were thronged, and traffic was at a standstill. It was topped off, the last day of our leave, by the Chinese government implementing a change in traffic direction of motorized vehicles in all of China, from the left, British-style, to right, American-style. We left leaning on the ship's railing witnessing the biggest traffic jam in the history of the world—nobody had gotten the word.

Ambassador Macomber was very interested in the tales I related, since his brother was part of them. He said he never knew much about his brother's war experiences, and appreciated hearing about them. He then confided that he was very close to his brother and thought of him more as a son. This meeting inducted me into the Macomber family and resulted in the following response: Of course I could come to Amman; of course I could meet with the king; and last but not least, he trusted me.

The trust that developed between Macomber and me was mutual and the working relationship harmonious. The coincidence would change the course of my life.

Chapter 3

CALM BEFORE THE STORM

Amman was still a sleepy desert backwater in the summer of 1963 when I arrived as chief of station with Katherine, Kelly, and Sean. The city, a far cry from cosmopolitan Beirut, still brought back fond memories of the summer of 1958. Amman is built on seven hills, called *jebels*. They rise from the center of the city. The most modern and largest is Jebel Amman, a long, one-sided hill that rises and then flattens out for miles outside the city. On top, there are a series of numbered roundabouts in the road. When I arrived in Amman, the Third Circle was the final circle. Now, there are nine circles. The British Embassy was at the Third Circle, but there were also shepherds herding sheep at the Third Circle. I lived in the oldest section of Jebel Amman, near the First Circle. My house was on an acre of land. It was surrounded by a seven-foot stone wall, except for a solid iron gate entrance, which was low enough so you could see over the top. It had a squash court, made of tile; a big flower garden; and a vegetable garden. Casey prowled the grounds. The house was made of stone, about a foot thick, which helped keep it cool in the summer and warm in the winter. Once again, I put my shotgun in my bedroom closet, for all my household staff to see. The gun provided little protection against a bomb that incinerated my living room, but now I'm getting ahead of myself.

Not long after we arrived, I looked out over the gate and saw a man halfway down a side street watching my house. I looked out again a little later, and he'd been replaced by another man, also trying to look inconspicuous. I thought to myself, My buddy Rasul has got me under surveillance. He wanted me to know he had been paying attention when I'd told him five years earlier always to watch when intelligence officers changed over if he wondered who the agents were that they were inheriting. So I called Rasul, who had become the first head of Jordan's General Intelligence Service since last we met.

"I'm watching your guy out here; give me a break," I said.

He didn't admit to what he was doing, but each of us knew. Rasul was thinking all the time. He always had some complicated scheme for what was happening. He was disliked by some people—too arbitrary and conspiratorial—but they didn't know him very well. They thought he was a bit weird, and he was. One time, he arrested a Jordanian American, with dual citizenship, because the man had been in the outlawed Jordanian Communist Party years earlier, before emigrating to the United States. The ambassador asked me to look into the arrest because it was a political case. I called Rasul and went down to see the prisoner.

"Are you mistreating him, Rasul?" I asked.

"No."

"He's an American citizen and we'd like him released," I said, noting that he was only back in Jordan to visit his family.

"As far as I'm concerned," Rasul said, "he's a Jordanian citizen and a member of the Communist Party and I arrested him and I'm interrogating him."

I turned to the prisoner. "Are you being harmed in any way?" I asked.

"No."

"Let me see your body. Take off your shirt," I said, though I knew

Rasul was too smart to beat him in a way that would leave welts on his torso. I looked down at the man's feet.

"You don't have any shoes on. Take off your socks and let me see your feet," I said.

The man bent down and peeled off his socks.

"Show me the bottom of your feet."

When he did, I could see the soles were covered in dark blue welts.

"Rasul, you've been beating this guy on the bottom of his feet," I said. "I'm going to lodge a charge against you with the American government. You've been beating an American citizen. But if you release him, I won't press it."

Rasul released the man immediately, knowing there was no point, or value, in holding him. Rasul and I played games like this. He concocted his theories and strutted around town. But he did a good job. There was no question about it, the king was safer because of Rasul. We worked together. The Jordanian government wasn't really an intelligence target for us. Since my job was to keep King Hussein in power, our primary targets were those groups that conceivably posed a threat, such as the Communist Party and other radical opposition groups. The Palestinian Liberation Organization was certainly a target after it was created in 1964. The Soviets and their satellites had arrived when I was in Amman, which presented us with a whole new set of targets.

The Egyptian Embassy, for one, was a target. When the Egyptians and the Jordanians broke relations at one point, the Egyptians vacated their embassy. We decided to bug the place while they were gone. I put in a request for the CIA's black-bag genius in Athens. We gave the agency's technical gurus from Athens more business than anyone else in the region. You might even say we went bug-crazy during my years in Amman. Rasul soon put two and two together. He showed up at my house and asked what was going on.

"I think you're trying to bug the Egyptian Embassy," he said.

"You're absolutely right, that's what I'm trying to do," I admitted. "Do you want to help me do it? You can find out what they're saying, too. We can make it a joint operation. I won't have to worry about you."

Once he'd agreed to participate, we realized that a chief obstacle to breaking in, beyond a guard posted at the front door, was a streetlight that illuminated the building's facade sharply. I was surprised, needless to say, when Rasul picked up a water gun that belonged to my son Sean and headed down the street to the nearby embassy.

"What are you going to do?" I asked.

"I'm going to shoot this water gun at the light, and the cold water will make the light burst," he said.

Before I could even protest, we had the Jordanian head of intelligence, hiding behind a bush with my son's water gun, shooting at the light.

"If somebody takes a picture of this," I said, "both of our careers are over."

It didn't work. But our man from Athens eventually broke in and wired the place for sound. When the Egyptians came back, they moved into a different building. The old embassy sat there with all these bugs, and no one to talk to them.

Rasul came to the rescue another time when we couldn't turn off a bug we'd placed in the living-room wall at the home of a Soviet intelligence officer. A KGB sweep team was coming, and unless we could deactivate the device, it would surely be discovered. We consulted with Washington, and the technical experts at headquarters suggested turning off the power going into the house, in the hopes of disarming the bug. To do this, I knew I needed Rasul's help.

"I've bugged a Russian intelligence officer's house," I told him, "and I can't turn the bug off."

"You did?" he said. "Why didn't you tell me?"

"I didn't think it was any of your business. But I need to turn the thing off. So I wonder if you could turn off the electricity in that part of the city?"

"Are you out of your mind?"

"No. I'm asking you as a favor, will you turn off the electricity in Jebel Amman, for five minutes, at noon? Will you do that for me?"

Rasul went to the power company, told the people there he was running a major operation, and needed the power turned off at noon. At the appointed hour, the lights and air conditioners, radios and televisions in the heart of Amman all shut down for five minutes. The bug still didn't deactivate. Undeterred, we waited for a weekend when the Soviet spy took off with his wife and kids for a picnic. We broke into the house and removed the device. We lost a good bug, but at least the Soviets never found it.

As with Rasul, my relationship with King Hussein was trusting and close from the moment I returned as chief of station. We were able to pick up where we had left off five years earlier, when I'd handed him the signed confessions of all twenty-two coup plotters. I was very patient in this relationship and didn't even realize at first that I was becoming his main point of contact at the embassy. Part of it was that he liked dealing with CIA. I think he found it more efficient than managing his relationship with Washington through the more formal State Department. But part of what quickly became a special relationship was my own sense of discretion. I think the king appreciated the fact that I didn't push myself with him, that I didn't try and get in pictures with him. I always stood back, outside the frame. As a CIA man, I could have easily become an embarrassment to him. So I tried to diminish this relationship, both in his eyes and the eyes of everyone else.

I still vividly remember the king sitting in my living room in Amman with his feet up on a stool, as relaxed as could be. He told me his brother Hassan was coming home from Oxford, and he was thinking about retiring and turning the country over to him. "I've had it," he said. "Things are quiet, and I'd like to just go, not be worried about all of this." I didn't know if he was serious and wondered whether I needed to report his ruminations to Washington. Even before Hassan returned from Oxford, Hussein formally changed the line of succession, making Hassan crown prince in the place of his own son, Abdullah, who was just three years old. Hussein did this to shore up his position as relations deteriorated with the PLO, whose creation Nasser had sponsored in 1964. But for the most part, until tensions with Egypt, Israel, and the PLO escalated in late 1966, there were no crises to contend with in Jordan.

Ambassador Macomber left in December 1963, and was replaced by Bob Barnes, a career diplomat. Barnes soon found himself caught in the middle of struggles between Jordan and the bureaucracies in Washington and took a beating from both sides. In the course of these struggles we became very close. During one six-month period, Jordan's prime minister, Wasfi Tal, a tough, often impetuous, dynamic person, refused to see Barnes because of the consistently bad news he brought to their meetings. When Barnes needed to pass information to the prime minister or ask him questions, he sent me in his stead. Tal reciprocated. We never told Washington, for fear Barnes would have been withdrawn. His problems notwithstanding, the mood in the Political Section brightened considerably when a young Foreign Service officer named April C. Glaspie arrived, with her British mother and dog in tow. Born in Vancouver, British Columbia, she had become interested in the Arab world through relatives on her mother's side, who were soldiers in the British military in British-mandate Palestine. I saw her every day. She had a lot of spirit, wanted to do a job, was excited about being the first female Foreign Service officer in the Middle East—and didn't want to blow it. I liked her spunk. I liked the way she talked: short sentences. As a single woman, it was hard for her to socialize. All the important people in the country were married, and she couldn't invite them out to lunch very easily. I introduced her to people. She appreciated it. We became close friends and remained so a quarter of a century later when April found herself at the center of a very big storm—Desert Storm—as ambassador to Iraq in 1990.

Much of the embassy's time was spent battling Washington over military and economic assistance issues. With Nasser pushing King Hussein to purchase Soviet arms as a member of the United Arab Command, I lobbied hard with Washington for an arms deal to gird Jordan's army, which was the country's security blanket. Modern equipment helped keep morale and loyalty high. The United States had to try to balance Jordan's military needs and Israel's opposition to any plans we had for selling arms to Arab countries. The problem for any U.S. administration was that Israel had virtual veto power over such deals through its clout in Congress. The danger always existed that, if the Israeli constraints were too tough, Jordan could turn to the Soviets. While we didn't want that to happen, Israel didn't seem to care. Many Israelis felt that polarizing the area between the United States and the Soviets was in Israel's interest. True or not, it enabled Israel to virtually blackmail the United States into providing its military with top-of-the-line equipment that it otherwise would not have gotten.

Phil Talbot, assistant secretary of state for the Middle East, visited Jordan as these negotiations were taking place. Ambassador Barnes asked me to include the military supply problem in my intelligence briefing. He was afraid he would lose his temper, and/or his job, since he had already been shot down by Talbot and others in the Johnson administration for pleading Jordan's arms case too strenuously. As an agency employee, I wasn't under Talbot's control and could speak more freely, which I did, much to Talbot's dislike. But the embassy staff was with me. It was the frequent case of field personnel being more supportive of the country in which they were serving than Washington, which was dealing with paper, not people, and politics, not projects. The arguments for supplying arms to Jordan were simply much stronger than those against.

Talbot didn't even try to answer the arguments. "Young man, don't you know we have a Democratic administration in Washington. Jewish members of the Democratic Party provide sixty percent of its funds," he blurted out in public at one point. "And they don't want the United States to arm any Arabs. It's that simple." The gathering was stunned by his admission. I replied only that Jordan was going to rearm; the king could not afford not to. It was just a question of whether they would be American or Soviet arms—and influence. Ultimately, U.S. negotiators agreed to sell one hundred tanks to Jordan as part of a deal with Israel, in which a pattern was established: whatever weapons Jordan received, Israel received more advanced models, which the United States had sold to no one else. Completing the deal was a cliff-hanger that took too long, was too painful, and earned no one's goodwill.

Matters were only slightly less contentious when it came to negotiations with the U.S. Agency for International Development, or USAID. On one occasion, the Jordanian government was in the process of purchasing two small, secondhand commercial airliners from Spain. King Hussein wanted a national airline. When USAID headquarters got word of this, they threatened to cut off all economic assistance if the deal went through. They thought it was a luxury Jordan couldn't afford. Everyone in the embassy thought this was well over the top, but the ambassador had to pass the message to Prime Minister Tal, who hit the roof when he heard it. As far as he was concerned, the United States could keep its aid. Tal told the ambassador he would talk to the king and get back to him. But he was recommending Jordan purchase the aircraft.

Tal immediately hosted a meeting of the top government figures, including the military, to present the problem to them and obtain their support for his position. For some unexplained reason, he invited me to attend; perhaps to attest to the unanimity of the government on the issue. The meeting was highly emotional. Tal was eloquent. Everyone agreed with him: Purchase the aircraft.

I thought to myself that this was not a big enough issue to break economic development ties between the two countries. I raised my hand. I said I had seen the USAID cable and it had read that if Jordan purchased the two aircraft, economic assistance would be cut off. What about purchasing one and leasing the other? Or better yet, lease them both. Simply tell Washington you decided not to buy the aircraft. To make a long story short, that's what the Jordan government did. Washington was never the wiser. Economic assistance continued as usual. Jordan now has one of the finest international airlines in the Arab world and one of the few in the world operating at a profit.

Against this backdrop of bureaucratic battles and political tension, more ominous forces gathered in the region. In 1965, Yasser Arafat's militant Fatah faction, beyond the control of the PLO at this point, staged its first guerrilla raid on Israel from inside Jordan. Syria mounted several raids. Israel retaliated against the Syrian raids by attacking the Palestinian village of Samu on the West Bank in Jordan, leveling ninety-three houses and killing fifteen Jordanian troops in November 1966. King Hussein saw the attack as a first step by Israel toward annexing the West Bank, should tensions rise and create a pretext for the takeover. He noted that every time there was trouble in Jordan, Israel went on military alert. The Samu attack came the same day the king received a friendly letter from the Israelis. The attack destroyed whatever trust or hope he had in Israeli intentions. The attack came after Syrian raids, which meant that to Israel all Arabs were the same: mortal enemies.

Hussein felt betrayed and explained why in an anguished conversation with me and the new American ambassador, Findley Burns, Jr., who had replaced Barnes in May 1966. Hussein had been secretly meeting with an authorized senior Israeli, Yaacov Herzog, for three years in an effort to find out Israel's terms for a durable peace—without success. I had no knowledge of these meetings and was surprised, to say the least. The risks in meeting with the Israelis were enormous. The king said his purpose was to find out what Israel wanted and whether their difficulties could be negotiated. The Israelis never gave him a straight answer. Indeed, a period of turbulence had begun that only escalated until Israel, Egypt, and Jordan went to war in June 1967.

After the Samu attack, two Democratic senators, Ted Kennedy of Massachusetts and John Tunney of California, accompanied by their wives, came to Jordan on an official visit that also would include a stop in Israel. I was their escort officer. The first thing Kennedy wanted to do was visit a Palestinian refugee camp. The head of police, Colonel Radi Abdullah, whose test I had passed back in 1958 when I'd shown up to meet him just before his arrest, was adamantly opposed to the idea. He didn't know how the Palestinians would react, especially in the heated aftermath of Samu, and wasn't sure he could guarantee the senator's safety. But Kennedy was on an oversight committee involved with the Palestinian issue and wouldn't take no for an answer. He was very relaxed, but determined to go. I told Radi, "He's going to the refugee camp. You had better be prepared." So, without the senator knowing, Radi moved all the refugees out of one part of a camp and brought in a bunch of his own people. He dressed them up and briefed them on how to act and what to say. When Kennedy arrived, Radi warned him not to go too far inside the camp. Kennedy talked to the supposed refugees without ever knowing that he was interviewing a group of policemen.

Next, Kennedy wanted to go to Samu, which the king was all in favor of. On the way, the senators, who had been classmates in law school, were going to have lunch with the king at a hotel on the Dead Sea. Hundreds of reporters were trailing their helicopter across the desert in taxis, but Kennedy did not want to speak to the press, given all of the sensitivities related to the Israelis and the Palestinians in the wake of the attack. Since I was the senators' designated liaison, many of the reporters approached me and wouldn't accept Kennedy's decision not to hold a press conference. They were so adamant that I went to the senator.

"This is not my job. I don't do this and I can't judge this," I said. "But they've come all this way, and they want you to say something. I don't know what to tell them, other than that you don't want to do it."

He thought for a moment, then went over and sat in a chair in the hallway outside his room and put his head in his hands. All by himself, he sat there, and I stood and watched him. He sat for five minutes. Then he got up and said, "I'll talk to them. Tell them I'll be out in five minutes." So I went out and said, "Okay, everybody, be quiet, move back, the Senator will be out and he will address you." In five minutes, he came out, and to my mind, knowing that he didn't want to do it, he gave an exceptional speech—a speech to which neither the Israelis nor the Arabs could take exception. His calculation was perfect. I thought to myself, This guy has got something extra. My God, for all he'd been through, chased by the reporters, he handled it beautifully.

Before he left for Israel, he asked that we send a proposed itinerary to Ambassador Walworth Barbour. When Barbour sent back a list filled with changes and other potential stops for the senator, Kennedy became incensed.

"I want to dictate a telegram I want you to send to the Secretary of State," he told me. "I just sent Ambassador Barbour a list of things I want to do in Israel, and I get back an answer suggesting a lot of other things. I want you to tell Barbour that I don't want to have anything to do with him. Frankly, I would recommend that he be changed. I'm going to go do the things I want to do, and the embassy better either prepare for it, or you're going to be hearing from me about that place, and about Barbour."

"You want to send this to the Secretary of State?" I asked.

"Yes."

Mrs. Kennedy and Mrs. Tunney headed back to the United States as their husbands departed for Israel. As keenly interested as they were in Jordan's relations with Israel and the Palestinians, nothing could have quite prepared them—or my colleagues at the embassy in Amman—for what was to come the following year.

For years King Hussein was convinced that a major Israeli goal was annexation of the West Bank as part of a Greater Israel. After Samu it became a certainty for him. Events have borne him out.

Chapter 4

THE PRELUDE TO WAR

As the rush toward war in the Middle East quickened in May 1967, I watched with unease as King Hussein moved to engage Egypt's friendship at whatever cost. His isolation from Gamal Abdel Nasser had only deepened in recent months, and relations were no better with Syria or the PLO. He felt war with Israel was imminent. He did not think it was in Jordan's interest to sit on the sidelines. Tension had begun to mount in a serious way two weeks earlier, when Nasser maneuvered Egyptian forces into the Sinai on May 14, a move that was clearly provocative to Israel. Two days later, he asked UN Secretary-General U Thant to remove UN Peacekeeping Forces that had been in place on Egyptian territory since the end of the 1956 Suez War, separating Egyptian and Israeli forces. U Thant immediately—and foolishly—complied with Egypt's request. Critics contend that he could, and should, have delayed. It removed a barrier to war. The peacekeeping troops were stationed on Egyptian soil, at Egyptian sufferance, so Egypt could legally remove them any time it wished. While the original purpose of the troops' presence had expired—the separation of troops—Nasser never wanted them removed. They were, indeed, a force for him to hide behind as protection from a war with Israel. Arab pressure forced Nasser to act against his own interests. But removing the UN peacekeepers was not illegal, or a casus belli, as Israel claimed.

Nasser's second provocation was trickier. On May 22, he announced the closure of the Strait of Tiran, between the Sinai and the Egyptian island of Tiran in the Red Sea, to Israeli shipping. The strait had been closed to Israel for ten years before Suez, on grounds that it was under Egyptian sovereignty. One of the provisions between Israel and the United States in the Suez Settlement Agreement in 1956 was that the United States would support Israel's right to sail the Strait. The Egyptian position was that the strait was Egyptian by law and could be closed, especially in time of war, against an enemy. It is a legal issue. The United States does not have the authority to nullify the law. Whether Egypt is the sovereign has never been adjudicated. Egypt only announced Israeli shipping would be banned; it was never tested. From Egypt's point of view it was operating within its rights in closing the strait.

On May 26, President Johnson made it clear to Israeli foreign minister Abba Eban during a White House meeting that the United States was vigorously pursuing measures to keep the strait open to shipping. "I must emphasize the necessity for Israel not to make itself responsible for the initiation of hostilities," Johnson told Eban, according to an official aide-mémoire of the conversation. "Israel will not be alone unless it decides to go alone. We cannot imagine that it will make this decision." But after the meeting, according to aides who were present, Johnson said he expected Israel to go to war.

On the morning of May 30, when King Hussein was scheduled to fly to Cairo and meet with Nasser, I found in my in-box in Amman two top secret reports of messages between Nasser and Syrian leaders. As chief of station, there were moments when U.S. intelligence provided me with remarkable prescience—and this was one of them. I picked up the telephone and called airport officials, trying to reach the king before he took off. But, piloting his own airplane, he was already airborne.

The intercepts were revealing. Syria was irate that Nasser was meeting with the king, whom they had agreed to ostracize, and asked for an explanation. Nasser replied immediately, telling the Syrians to calm down. He said he had something in mind which would please them. He knew what he was doing and the Syrians could relax. He'd brief them later. It looked like a trap, but there was nothing I could do. What ensued in Cairo, on the surface, was a reactivation of the Arab Mutual Defense Pact, in which each Arab country agreed to come to the defense of the other if it were attacked. This was a normal and legitimate practice among states, recommended by the United Nations as a deterrent to war. For Nasser it also meant, in terms of military tactics, that if Israel attacked Egypt, Israel would also have to commit forces to defend against the Jordanian front. Jordan's role in the present crisis was to station troops on the Jordan-Israel border, forcing Israel to counter, thereby weakening its forces facing Egypt.

One might argue that this was a price worth paying for Jordan to mend its fences with its hostile Arab neighbors. Hussein thought if he made peace with Nasser, then at least the Arabs would be of one voice, and they should be of one voice if Israel was threatening them. But the king, at Nasser's behest, made a concession which sealed Jordan's fate: he placed the Jordanian Army and Air Force under Egyptian military command. This may have been what Nasser told the Syrians would please them. Three days later, Lieutenant General Abdul Munim Riad, one of Egypt's finest generals, arrived with staff to take over the Jordanian forces. Jordan's hands were tied from then on.

I was at the airport when the king and his party returned, and it was really quite a sight. One of the demands Nasser had made on Hussein was to improve relations with the PLO. To that end, he asked the king to bring PLO chief Ahmad Shuqeri back with him to

Jordan. So when the king unloaded at the airport, out came Shuqeri, who the day before had been public enemy number one in Jordan. I began to wonder, What the hell is happening? How much has the king given up?

I tried to see the king that night at the palace but was told he was out. So I drove to see Prime Minister Saad Juma'a, who lived in Jebel Amman at the Fourth Circle. He told me everything that had happened. He was elated. In fact, he said, "This is the first time that I can remember that I'm going to sleep peacefully tonight." The Jordanians were happy. They had made peace with Nasser, and that had been one of their great concerns. If there was going to be a war, they'd be left on the sidelines, and they'd be trampled as a result of the failure to join the war, especially if the Arabs won. They were more concerned with their Arab credentials and gaining Nasser's favor than they were with the consequences of war and defeat. They were trying to put out what they considered was a fire, and they did. But they didn't realize that that just started another fire, a blaze that brought war closer to them—and ended up costing the king the West Bank and East Jerusalem, half his kingdom. In other words, this turned out to be an incredibly shortsighted assessment on their part.

I tried to digest and dissect what I was hearing, because it was complicated, especially in light of the intercepts I'd read that suggested a trap by Egypt and Syria. But I wasn't sure, at this point, that there was going to be a war. I knew Nasser didn't want one. Perhaps if I had been able to brief the king on the Egyptian-Syrian intercepts before he departed for Cairo, he might have been more wary and not agreed to place his army under the command of an Egyptian general. There were two unknowns hanging over all the decisions Jordan had to make: Would Israel take the West Bank regardless of what Jordan did, in the same way it took the Golan from Syria, without provocation? And would the Palestinians in the West Bank have revolted against the king if he'd stayed out of the war? King Hussein consistently erred on the side of Arab unity. He continually took the lead in making peace with Nasser and Yasser Arafat, as they continually attempted to overthrow him.

Two days after the king's fateful trip to Egypt, Meir Amit, chief of the Israeli Intelligence Service, met with Dick Helms, the director of Central Intelligence, at CIA headquarters in Langley, Virginia. Amit was on a vital mission on behalf of the hard-liners in the Israeli government, seeking U.S. approval or, at the very least, acquiescence for a surprise, preemptive attack on Nasser. The hawkish Moshe Dayan had become Israel's defense minister the same day, adding to the sense that war in the very near future was all but a fait accompli. They met in secret, and what they talked about was shrouded in mystery for many years. Helms wrote a memo to the president on the meeting the following day. Johnson then sent a letter to Israeli prime minister Levi Eshkol in which he reiterated that Israel should not be responsible for initiating hostilities. The president added a line that has intrigued scholars ever since his letter became public years later: "We have completely and fully exchanged views with General Amit."

The exact meaning of this sentence was still the subject of debate in the late 1990s when I was beginning the research on this book in collaboration with Dick Helms. I told him I thought his meeting with Amit was critical and asked what he remembered about it. He said he didn't remember much, but would look into it. A couple of weeks later, he called me and asked if I wanted to meet him for lunch at the Sulgrave Club on Massachusetts Avenue just off DuPont Circle. After we sat down, he showed me two memos to the president on his meeting with Amit.

Helms would not give me a copy of either document, saying he was on record as having checked them out of the CIA archives. But he let me take notes. Later, after he decided that he could not incorporate the points King Hussein wanted made in his memoir, he wrote me the following memo on his meeting with Amit, which he dated June 20, 2001, and signed in ink. It reads:

> The following is, to the best of my recollection, an accurate account of statements made during my meeting with General Meir Amit. . . .
>
> General Amit made no claim that Egypt planned to attack Israel. On the contrary, he dismissed Egypt's eviction of UN Peacekeeping Forces from the Sinai and its threat to close the Straits of Tiran as saber rattling. Its main significance, he said, was that it gave Israel a pretext to carry out its larger mission—the destruction of [President] Nasir's power—an objective he said was more in the US interest than Israel. Amit said that, if Nasir were not destroyed, the domino theory would soon eliminate US presence in the area, and the Soviets would take over. Amit stated that Israel should have attacked Egypt earlier to take advantage of the disarray within the Egyptian army at the time, but wanted to be sure the US would not attempt to thwart the attack.
>
> General Amit predicted the war would last 3–4 weeks, with Israeli casualties of 4,000. Helms countered that the war would last a shorter time, probably one week, with many less casualties. Amit said he intended to recommend that Israel immediately undertake an all-out war against Egypt. He wanted to obtain a positive response from the President, whose acquiescence and political support Israel considered essential, in order to keep the Soviets out of the ring.
>
> Meir Amit, in official exchanges with the US Government on the eve of the war, dismissed the reaffirmation of the Egypt-Jordan Pact as a measure Jordan had to take to maintain its Arab credentials. He admitted Israel did not consider Jordan a significant military threat.

The documents Helms showed me in 2001 became public early in 2009 when they were posted by Patrick Tyler on the Web site of the National Security Archive at George Washington University. He noted that they were obtained from a private collection. They were among Helms's papers that had been donated to Georgetown University following his death. My assumption is that Dick never returned the documents to the CIA after he showed them to me at the Sulgrave Club and let me take notes of their content. They went to Georgetown University instead.

Helms's June 2 memorandum for the president, and an attached memo on the "Views of General Meir Amit," were copied to Secretary of State Dean Rusk, Defense Secretary Robert S. McNamara, and national security adviser Walt W. Rostow. "Amit thinks the Israelis' decision will be to strike . . . ," Helms wrote in his memo to Johnson. "Again, Amit said Israel wants nothing from the U.S.—except to continue to supply weapons already arranged for, to give diplomatic support, and to keep the USSR out of the ring. He indicated they have everything they need." Helms wrote that Amit had told a senior CIA official that "the time of decision has come for the Israeli government." He noted that Amit "almost certainly" shared the views of General Dayan, Israel's new defense minister.

"It seems clear from Amit's remarks that the 'tough' Israelis, who have never forgotten that they are surrounded by hostile Arabs, are driving hard for a forceful solution, with us and with their own government," Helms noted. Dayan's appointment and Amit's message "can be interpreted as an ominous portent, considering the Israelis' military capability to strike with little or no warning at a time of their choosing."

Helms's second memo, the summation of Amit's views, begins with a warning: Nasser, "if left unimpeded," would trigger a domino effect and eventually drive the United States out of the region: "The first sign of the domino reaction was Jordan's forced accommodation with Egypt." Nasser's closure of the Strait of Tiran was not a "real issue," according to Amit, but "a pretext for Nasser's moves to dominate the Middle East."

Reiterating that Israel was not seeking "collusion" with the United States in any war against Egypt, Amit said that a preemptive strike would be "as much, if not more, in the interests of the United States than of Israel that Nasser be defeated." Amit's final point, according to Helms's memo: "The commitments of the United States in the Middle East are no less than those in Vietnam, but the Middle East offers the United States a chance to demonstrate its commitment at a much lower price than in Vietnam. In Israel, the United States has people on whom it can rely."

One must conclude from a reading of these memos that the president's handwritten insertion in his June 3 letter to Eshkol—"We have completely and fully exchanged views with General Amit"—was in fact a green light. The ostensible purpose of his letter, which arrived in Israel the following day just as the cabinet was voting to go to war, was to caution Israel against launching a preemptive war. But the added reference to Amit is clear evidence that Johnson knew exactly what Israel was planning to do, and acquiesced.

Israel waged preventive war against Egypt to destroy Nasser's military power and has occupied half of Jordan for over forty years. Jordan's defense of Egypt was a legitimate act of defense. Israel only had the right to employ enough force to repel Jordan's attacks—not occupy half the country for forty years. The United States acquiesced in Israel's illegal attack on Egypt and did nothing to restrict Israel or protect Jordan from an Israeli attack, despite knowledge of Jordan's mutual defense pact with Egypt. What a multitude of disasters Lyndon Johnson wrought for his own country, as well as others, by condoning a war that was both illegal and unnecessary.

Chapter 5

THE SIX DAY WAR

On June 4, 1967, I was working late in my office on the second floor of the U.S. Embassy, a rambling old mansion on Jebel al-Webdah, when an assistant military attaché stuck his head in my door around 7 p.m.

"I think we're going to have a war, Jack," he said.

The officer proceeded to tell me that the Israelis were going to demolish Egyptian airfields as well as destroy planes on the ground the following morning at 8 a.m., then invade the country by land. He had been told all of this on back channel by a buddy in the attaché's office in Tel Aviv.

"Did they say anything about Jordan?" I asked.

"No, nothing," he said, and left.

I immediately called the palace to find out where the king was. I was given the address of a home in the Shmeisani section of Jebel Amman and told he was attending a small gathering there. I drove off in my tan Chevrolet Sedan, knocked on the door, and asked if I could speak with the king outside. I told him the attaché's story.

I admitted I was not authorized to tell him any of this. But I believed the information was solid. I said: "Your Majesty should know, the CIA estimate is that the Israelis can defeat all of the Arab armies in one week. You don't want to get involved in this war; you will lose.

You don't have to be more Arab than the Syrians. Until the Syrians go to war, in support of Nasser, you don't have to go."

He nodded. I said, "Okay," and that was it.

I didn't report this to CIA headquarters in Langley, Virginia. I've never told this to anyone in Washington. "Need to know" governed my behavior, so I felt it was my duty to tell only Ambassador Findley Burns. I have no idea who he might have told. I felt no purpose would be served by telling anyone else. I didn't know how serious Washington would have judged the matter to be. If, for example, the king had informed Nasser—and I didn't know whether he had or not—and the Israelis were thwarted, I'm sure I would have been the target of pro-Israelis in Washington. My job at CIA was to keep the king in power, and I felt as a friend of the United States he needed to know that a war in which Jordan might become involved was going to start the next morning.

As predicted, Israeli aircraft took off at 8 a.m. on June 5. Within the hour all Egyptian airfields were inoperable and the Egyptian Air Force destroyed. The Six Day War was actually over in thirty minutes. The Israelis had also attacked and destroyed the airport in Amman. I got a call from the Jordanians that morning that the Israelis had bombed the palace. I drove down there and went to the king's office on the second floor, which was notable for a large picture window that took up much of one wall. An Israeli pilot had fired a rocket straight through it, blasting a big hole down the middle of the office before it went out the other side of the building. If the king had been there, he would have been killed. I immediately went back to the embassy and sent a FLASH message to Washington saying the Israelis had attempted to assassinate the king. Maybe they knew he was someplace else, given the war, but they had taken this shot. I made a big thing of it. I said in my telegram, "Tell the Israelis to knock it off." Somebody in Washington, probably the CIA or the State Department, told them to do just that. And they stopped. Assassinating the king wasn't part of this game.

Once the war began, I knew there was no longer any point in sending Zakharia Muhuiddin, Egypt's vice president, to Washington in an attempt to broker a truce in what had been an escalating war of words. Dean Rusk told members of the State Department Middle East Bureau he believed Israel started the war sooner than planned to ensure Muhuiddin did not get to Washington to broker an end to the confrontation. Israel wanted theatre, and its justification for the attack was constantly changing. First, it was defending itself against an Egyptian tank attack. When that was debunked, it was waging preventive war against the threat of attack posed by Egypt, which did not exist. Then it was to prevent a Soviet takeover, although Meir Amit had told Dick Helms the real reason at their Washington meeting: To destroy Egypt and Nasser as a future military threat to Israel.

No one was more surprised by Israel's attack on Egypt than Nasser, who believed that the United States was pressuring both sides to back off, and that this would enable them to end hostilities. He later told Hussein that he had no intention of attacking Israel. On the first day of the war, it was too late for the king to consider last-minute offers transmitted by Israeli prime minister Eshkol through the United Nations and the U.S. Embassy saying that if Jordan stayed out of the war, Israel would not attack Jordan. The king had already placed his troops under the command of Egyptian general Riad. Nor, having done so, could the Jordanians reject his disastrous deployment of Jordanian troops on the West Bank. On the battlefield, Jordan had no options and was defeated in four days. Jordan's air force was destroyed in one day. Jordanian troops were moved around the West Bank in confusing manner by General Riad and became sitting ducks for the Israeli Air Force. Jordan lost 5,000 men, most of its armor, artillery, and weapons, and all of the West Bank. The king admitted afterwards that he might have played his cards differently had he known that Israel had destroyed the Egyptian airfields and air force in the first sixty minutes of the war and that the Egyptians were lying to Jordan about Egyptian successes on their front.

Early on the second day of the war, Washington obtained a report of a conversation between the king and Nasser—widely reported at the time in the press—in which the two leaders agreed to state publicly that the United States and Britain had been involved in the surprise attack. They were immediately denounced by the Americans for propagating "the Big Lie." But King Hussein had some reason to believe that an outside power could have been involved. On the second or third day of the war, he asked me to meet him at Zaharan Palace, the home of his mother, Queen Zein al-Sharaf. I was taken to a sitting room where the king; General Kurdi, head of the Jordanian Air Force; and some technicians were waiting. A movie screen and projector had been set up. The king said General Kurdi wanted to show me a film that had been taken from Jordan's radar recordings on the first day of the war. On the screen waves of aircraft were seen coming toward the radar. Kurdi explained that they were coming over the ocean toward Egypt from the west, not the east, where Israel is located. He said it raised a serious question whether some Western country (read the United States) assisted Israel in the attack on Egypt.

I replied that I was not competent to comment, but if they wished I would request that CIA headquarters arrange for an expert from the United States to come out, view the film, and give them an answer. I suggested that U.S. satellite and Sixth Fleet surveillance may have supporting data to share. They wanted the expert. Washington sent a pair, who met with Jordan's air force. I did not attend the sessions. When they finished, both the experts and the king told me the Jordanians were satisfied that other countries were not involved in the air attacks. I do not know the details, but one revelation was that the Israeli attack planes flew west from Israel around Egypt at high altitudes and then came in low attacking from the west—not from Israel to the east. So, the charge was not entirely concocted. It had a basis in fact. But in the end, suspicions were allayed.

Four days into the war, the CIA received word of a different attack on the sea to the west—Israeli fighter jets and torpedo boats had opened fire on the USS *Liberty*, a spy ship that was in the eastern Mediterranean off the Sinai Peninsula to gather intelligence on the possible presence of Soviet weapons and troops in Egypt. In what has been called the "gravest incident" in U.S.-Israeli relations, 34 Americans died and 170 were wounded. Israel immediately apologized for what it described as a tragic mistake, and numerous official U.S. and Israeli inquiries have reached the same conclusion. But many at CIA, the Pentagon, and the National Security Agency, whose employees were killed, believe the attack was deliberate. Theories for why Israel would attack its chief ally have varied. Some believe the *Liberty* had collected intelligence about an alleged Israeli massacre of Egyptian POWs in the Sinai. Others have argued that the ship had intercepted communications indicating that an Israeli attack on Syria's Golan Heights was imminent and had to be silenced, lest the attack be thwarted. In his memoir, Dick Helms said he had no role in a board of inquiry that concluded there could be no doubt the Israelis deliberately attacked an American warship. But Dick told me he had good reasons to believe that the Israelis involved knew what they were doing. It was not an accident. That's all he said, and I did not question him further. Alan Wolfe, a Middle East Division chief at CIA, believed the attack was not malicious but an act of gross stupidity.

Once the war was over, with Israel victorious and in possession of the Golan Heights, the Sinai Peninsula, the Gaza Strip, and the West

Bank, Israeli defense minister Moshe Dayan contacted Jim Angleton at CIA headquarters and said, in so many words, "My fellow cabinet members are planning to keep the West Bank, and that's going to be a disaster for Israel. We have to stop it. I would suggest that I meet with King Hussein someplace, with the Americans, and we plot out a different solution to this problem." A recently declassified secret CIA history of Helms's years as director of Central Intelligence said that Angleton "found himself increasingly disturbed by the prospect of an endless cycle of war and more war in the Middle East." He and Jim Critchfield, chief of the Near East Division, went to Helms and proposed a secret meeting in Geneva between Dayan and King Hussein, with CIA present. Helms liked the idea and arranged for them to brief former national security adviser McGeorge Bundy, who'd been called back as a consultant during the Six Day War, and Nicholas Katzenbach, deputy secretary of state, who was sitting in for Secretary of State Rusk. Katzenbach vetoed the plan based on the belief that the king, having lost his army and the West Bank, was too weak to negotiate with the Israelis. "In the embittered views of both Angleton and Critchfield," the secret CIA history concludes, "an opportunity of possibly historic proportions had been allowed to slip away."

Critchfield told me the story, and I've seen a memo that he wrote to Dick Helms. Dick has mentioned this in his memoir. In fact, this missed opportunity was one of the few things he did mention about the Middle East. He wrote: "I thought at the time that this was a mistake, and I believe that events since have confirmed the possibility that in the prevailing atmosphere, secret negotiations involving the exchange of land for substantive peace treaties might have been productive." I feel the same way. If somebody had met with the king then, and wanted to make peace, they could have done so. The king had been weakened; he'd lost his army and half his country. But he wasn't too weak to negotiate with Israel. I thought a meeting in Geneva was a very good idea. It could have offered Israel peace for a return of territory; the same deal Israel offered Egypt and Syria.

The interesting thing about this story is that, throughout the overt history of the Middle East after the 1967 War, Dayan was very much a hawk on keeping the West Bank and not having anything to do with King Hussein. He refused to go to the meetings. When the other Israelis would say, "Why don't you join in?" Dayan would say, "I'll walk out on him after two or three minutes, so there's no sense in my going." So his overt behavior was totally inconsistent with this message he sent to Angleton. He was playing a game, obviously, by being so openly anti-Jordanian publicly, but conniving with Angleton to save Jordan and the king.

How King Hussein might have played his cards, if he knew Nasser would be defeated in thirty minutes, he did not say. He had some options. And his advisers offered several opinions.

The first option was not to have gone to Cairo in the first place, and not to have reactivated the Arab Mutual Defense Pact with Egypt. Would Jordan's security have been threatened if the king had not gone to Nasser's aid? No other Arab state went to Nasser's aid, not even Syria, which was also a signatory to the Arab Mutual Defense Pact.

The second option was to revive the Mutual Defense Pact, but not to place Jordan's armed forces under Egyptian command. This would have satisfied Jordan's Arab obligation, but not tied its hands. Jordan could have regulated its involvement in the war and limited its liabilities. By placing its troops on the border, it could have served its primary function of tying up Israeli forces, without firing a shot. Perhaps, if I had been able to brief the king on the Egyptian-Syrian message intercepts before he departed for Cairo, he might have been more wary and not agreed to an Egyptian commander. The defeat was not only humiliating for the Arabs but numbing. A big loser, along with Jordan, was Nasser and Egypt, whose hegemony over the Arab world and threats to Israel were demolished. Nasser himself was stunned. Not that the Arabs had lost the war, but that Israel had attacked Egypt. Nasser trusted Israel when he should not have, and he failed to trust King Hussein, over the years, when he should have. To his credit, Nasser realized the latter after the 1967 War and spent the last three years of his life trying to make it up to the king.

A fascinating postscript came years later after I'd retired from the CIA and become Jordan's lawyer in Washington, a position I still hold. I had arrived at the old airport on a trip to Jordan and was immediately summoned by an aide to the king.

"Jack, His Majesty is over there with his private plane, and he wants you to join him."

I proceeded to the king's plane, with props running. Queen Noor and one of her daughters were on the tarmac with someone I thought was an Englishman. The queen introduced us, but the engines were roaring, and I didn't hear his name. I said, "Hi, how are you?" When I got on the plane, Noor reintroduced us: "Jack, this is His Majesty, King Constantine of Greece." We were going to Aqaba, where King Hussein had a beach house. We stayed for three days. There was no one else there—just the two kings and Noor, her child, and me. The two kings and I ended up sitting outside on the deck chatting much of the time, except for an overnight boat trip and a series of dune buggy races. At one point, apropos of nothing in particular, King Hussein told King Constantine: "Jack tipped me off in '67 about the war. And I sent two messages to Nasser warning him."

The Greek monarch looked surprised, but I was astonished. "Your Majesty, you sent two messages to Nasser?" I asked.

Finally, after all these years, he was telling me what he'd done with the information I had provided him.

"Well," I said, "why didn't Nasser do something?"

"That's the first thing I asked him after the war," Hussein said.

"What did he say?"

"He said, 'I didn't believe you.' "

As a postscript to a postscript: Years after this outing, I began researching the period. I spoke to a colleague, Richard Parker, who had served as a political counselor at the U.S. Embassy in Cairo during the 1967 War. We talked about Meir Amit's meeting with Dick Helms and other events related to the war. I told him at one point that I had warned King Hussein of the attack the night before it took place. But he said to me that he did not believe that I or the king could possibly have had advance warning. In this case, I have a witness, because King Hussein not only told King Constantine, he told Dick Helms. The king said he did not mention my name for fear it would get me in trouble.

Later, after the king's death, Dick wrote this memo to me, dated June 20, 2001, and signed his name:

> The following was related to me by King Hussein: On June 4, 1967, Jordan learned that Israel planned to launch a surprise attack against Egyptian aircraft and airfields at eight a.m. the next day. The King sent two urgent messages to Nasser warning him of the impending attack. Nasser disregarded both. He admitted later that he did not believe the warnings and was dumbfounded by Israel's attack.

Chapter 6

MAKING THINGS UP
AS WE WENT ALONG

There was no precedent for the situation in the Middle East after the war. There had never been such an upheaval. It affected everybody, and nobody knew where it was going to end or what was going to happen. Nobody had a plan. We were all making things up as we went along. The Israelis offered peace to Egypt and Syria within two weeks of the war—and they still haven't made peace with Syria. About the only thing that was clear was that the Israelis were euphoric and maybe a little intoxicated by their victory so quickly over the Arab world. That was the overwhelming fact. But they couldn't permanently control the Arab lands they'd captured, so what were the Israelis going to do? And what were the Arabs going to do? They really weren't defeated. They didn't surrender, and Israel only occupied parts of each defeated country, some of which it obviously didn't need, like Egypt's Sinai Peninsula. The Golan Heights, seized from Syria, was advantageous because it gave Israel a buffer zone against Syria. But nobody seemed to realize at the time that the West Bank was something special. To the Jewish people, the West Bank was their biblical homeland, and the Israelis revived their claims to the land, which had been dormant for I don't know how long. The king kept saying, "They want the West Bank," and I thought, Who the hell wants the West Bank? Is he exaggerating this?

I had traveled to the West Bank, and there wasn't anything there. But the king clearly read the situation better than I did.

In late June 1967, Israel sent messages to Egypt and Syria through the United States stating that in return for a full peace it would give back the lands occupied during the war. Nasser turned down a separate peace, living up to his promise to Jordan that Egypt would not make peace until Jordan's lands were returned. Syria refused to discuss a settlement, and it is doubtful the message was ever officially passed to the Syrian government. Both offers were later withdrawn by Israel. "But what about Jordan?" the United States asked Israel's foreign minister, Abba Eban. He replied that Jordan was different; Israel had historic and nationalist interests in the West Bank, which would require special negotiations.

When cease-fires ended the war, the State Department and others in the U.S. government assumed Israel would withdraw its forces from the territories it had occupied. The assumption was based on the fact that, despite questions regarding the legality of the war, Israel had accomplished its purpose by destroying the power and threat of Nasser's Egypt and Syria. But it soon became clear why that wasn't happening. Roy Atherton, chief of the State Department Middle East Bureau, was nonplussed when Eugene Rostow, the White House aide to President Johnson, told him that Israel would not withdraw from any of the occupied lands until peace terms had been finalized. I remember Atherton telling me after Rostow told him this, "Can you imagine, Jack, they don't want to withdraw until they make peace." That's not the way we were programming the thing.

Atherton asked Rostow how, when, and why that decision had been made. Atherton said he had seen no papers on the subject and there had been no meetings about it, as far as he knew, and if there had been meetings, the State Department should have been included. Rostow replied that there were no papers, but there was a private meeting with only three persons present: President Johnson, Foreign Minister Abba Eban, and Rostow himself. He reiterated that the policy now was this: Israel would not be pressured to withdraw from the West Bank until the parties had agreed to a peace plan. And the State Department would be expected to follow it. Rostow said that peace must precede withdrawal because the United States did not want to return to the "unpeaceful conditions" which had existed before the war.

However noble this rationale appeared, it was badly flawed. First, there was no way the situation prior to the war would be repeated. Israel's two major enemies had been destroyed and were no longer a threat. Second, if Israel preferred the lands it occupied to peace, it would keep the land and forgo peace—in perpetuity. Third, if Israel could make a separate peace with Egypt, it would have little incentive to give up coveted land for peace with the Palestinians, Syria, or Jordan, none of whom represented a threat.

As history now tells us, all the flaws came to fruition. What was labeled as a path to peace turned out to be a dead end. And returning to the "unpeaceful conditions" prior to the 1967 War would be a godsend compared to the conditions that exist today.

Some of those who were in close contact with the king immediately after the war have commented on his fragile emotional state, his depression, and his frail health at the time. I probably had as much contact with him as anyone, but I never sensed anything nearly that dramatic. The king accepted personal responsibility for the losses Jordan had suffered, but I was surprised that he wasn't more depressed. While nobody knew what would happen next, the people around the king remained optimistic that this unsettled postwar situation would be resolved. They had all agreed with his decision to join the Mutual Defense Pact with Egypt and so were reinforcing the notion that he was not mistaken and had done what he had to do. The alternative, had he not gone to war, they tried to convince him, would have been a revolt by the Palestinians on the West Bank. The king felt safer going down with the Arabs than being an outcast. I didn't agree with him. I didn't think that anybody was going to overthrow him when he didn't enter a war that only lasted six days, and I still don't. He could have helped Egypt simply by moving his forces closer to the Israeli border, thereby drawing Israeli troops away from the Egyptian front in response. He didn't have to go to war.

By late June, he resumed the peacemaker's mantle at a meeting at the UN General Assembly in New York, where he offered peace with Israel on behalf of the Arab states in return for the territory Israel had captured. The king then went to Washington, where he met with President Johnson and was advised to seek a bilateral peace with Israel. On his way home, Hussein stopped in London and met secretly with Israel's Yaacov Herzog. In July, after his return to Amman, I remember what he said: "I'll make peace, and I'll do it alone, but I have to get everything back to do it." All the territory back, and he'd make peace—openly, even if the other Arabs didn't go along, as long as he could say to his people, "We've got back what we've lost, and I'm making peace with Israel." He was trying to find out what he needed to do to make peace with Israel. But the Israelis weren't willing to give him everything back to make peace. They never did tell him what they would give him.

A few weeks later, a bizarre incident took place as the king was entertaining a group of guests at his resort home in Aqaba. Among the guests were Linda Christian, an aging actress who had been married to Tyrone Power, and her daughter, a sexpot, I was told. I would imagine that she would have found it interesting if somehow the king and her daughter hooked up. I don't think he would have had much interest in Christian, who was twelve years older than the thirty-one-year-old king. I wasn't there, but I got an emergency call saying that

Christian had apparently laced the king's drink with LSD. The way his aides described it, the king was seated in a chair but was no longer capable of discerning where his body ended and the chair began. He wasn't making any sense talking, either. They needed medical help. I immediately sent a FLASH message to Athens, where we had medical people. They flew in the next day, and went directly to Aqaba, with headquarters' approval. I don't know what they did to clear his situation, but he pulled out of it. I don't think he remembered much. It didn't amount to much in the end. It was just a bizarre act.

Thankfully, this episode had been long forgotten by the end of August, when the Arabs gathered to assess their wounds and chart a future at a conference in Khartoum, Sudan, sponsored by the Arab League. The invitees were leaders of the twenty-two Arab states and the Palestine Liberation Organization. In the closed sessions each leader could be accompanied by only one aide. All were sworn to secrecy. No note-taking was permitted. The Arab foreign ministers had met in Kuwait before the conference to draft an agenda and proposed policy positions, mostly seeking revenge for Israel's aggressions. But once the conference got underway in Khartoum, Nasser wryly asked at one point who the bellicose foreign ministers were representing and who had drafted their position papers. He tossed them aside, stating that the Arabs were in no position to avenge their defeat. They had been beaten badly and it would take years to recover.

Nasser apologized to the leaders, said he accepted full blame for the defeat, and urged each country which had suffered to serve its own best interests in recovering what it could. He said Egypt was in the United States' bad graces and was, unfortunately, in no position to help anyone.

The other Arab leaders, when they had their chance to speak, were very critical of Nasser. King Hussein felt sorry enough for the abuse Nasser was taking to come to his defense. In the end, everyone agreed that the Arabs were not in a position to seek revenge and they all should make the best deal they could. The only significant exception was Ahmad Shuqeri, chairman of the PLO, who was defiant in his speech, ending up with three "no's"—no recognition, no negotiations, and no peace. No one wanted to challenge the PLO, so they let it ride on the grounds that the decision to give Jordan, in particular, the right to seek its own solution had already been taken.

The public understanding of what took place, however, was badly distorted by Shuqeri. The other delegates had been sworn to secrecy as to the conclusions they had reached—that they were too weak to confront Israel and were anxious to make peace. Secrecy was required in order to preserve some bargaining power in negotiations with Israel. The only caveat was that none would make a separate peace without prior consultation and approval. Shuqeri, on the other hand, appeared at multiple press conferences, loudly repeating his three "no's."

Luckily, CIA had a clear sense of what had transpired at the secret conference. I made sure of that. CIA's very best technical people managed to tape the meeting. I received a copy of the English translation and the Arabic tape and gave copies of both to the Jordanians for their records. Jim Angleton gave Mossad a copy of the CIA transcript, and the British received a copy. The recording was illuminating. If there were three "no's" at the conference, they were "No war. No limit on deal making with Israel to get back land. And no separate peace without approval." We knew this, and the Israelis knew this.

And yet, ever since, Israel has trumpeted Shuqeri's three "no's"— no recognition, no negotiations, and no peace—rather than the three "no's" of the Arab countries reflected in the transcript they received from the United States—no war, no limits on negotiations, no separate peace. King Hussein also told the Israelis repeatedly when he met with them that he had a blank check from Nasser and the other leaders to negotiate a peace settlement. It puzzled the king why Israel chose to lie to its own people about it—and why the United States remained silent. It was further evidence that neither seemed to want peace, despite their contradictory rhetoric. The king could only conclude that land was more important to the Israeli leaders than peace or that the leaders lacked the political fortitude to take on the "Greater Israel" extremists in the country. He felt the U.S. administrations were equally spineless in taking on the Israeli lobby and major Jewish supporters of Israel in the United States. The king contended the United States was doing Israel a disservice, if it wanted peace. The Israelis claimed their goal was security, not land, and spent years trying to marry the two, without success. In truth, the occupation of the land is the major source of Israel's insecurity. King Hussein believed security is the product of peace. Israel had turned the equation on its head, which is why it was flawed. He concluded after so many years that most Israelis were too close to the problem to see it accurately, and too emotional about it to deal with it rationally.

There was no lack of peace partners, only a lack of will. Khartoum was not a call to war. It was another lost opportunity.

Another major post–1967 War Israeli provocation was the blanket Israeli bombing of the Jordan Valley, on the grounds that known insurgents in the area were committing terrorist attacks against Israel. Israeli bombing and Jordanian security sweeps had vacated the area, yet the Israeli bombings continued, destroying all the homes, orchards, and infrastructure. The king complained through the embassy to Washington, which replied that Jordan knew who the insurgents were as well as Israel did and the bombing would continue. I requested Jim Angleton, in charge of the Israeli desk at CIA headquarters, to provide the Amman station with Israel's list of the insurgents so that we could vet them with the Jordanians. It was more of a bluff than anything else. I never expected to receive a list.

Two weeks later, a list of over one hundred names arrived, many with Valley addresses. I turned the list over to Jordanian General Intelligence, which formed a large working group to investigate people on the list, almost all of whom turned out to be identifiable. The intelligence staff did a first-class job. They literally ran down everyone.

The Israelis must have obtained their list from an old Jordan Valley telephone directory or some other public document. Many on the list had died; most had moved and were contacted at their new residences. The activities of almost all could be confirmed. None was involved in terrorist activity. I sent the list back to Angleton. I was told that he raised hell with the Israelis for setting up the agency with such misinformation. Until the disclosure the U.S. ambassador to Jordan was, on Washington's instructions, excusing the Israelis' bombings in his meetings with the king. That stopped immediately when the king and the ambassador received a copy of the General Intelligence report. The bombings stopped after Israel received its copy.

Chapter 7

"CAN I TRUST THIS LITTLE KING OF YOURS?"

By November 1967, the center of activity had moved from the Middle East to New York City and the United Nations. Israel was basking in the glory of its stunning victory and digesting its conquests. The Arabs were in various stages of self-delusion, denial, and bitterness. But the time had come to pick up the pieces and try to settle the differences. The United States and Great Britain, in particular, had decided that the UN Security Council must preside over some kind of political or diplomatic ending to this war. Nobody had made peace, nobody had surrendered, nobody had done anything. They'd just stopped fighting. The United Nations had only passed a cease-fire, so this meeting of the Security Council was a follow-up, based on the proposition that a peace treaty, or treaties, could flow from whatever was decided.

King Hussein arrived at the United Nations in New York in early November to lead the Arabs in negotiating a resolution for peace. Nasser had no interest in attending, humiliated by his defeat and uncertain what kind of peace arrangement he might be forced to accept. The Syrians, who never participated in anything, were unrepresented. The king, if not humiliated, was deeply saddened by what had happened to the Hashemite Kingdom. "Jack," he told me at one point, "I've lost half my country." He was bitter. But it wasn't as though he was falling apart emotionally, as some historians have suggested. He remained very much in control. The king was meeting with people all the time, a lot of whom would have noticed if he were depressed, or worse. I thought that whatever he was demonstrating was normal for the situation.

The document produced by this meeting, Resolution 242, was well crafted and unanimously adopted by the Security Council on November 22, 1967. It still comprises the framework and principles for peace in the Middle East, calling for Israel to return the lands it captured during the 1967 War in return for peace with its neighbors, Egypt, Jordan, Lebanon, and Syria.

UN Security Council members went through several drafts and negotiations before the British version was adopted. The most important of these negotiations, and the least publicized, were the private negotiations between Israel and the Arabs on the critical parts of a proposed text, mediated by the American delegation, headed by Arthur J. Goldberg, the former Supreme Court justice who was U.S. representative at the United Nations. Israel was represented by Abba Eban. The Arabs were represented by King Hussein and Egyptian foreign minister Mahmud Riad. It was shuttle diplomacy conducted between floors of the Waldorf-Astoria Towers. Judge Goldberg's home apartment and an accompanying office were located there. The Israelis and Arabs were located on different floors. Goldberg spent a lot of time in the elevator.

Goldberg's principal staff consisted of Joseph J. Sisco, assistant secretary of state for International Organization Affairs, and Ambassadors-at-Large William B. Buffum and Richard F. Pedersen. Goldberg took them to meetings with the Arabs, but he went alone to meet with the Israelis, which created general suspicion of his motives.

Judge Goldberg (he preferred "Judge" to "Ambassador" from his Supreme Court days, even though he was technically a "Justice") had one major handicap in negotiating between Israel and the Arabs. He was a high-ranking, well-known, pro-Israeli Jew. The Arabs did not trust him. To compensate for that, I was added to his team. I was back in Washington for consultation when I was given the assignment. Helms called me up to his office on the seventh floor at CIA headquarters. "The State Department wants to borrow you to go up to New York for these negotiations," he said. "We've approved. So you go up and meet with them." My secretary from Amman was back in town as well, and I asked to have her come up in case I needed to send messages. She took a room at the Waldorf Towers, as did I. I'm sure adding me to the diplomatic team was Sisco's idea, since he was the only person in the group who knew me, and he knew I was close to King Hussein. Sisco was brusque and aggressive. He was a burly man, around six feet tall, who looked like he could have been a prizefighter. But when he talked—and he was a big talker—there was a softer, more thoughtful side to him. My role was to present the U.S. view to the Arabs before Goldberg met with them. Goldberg would only show up after I had negotiated language which was acceptable to the United States and the Arabs—and, according to Goldberg, Israel. Then Goldberg and his team would meet with the Arabs to ratify the agreement. That way Goldberg never needed to pressure the Arabs or arouse their sensitivities. It was a clever idea. I knew I was being used, but it worked—for the time being. It unraveled later.

My first meeting with Judge Goldberg was quite eventful. He was like a little bantam rooster—his chin always out. I was met at the door of his Waldorf quarters by a servant and shown into a large sitting room. The judge was standing in the middle of the room. Sisco, Buffum, and Pedersen were standing, at attention, in a line on his right. He had a Napoleon complex, always wanting to come across as a tough guy. They were afraid of him, and deferred to him, which he expected. I walked up to the judge, who, despite his small size, had a commanding presence and was intent on imposing it. I stuck out my hand. He ignored it and asked, "Tell me, O'Connell, can I trust this little king of yours?" I was so taken aback that I forgot my manners. I said, "He's nobody's king, and he's completely trustworthy. The question is whether he can trust you."

Goldberg did not respond directly. He paused a long moment, then took me by the arm and introduced me to Buffum and Pedersen. We all sat down to discuss the logistics of our efforts and agreed to meet the following morning to commence shuttle diplomacy. As we dispersed, the judge asked me to stay behind. When we were alone, he said, "O'Connell, you don't trust me, do you?" I replied, "Judge, I don't even know you. I have no reason not to trust you." He replied, "No. I can tell you don't trust me."

He then directed me to an L-shaped seating area, where we faced each other at right angles. Between us was a side table with lamp and telephone. He picked up the telephone, asked the operator to get the president on the line, and hung up. He smiled at me as we awaited the connection. Within a minute the phone rang and he was back on the line. "Yes, Mr. President. How are you, sir?" he said. "I just wanted to report that we are on top of things. I'm sure we will reach an agreement that will please you. I have with me a CIA man who will be helping. He is a friend of King Hussein's. I want to confirm to him that I have a blank check from you to work out an agreement between the parties. Yes, sir. I appreciate that. I didn't want there to be any misunderstandings within our group. Everything will come out all right. Don't worry. Thank you, Mr. President."

I wondered as he was talking whether it really was the president. It could have been the hotel concierge. It was a man's voice on the other end; I made out that much, and he would have had to rig the call with his secretary before I arrived, which seemed far-fetched. I assumed it was the president and that the call was made to ensure Goldberg's control over me and to impress the Arabs. When he hung up, he said, "Well, O'Connell, as you can see, I have a blank check from the President. I also have a blank check from the American Jewish community. They will buy whatever I decide upon. Your king and the other Arabs should know that I hold the key." I told him I was impressed and would tell the king.

The shuttle diplomacy began the next day and followed the same routine for several days, until agreement was finally reached on the critical language of the resolution. The first step was for me to relate to the king the language Goldberg wanted and the reasons. Goldberg had already cleared it with the Israelis. Sometimes Mahmud Riad, the Egyptian foreign minister, was present. Otherwise, the king briefed him. There was little controversy over most of the provisions. If the king suggested changes in the wording, I would take his suggestions back to Goldberg to reconcile, whereupon Goldberg and company would meet with the king to ratify the agreement, orally.

The only truly difficult issue was the "withdrawal" provision. It was finally boiled down to "the withdrawal of Israeli forces from territories occupied in June, 1967." The king agreed that there should be adjustments in the prewar borders, since some ran through the middle of villages or were otherwise flawed. However, his main concern was not the wording but the interpretation the United States applied to it. In the final go-around, Goldberg said I could tell the king that the United States would support the following interpretation of the withdrawal provisions: any changes in prewar boundaries must be "minor reciprocal border rectifications." He added that the rectifications need not be in kind, citing as an example the Latrun salient, a strategic overlook in the Ayalon Valley twenty-five kilometers west of Jerusalem, which Israel had captured during the war. If Jordan relinquished its claim to the Latrun salient to Israel, Jordan could receive, in return, access to Israel's Mediterranean port of Haifa. He said that

Israel was "on board" with this interpretation, but he was not sure how long he could keep them "on board" if Jordan didn't accept.

I took the message to the king and he agreed to it. On the way back to Goldberg's suite, I had an uneasy feeling. I had been the go-between on some very important issues, but nothing was in writing. Everyone could deny everything and, as the lowest person on the totem pole, I would undoubtedly be blamed. So, I contacted my secretary, who was waiting to help with just such an issue. I went to her room and dictated a two-page account of what I told the king and what he agreed to, which she typed on Waldorf stationery.

I took the paper with me to Goldberg's suite, where he and his three senior advisers were waiting. I told them that I thought the issue was important enough to reduce to paper. I said the king had agreed to what I had presented on Judge Goldberg's behalf, but, if I misquoted him in any way, they should point it out and I would correct it with the king. I handed the paper to Goldberg, who read it and passed in on to the other three. After they read it, they all agreed that it was an accurate representation of the instructions Goldberg had given me. I then went into the next room and asked the secretary who was on duty to type at the bottom of the paper that Judge Goldberg, Assistant Secretary Sisco, and Ambassadors Buffum and Pedersen agreed to the above. I put the paper in my pocket.

From their demeanor, I am not sure Goldberg or Sisco was that happy that the agreement was on paper. However, an agreement had been reached, and they set off for the king's quarters to ratify it.

I returned to Washington the next day. The king followed a day later for a lunch with Secretary of State Rusk, and a meeting with the president. He called me before the lunch and said he wanted Rusk to confirm that what Goldberg had promised in New York was the United States talking, not Goldberg. I arranged a rush meeting with Sisco to relay the king's request. Sisco asked to see the paper I had written on the matter. I had it with me and showed it to him. He read it and sighed. "My God, did we say all that?" I replied that he had authored it. I was only the messenger. He said he would tell Rusk, and I went on my way.

About four o'clock in the afternoon, the king called and asked me to come to his hotel suite. He told me that he had sat next to Rusk the entire lunch and he never raised the subject. I called Sisco and relayed what the king had told me. Sisco cursed and said, "I don't know what the story is, but I'll find out." About a half hour later, Katzenbach, the deputy secretary of state, called the king back on Rusk's behalf and apologized for Rusk not answering the king's query at lunch. He had just forgotten. Katzenbach said the answer was: Goldberg was speaking for the United States.

The next day, the king met with the president. One of the U.S. participants told me the president told the king that he would not get back all the territory he lost and the king took no great exception to this. Now, I thought the king should have said, "What do you mean, Mr. President? I have a commitment from the U.S. UN delegation and the State Department." But he figured he had that, and maybe the president hasn't gotten the word yet, and he didn't want to fight with the president. Maybe the president didn't know and the king had already received the U.S. position from Goldberg and Katzenbach—"minor reciprocal border rectifications on a reciprocal basis."

A few years after I retired from the agency in 1972 and was Jordan's lawyer, "trust" became a critical issue. I read in *The Washington Post* that Arthur Goldberg, who had retired from government, had denied, in a press interview, that he had ever promised the king "minor reciprocal border rectifications." I wondered what would happen if the king heard that. I met with Hal Saunders, assistant secretary of state, the same day, asking that the State Department publicly refute Goldberg's statement. He said he would check the files first. I said the language had been negotiated in November 1967 at the UN, as part of Resolution 242. The negotiations involved Goldberg, King Hussein, and Abba Eban. Saunders said he would check on it and give me a call. One week later, Hal's secretary called and asked me to come in the next day. Hal's face was grim when I walked into his office. After I sat down, he looked up, and said, "The files are missing. We've searched everywhere. I don't think we will find them." He was angry. I could only think back to my first encounter with Judge Goldberg and our comments about who could be trusted.

Early during his tenure, President Jimmy Carter requested that the State Department provide him with a report citing all the promises the United States had made to all the parties regarding the territories Israel occupied in 1967. He received a lengthy report. The promises Goldberg made to the king as to whether Israel was "on board" were not included. Obviously, they never found the missing file. Equally obvious, some people in the U.S. government were only interested in adopting a Security Council resolution, not implementing it.

King Hussein summed up the problem as succinctly as anyone has in a speech before the UN General Assembly shortly after the 1967 War. "Israel can have territory or peace," he said. "But it can never have both." The king at first thought Resolution 242 was going to work. He thought he'd negotiated a good deal, and he thought that the United States would support it. But the U.S. position eroded. Immediately after the war, when U.S. officials were questioned at the UN, they said withdrawal included Jerusalem, which was part of the West Bank. But then Israel annexed Jerusalem, and slowly the United States reneged on that. American officials never said that they'd abandoned 242, but in defining it, they started calling the occupation an obstacle to peace, not terming it illegal. However, they still have to admit it's illegal. Under the Geneva Conventions, it's illegal. It's a violation of the rules of occupation. The World Court has ruled overwhelmingly that Israel's settlements are illegal and should be dismantled. You can't transport your people into their territory, and there's now a quarter of a million Israelis living on the West Bank, not counting Jerusalem. That's where it still stands. In the long run there were no winners—everyone lost.

As a footnote, Zaid Rifai, the king's private secretary, told me that upon his request, the king received a letter from President Johnson confirming the interpretation of the withdrawal clause in 242, in which Goldberg had recited "minor reciprocal border rectifications." I have never seen or heard any reference to such a letter. There is no record or mention of it in any of the official U.S. documents. But Rifai, who accompanied Hussein to New York and Washington in November 1967, would have been one person who would have known whether the king had received such a letter. The king had his own filing system, so the fact that the Jordanians cannot locate the letter is not extraordinary. There is, in any event, no doubt in Rifai's mind—or mine—about Goldberg's commitment and Katzenbach's confirmation.

Chapter 8

JOUSTING WITH THE SOVIETS, TALKING TO THE ISRAELIS

It dawned on me early in 1968 that the king was starting to give up on the United States. Despite the commitments we made just two months earlier in negotiating UN Security Council Resolution 242, we weren't acting on them. But what made him even angrier was the United States' unwillingness to replace the military equipment lost during the 1967 War, due to intense pressure from Israel and the American Jewish community against rearming any Arab state. The Jordan Army and Air Force had lost all of their equipment. They were without tanks or planes, and you couldn't have an army without tanks, or an air force without aircraft. As months passed, morale within the army plummeted dangerously. The bastion of the kingdom's security was on the verge of revolt and the king was losing his grip on this pillar of his support. The king was embarrassed. He had to get weapons. The U.S. Embassy in Amman was warning Washington that not only was Jordan facing a crisis, but the United States was losing a strategic ally. The argument fell on deaf ears.

Still, I was stunned a short while later when I learned that the king had secretly invited a high-level Soviet military delegation to Amman to negotiate a major arms deal. They would arrive in early January. I immediately informed Ambassador Harrison M. Symmes, the dean of the Arabists at the State Department. Stern and somewhat cold, he had replaced the likable Burns as ambassador in late November 1967, a difficult period in Jordan. Despite the negotiations at the United Nations, Israel and Jordan were still feuding over Israeli bombing of alleged terrorists in the Jordan Valley, whom Jordan claimed didn't exist. Jordan and the PLO were at loggerheads, a feud that would only intensify and come to threaten the king's hold on power in 1970. And the army, while lacking arms, was nonetheless unhappy with the king's failure to confront the PLO.

Symmes and I may have differed at times, but he was the boss and I never challenged him. On the Soviets we were in complete sync: a threat that could easily have derailed America's position in the Middle East. We quickly arranged to meet with the head of the army, General Amer Khammash, at his home. We finally located the king at Intelligence Headquarters, left a message with an aide that we would be with Khammash, and would like to see him.

Khammash was hardly comforting. The Soviets were coming, he said. The king was bitter. He was prepared to rearm the military with Soviet weapons. The big question for us at that moment was whether the king would go home when he left the headquarters or join us. A carload of staffers followed the king out of Intelligence Headquarters. They knew what the stakes were, too. There was an intersection ahead. To the left was the road to the king's home; to the right was Khammash's. It was a moment of truth. He turned right, thankfully. We weren't out of the game, at least not yet.

When the king arrived at Khammash's, he was as stern as I'd ever seen him. He hardly greeted us. He sat down, almost at attention, and asked Ambassador Symmes coldly what he wanted. The ambassador explained that he had just learned that the king had invited the Soviets to Jordan to negotiate an arms deal and he would like to discuss it. The king as much as said there was nothing to discuss.

The ambassador then gave the best presentation I have ever heard as to why Jordan should remain allied with the United States. He asked for patience; the arms would come. The Soviets were not the answer. When the ambassador finished, I thought he had convinced the king. Instead, the king said that he had heard all that before. The Soviets were coming and he was leaving. For one brief moment, my heart sank. Despite all our efforts over the years, Jordan was dumping the United States and joining the Soviets. I'm sure the ambassador felt the same way.

I hadn't said anything to the king, but I knew I couldn't let him leave without trying. He wasn't interested in arguments, so I made it personal. "I've known you for ten years and I've never asked you for anything," I said. "I'm asking for something now. Give us one more chance to resupply your forces before you go to the Soviets." It was a dirty trick. And for it, he gave me a piercing dirty look. But he knew that I had been very helpful to him, behind the scenes. I think he felt he owed me one, on a personal basis. And that's why he listened. He was honoring something.

The king said nothing but he took Khammash's arm and steered him into another room. Symmes and I sat back and waited, not knowing what was going to happen. The next thing we knew the prime minister, the head of the Royal Court, and other leaders of the government began to arrive and join the king and Khammash. Half an hour later, they left as quietly as they had come. Then, the king and Khammash rejoined us. Neither of them sat down. We stood up. The king addressed Khammash for our benefit. He said he was sending Khammash to Washington in three days with Jordan's military shopping list. If he didn't come back with approval for everything on the list, Khammash would lead the Jordanian delegation to Moscow. Then the king left.

I learned later that the prime minister had asked the Soviet ambassador to delay the Soviet military delegation's visit. I thought to myself how fortunes had shifted so rapidly. One minute the Soviet ambassador was dreaming of the medal he would have surely won, if Jordan had shifted to Soviet arms. The next minute, Symmes and I had lost Jordan to the Soviets, and probably our jobs. Then we won them both back.

General Khammash and I stayed up all of the next night drafting rebuttals to any argument policymakers back in Washington might muster for rejecting Jordan's arms requests. Then Khammash went off to Washington, met with McNamara, the secretary of defense, to make his case, and received approval for all the items on his shopping list. The fact that the king was prepared to turn to the Soviets was enough to trump the naysayers and the Washington bureaucrats, who often take friends for granted and tend toward arrogance in the exercise of power.

Even as we held off the Soviet military delegation, there was no denying that the Soviets' diplomatic and intelligence presence had increased dramatically during my years in Amman. We responded by going bug-crazy, placing listening devices in more Soviet satellite facilities than most places in the world. It was an easy environment in which to operate, and we took advantage of it. Some jobs, though, were more artful than others. I was walking home late one night with another officer from the station when we passed a duplex under construction. We knew a Soviet military intelligence officer would soon be moving in. There was a watchman, an older man, maybe seventy, by a gate out front. But we'd had a couple of drinks and couldn't pass up an opportunity to bug the place. The officer with me was fluent in Arabic and told the watchman he owned the property and would like to look around inside the compound. Once inside, we found a transom above the locked front door that was open. I pushed my colleague through and he unlocked the door. We knew the techs from

Athens had left lots of spare eavesdropping equipment back at the station. "Let's go get some," I said.

We walked back to the embassy, got a bug, and returned to the duplex. We installed the bug in a window frame without really knowing what we were doing, a real Rube Goldberg job. We were proud of ourselves, but not quite proud enough to report the bug to headquarters. When it came on the air, technicians listened in, but they couldn't hear very much, because there was so much outside noise coming through the window. I didn't think too much more about the bug until I was summoned a little while later by King Hussein.

"The Russian ambassador has just left the Foreign Ministry," he said. "He has just presented the Foreign Minister with some kind of mechanical contraption, which he said was found in the living room of a member of the Soviet Military Staff [the GRU chief]. He accused us of having bugged the officer's living room. The Foreign Minister told him, 'We don't do that sort of thing. It had to be the Americans or the British.' The Soviet ambassador replied, 'This is an amateur's job. This is not the Americans, or the British. This is you.'"

The king paused. "Jack, did you do that?"

"Yes, sir," I said.

"Why didn't you tell me?"

"I didn't think you'd want to know."

It wasn't a very suitable answer, but he never said any more about it.

A somewhat more successful operation involved our bugging of the Soviet ambassador's desk. My secretary was browsing one Friday at a shop that sold expensive furniture, artwork, fancy carpets, and pieces of jade. She saw an elaborate desk that was very beautiful and asked the proprietress whether it was for sale. She said yes, but it was already sold to the Soviet ambassador. His staff was going to pick it up on Monday morning and deliver it to the embassy. My secretary rushed back and told me what she'd stumbled upon. I immediately cabled Athens to send its top technicians and black-bag experts: We've got a job. They arrived the next morning. That night, they broke into the shop and inserted tiny listening devices into each of the desk's rear legs. They could be turned off and on remotely. After a quick test to make sure they were working, the CIA experts were gone. On Monday morning, we staked out the shop and watched the Soviets move the desk into the embassy. Where they were taking it soon became clear—the fancy desk, it turned out, was placed in the ambassador's office. So, we turned the microphones on, set up a listening post in a nearby house, and found that we had access to the Soviet ambassador's most intimate and sensitive conversations. The ambassador held most of his meetings there, including the morning embassy staff meetings at which he would tell them the latest news and what was on the day's agenda.

But about a month down the road, we heard the ambassador say that an audio sweep team was coming to town. We again tested the bugs but discovered we could only turn one of them off. When the sweep team arrived, we listened. They started going over the desk. When they turned on their receivers and channeled through various cycles, they caught the defective bug. We heard them narrowing the signal to the leg. We were hoping they might miss the bug in the other leg, which wasn't on. But they found that one, too. So we lost both bugs. We had it for a few months. It was one of the three Soviet bugs that we lost. Fortunately, there were others.

By the late 1960s, the KGB had developed a new class of agents who spoke English beautifully and fit in exceedingly well with Westerners. They knew all the latest dances, they were good-looking and usually had beautiful wives. We called them "the Golden Boys," real swingers. One of them, named Petrovsky, arrived in Amman with a blonde he said was his wife who was easily the best-looking diplomatic spouse in town. He was the first secretary in the Soviet

Embassy; that was his cover. He was related to the minister of health in the Soviet Union. He and his wife became part of a swinging group of young people in Jordan. They belonged to the few clubs that existed, raced cars, and went to all the right parties, including the king's. I didn't want to be part of that scene, and the king knew it, but I watched it closely. Soon, I thought Petrovsky was getting a little too close to the king. He and his "wife" were obviously sent out here to cultivate the king, and they had succeeded. This is dangerous, I thought. So after quite a wait, I went to see the king, and said, "Your Majesty, I've got to tell you something. You know Petrovsky and his wife?"

"Oh, yes."

"Do you know he's KGB, one of their Golden Boys? He's an intelligence officer, and his job is obviously to get as close to you as he can, to get as much as he can about what you think and do. And we're not even sure that his wife is his wife, they might just have paired them up for this purpose, and you're the target. And you've got a lot of other things on your mind. You might not have your guard up on this, or he might want to recruit people around you." I gave him my spiel and put him on the alert.

He nodded. Then he said, "Jack, instead of his recruiting me, I think he's courting me. He has just come back from a meeting of area KGB chiefs in Cairo, and gave me a rundown."

I said, "Really, what did he say?"

The king described the conversation. What Petrovsky told him was pretty general, so I don't think he was providing any intelligence. You have to give something to get something, and maybe this was just his way of ingratiating himself with the king, which is the way I saw it. The king saw it as a guy telling him things he shouldn't be telling him. Anyhow, I sent word of this back to Washington. But I put very high classification on it, so that it wouldn't be widely disseminated. And then I went on home leave. When I came back, Petrovsky was no longer there. I asked, "What's happened to Petrovsky?" I knew someone who lived on the same floor of his apartment building, and he said, "Jack, you wouldn't believe what happened. Some thugs came. Definite thugs. They said they were from Moscow. They ransacked his apartment, and shot his dog. They took Petrovsky out of the country, and he's gone. His wife was in Beirut shopping, and we understand that they grabbed her and took her back to Moscow." The Petrovskys had been kidnapped by their own service and taken back to Moscow. They didn't say good-bye to anybody or anything. The king said, "Jack, did you tell anyone what I told you?"

"Well, I told Washington on a very restricted basis," I allowed.

The king said, "The only person I told was my uncle, General Sharif Nasir, and he didn't tell anyone. I suspect some Soviet agent intercepted what you sent to Washington and Moscow overreacted by arresting the two suspects."

Neither the king nor I was sure Petrovsky had done anything wrong. Maybe he was just doing his job, and Moscow overreacted to what I wrote. The next time the king went to Moscow, he asked at a high level to see Petrovsky. They said they didn't know who he was talking about, but they'd find out. Nothing ever happened, and he never saw him.

I warned Washington about what had happened. "You've got a mole," I said. "Is there some way we could trace back who got the papers?" No, I was told that my report had gone out beyond the agency, making it hard to discern who might have had access to it. I said, "Well, let's look at it another way. It looks like all you have to do is write a negative thing about a Soviet intelligence officer who is in touch with us. We could send a report that he's told us a lot of things, send it off, mark where it went, and then watch this guy get in trouble, even though he doesn't belong in trouble, and they may come and get him. This way, we would be getting rid of their best officers by putting them under suspicion."

A colleague and I wanted this to be a program, but it never got off the ground. My concerns about a possible mole almost certainly would have ended up on the desk of Jim Angleton, the agency's obsessive (and some might say dangerously paranoid) chief of counterintelligence. But he never mentioned it to me, and I never knew whether a formal counterintelligence investigation had ever been opened on the incident.

I met with Angleton in the winter of 1968. After the Soviet arms crisis had passed, I was back in Washington on a two-week consultation at headquarters when I paid a courtesy call on him. Our paths were always crossing because of the other hat he wore, that of chief handler of the Israelis, a mission he guarded jealously.

In the course of our conversation, he told me I should talk King Hussein into meeting secretly with the Israelis to negotiate a separate peace. He said the Israelis told him they would give the king almost everything he wanted, if he would meet with them. I told him I doubted that, and with all due respect, I wouldn't even think of suggesting secret meetings to the king. He would be taking too great a risk. (I already knew he had been meeting secretly with the Israelis before the 1967 War, though I didn't know whether those meetings were still going on.)

Whereupon, Angleton picked up the phone, saying he was calling the Mossad chief at the Israeli Embassy in Washington. The chief was at a downtown spa. Angleton called the spa and the Mossad man came to the phone. I could picture him, dripping wet with a towel wrapped around his waist, wondering what the crisis was. "Our man from Jordan is here and I told him, if the King met secretly with you guys, you'd give him almost anything he wanted," Angleton said.

(Pause) "That's right. I just wanted to know if it was still on." He hung up and said, "See, the King should talk to them."

I repeated that this was not enough authority for me to suggest the king risk his life and kingdom in such an effort. Angleton asked, "How much authority would you need?" Hoping to close the matter forever, I said, "The President, and he would have to agree to support it, actively." We parted on that note. I thought it had been a little strange when he picked up the phone and called the Mossad chief at the spa. While he was very close to the Israelis, I didn't think his suggestion was part of some Israeli ploy. I thought he was probably pro-king, or at the very least not anti-king. I remembered how he'd wanted the king and Dayan to meet secretly after the war to negotiate a giveback of the West Bank.

While some people believe he practically ruined the agency by thinking everyone was a mole, I didn't mind dealing with Angleton, though I found him to be a suspicious character. He even looked suspicious. He wore a big black hat and black coat and looked almost sinister. So I wasn't going to take his suggestion about talks with the Israelis as the last word. At the time, I didn't find it strange that the agency's legendary mole hunter also managed the Israeli account as a personal, secretive fiefdom. Israel got special attention, from the president on down. They didn't want a bunch of Arabists in the same division where our dealings with Israel were going on, and I think the Israelis may have insisted Angleton be their point of contact. Israel is in the Middle East, it could be part of the Near East Division; but no, it's handled by the most secretive and most isolated group in the agency: counterintelligence.

A week after my meeting with Angleton, while consulting with the Jordan desk at headquarters, Jim Critchfield, the Near East Division chief, called and told me to meet him in front of the building, which I did. Angleton was also there. A car and driver were waiting. We all got in. I asked where we were going. Angleton replied, with a wicked grin: "The White House." I was impressed with Angleton's efficiency and power. I told him the king needed support from the president, and he called the White House and got an appointment. We ended up in the office of McGeorge Bundy, the national security adviser. He did all the talking. He said he had heard my conditions for suggesting that the king meet secretly with the Israelis to resolve their differences. He wanted me to know that he and President Johnson thought the Israeli offer was sincere and that it was in everyone's interest for the king to meet with them. I asked whether the president would support the king if he took this risk. Bundy said he had spoken to the president just before we arrived and he was prepared to give his support.

I told the group that on the basis of what I had heard, I would brief the king and relay the suggestion that he take up Israel's offer for secret talks. All smiled and we left.

I returned to Amman. The king was in Aqaba. I joined him there. At the first opportunity we walked to the beach and I told him the story. I said I could vouch for nothing, but we had gone to the top. He took it all in, but had no questions or comments, other than to thank me. I reported this to headquarters and never mentioned it to the king again.

In May 1968, the king and his private secretary, Zaid Rifai, met to brief me on a secret meeting they had with the Israeli foreign minister, Abba Eban, and Dr. Yaacov Herzog, the deputy director general of the Israeli Foreign Ministry, in London. Rifai had taken notes at the meeting, and at the king's request, gave me a copy to send to Washington. The conversation at the meeting had been in English, as were Rifai's notes.

The king said he wanted the president to know the results of the presidential suggestion that the king negotiate secretly with the Israelis and to provide the background, if the support the president promised was required. This was the first of over twenty reports on these meetings between May 1968 and the end of my tour of duty, the summer of 1971. I forwarded them "eyes-only" to CIA director Helms, who summarized them in "eyes-only" memos to President Johnson. My successor continued to receive the reports for another year.

The talks turned out to be a subterfuge by Israel to eliminate pressure from the United States, by claiming that progress was being made secretly with the king, without conceding anything to the Jordanians. The Israelis lured the king into negotiations by offering him "almost everything he wanted" in terms of territory. In the negotiations, the king constantly stuck to his guns on territory: the pre-1967 borders with "minor reciprocal border rectifications." This was the U.S. interpretation of the withdrawal clause of UNSC 242, regarding which Goldberg said Israel was "on board." The most the Israelis ever offered the Jordanians was the Allon Plan, which placed the Israeli Army along the Jordan River, which separates the East and West Banks of Jordan, splitting the country in half, with a bottleneck opening between the two, and ceding Jerusalem to Israel. The Israelis knew this was a non-starter, but it was part of the rhetorical game.

The Allon Plan was based on the Israeli contention that they needed to control the Jordan Valley militarily because it was a pathway to Israel for hostile forces. King Hussein contended that if Jordan and Israel were at peace, Jordan would not be a hostile force, and that, in any event, Jordan was no military match for Israel and did not pose a military threat. The Israelis argued that they were not concerned about Jordan's forces, but about Iraqi, Saudi, and other Arab forces who were stationed in Jordan or could come through Jordan on the way to Israel. The king said Jordan would ban foreign forces from Jordan as part of its peace agreement with Israel. Israel stuck to its contention.

King Hussein made sense. In addition, the Israeli premise was flawed. The U.S. Army conducted a study on the issue. It concluded that the Jordan Valley was not a pathway to Israel, but a "killing field" for any army attacking Israel through the Valley. The passageways were so structured that the attackers would be sitting ducks.

During his secret meetings with Israel, the king requested the president's intervention to help break the continuous deadlocks, as President Johnson had promised. But neither he nor President Nixon, who replaced him on January 20, 1969, responded or even replied to these requests. The secret talks served Israel's intended purpose: staving off for ten years peace negotiations regarding the West Bank and pressure from the United States. Israel missed its best opportunity for peace during the past forty-odd years. Jordan accomplished only one thing by talking: it reduced the possibility of further Israeli aggression.

Ironically, Israeli leaders most hostile to Hussein became his biggest fans after they met with him. He stuck to his guns in the talks. He would tell the Israelis, "You're supposed to get off the West Bank, with 'minor reciprocal border rectifications.' I have that from the American government. That's what I want." They would come up with all kinds of different schemes—the Allon Plan was one. But he was such a likable person, they all fell in love with him. Of course, right-wing Israelis don't want any moderate Arabs. That's their downfall. Arabs are terrorists, they're awful people, you can't make peace with them. But what happens when suddenly the Arab they're meeting with is friendly, honest, straightforward, and obviously not a terrorist. All he does is say nice things back while you're cursing him, and after a while all you do is look foolish, while he looks like a gentleman. And he was always a gentleman. He brings people up to his level. I mean, you just cannot dislike him.

Once, in May 1969, I received a call at home saying the king wanted me to go to Aqaba with him. I drove to the airport and found the king and his trusted aide, Zaid Rifai, on the tarmac. It was just the three of us. The king flew his own plane. Normally, we'd fly down to Aqaba for a meal at the king's vacation home. But when we arrived, there was no one there.

"Where is everyone?" I asked.

"We're going to a meeting," the king said. "The Israelis have decorated the old abandoned castle on Coral Island out in the bay."

I thought at first they wanted me to go with them. "I don't think I should go, do you? I mean, we don't want them to know we're doing this," I said, referring to our practice of sending notes from each meeting back to Helms in Washington.

"You're not going," the king said. "But nobody knows where we are, except you. So we want to be sure, if we don't come back, that somebody knows what happened."

He handed me a walkie-talkie. "You sit here on the sand dunes on the beach and wait for the boat to come back. Don't break radio silence unless you have to."

They motored out to the island on the king's 28-foot boat. I sat on the beach with a bottle of scotch from 8 p.m. until 1 in the morning, and waited, the only person in the world, other than the Israelis, who knew where the king of Jordan was. When they got back, they said they'd had a big dinner in a decorated banquet hall in the old castle. They said Golda Meir served the king. Abba Eban, Yigal Allon, and Yaacov Herzog were also there.

"It sounds like a party, not a business meeting," I said.

"We did have a good time," the king replied.

"Did you accomplish anything?"

"No," the king said. "Not really."

When I sent Rifai's minutes of the meeting back to Helms, I attached a covering memo in which I explained that the most precarious aspect of what I'd witnessed was not the king's clandestine meeting, but his 28-foot boat—the same boat that would be used to evacuate the royal family in the event of an emergency. I wasn't sure how far this vessel could get in rough weather. Helms, on his own, bought the king a secondhand, 50-foot yacht, and had it sailed to Aqaba as a gift.

Throughout this period, the Israelis would tell the Americans that they were meeting with the king and should be allowed to continue, uninterrupted. What they didn't know was that we knew they were stalling, because we were getting the minutes. Helms, in a memo to me in June 2001, when I first began work on this manuscript, wrote that he sent a memo to the president stating that the talks "had gotten nowhere and that, unless the U.S. intervened, further meetings would seem to be a waste of time." But it made no difference. Presidents Johnson and Nixon were indifferent. And there has been no apparent change in the White House attitude since then. The West Bank and Golan are still up for grabs and prospects for peace have sunk below the horizon.

For the risks the king took in this search for peace, he was betrayed by both the Israelis and the Americans. It was a price he paid to find out that the Israelis preferred land to peace and that the Americans didn't care which of the two the Israelis chose. In the king's mind, no good would come from this dilemma.

Two months after he helped turn back the Soviet arms delegation in early 1968, Ambassador Symmes recommended that the United States "stimulate a return to direct negotiations between Israel and Jordan," according to the State Department. But the king had a different impression of Symmes, whom he didn't see as a friend of Jordan's. It didn't help that Symmes was quoted all over town as saying, "Jordan had the West Bank for twenty years; what's wrong with Israel having it for the next twenty?" even if that wasn't what he was telling Washington. I liked most of the ambassadors I served with, and they seemed to like me. It was not a natural relationship. I was competition for them, as far as the State Department was concerned. But as far as they were concerned, I was working in their interests. Symmes was the only one I had trouble with, but there was no need for that—he simply misread my intentions. The king kept warning me that he was going to PNG Symmes—have him declared *persona non grata* and sent back to Washington. Symmes was often very stern in dealing with the Jordanians, more stern and callous than he realized. At one point, when he asked the king for an appointment, he was told to bring me to the meeting. The king and others in the palace told me they did this so I could see firsthand how the ambassador behaved. I had to admit they were right. He was not very friendly in his remarks or his demeanor. Still, I defended him whenever the king threatened to throw him out.

"He has an awkward way of questioning things," I said, "but it's more like he's playing devil's advocate. I see what he sends back to Washington, after meeting with you, and it's very well stated, and fairly stated, and he's supporting your position. He might not have done it at the meeting, but to Washington, he did. You're making a mistake kicking him out, and if you do, Washington will retaliate in some way that won't be helpful. Please don't kick him out."

The king relented, only to raise the issue again three months later after another Symmes insult. The straw that broke the camel's back came in April 1970, when a planned visit by Assistant Secretary of State Joe Sisco was canceled when he was already in the area, after Symmes told him that escalating tensions between the king and the Palestinian fedayeen, guerrilla fighters whose camps had proliferated in Jordan since the 1967 War, made it unsafe to come to Amman. The king had told Symmes to assure Sisco that the entire army would be there to protect him. When Sisco canceled, it was a slap in the face to the king. That's when I got the phone call.

"The Foreign Minister right now is PNGing your ambassador. I didn't tell you beforehand, because I didn't want to be talked out of it again," the king said. "This time he's going." The king told me the reason why, and away he went. Symmes arrived back in Washington, PNGed from a friendly country. Nobody had ever heard of such a thing before. He told people in the State Department that I was responsible for getting him kicked out.

Shortly thereafter, when I was back in Washington on consultation, Helms called me into his office.

"Jack, you're going to have to leave Jordan," he said.

"Why?"

"The State Department wants you out of there."

"They do?"

"Yes, they do," Helms insisted. "Jack, I'm not going to fight this battle for you, I have too many battles going on with the State Department as it is. I can't add this one."

"Do you mind if I be my own attorney on this one?" I asked.

"No, not at all," he said. "You make your case to the State Department. But I can't help you."

So I went over to the State Department and said I wanted to see Joe Sisco. My fellow negotiator from the fall of 1967 at the United Nations showed me into his office and sat down behind his desk.

"Joe, I understand from Helms that you want me out of Jordan," I said.

"That's right, Jack."

"Am I not doing a good job?" I asked.

"Oh no. You've just been there too long."

It went back and forth like this until I finally asked Sisco whether the real reason he wanted me out of Jordan was Harry Symmes's claim that I was responsible for getting him PNGed. Sisco admitted that it was.

"Well, I knew that, so I'm glad you told me the truth," I said. "You want to know something, Joe? The King wanted to kick him out nine months ago, and I talked the King into keeping him there, but he finally went over the brink. I couldn't keep him there any more. The King told me so. Now, if the King finds out that you have asked for me to be relieved because I'm responsible for Harry Symmes's demise, he probably will talk to the President about it. I don't know. But I'm sure he's not going to let this one pass, and I'm not either. You can try to get me out on whatever reason you want, but I'm not going out on a false charge."

Sisco didn't know any of this, and I assured him that the king would back me up.

"So at least you know the facts, because you've been dealing with a bunch of crap," I said.

"Okay, okay," Sisco said. "You can stay."

Chapter 9

SEPTEMBER 1970

By the summer of 1970, PLO militias had seized control of Amman. Unable to challenge Israel with raids from the West Bank, they had turned east, aiming to topple King Hussein and claim Jordan as their consolation prize. They assassinated the assistant U.S. military attaché at his front door in Amman with his family watching, kidnapped and terrorized my next-door neighbor, thinking he was me, and firebombed my house. There were roadblocks all over Amman that made even the most routine trip a harrowing adventure, and fedayeen guerrillas held forth at the Intercontinental Hotel as though it were part playground and part prison.

There had been no progress toward peace since the 1967 War, a period in which the PLO had grown substantially in size and power. About half of the population of Jordan was of Palestinian origin, so PLO chairman Yasser Arafat thought he had the ingredients for a successful insurgency. Ever the peacemaker, the king found himself in a familiar position: trapped. On one hand, he was left negotiating a series of cease-fires with Arafat. On the other, he tried to mollify his own army, which was furious over the way he had allowed the PLO to take over Amman. The king knew that if he went to war against the PLO, it would be Jordanians fighting Jordanians, and that would tear the country apart.

He wanted to avoid armed conflict if he could. He considered both the Palestinians and the East Jordanians members of the Jordan family, which he wanted to protect more than anything else. He feared the scars it would leave if the conflict was resolved by force, not negotiation. But his hope for a deal was unrealistic. It was wishful thinking on his part. That's the only way I can describe it. There was no way Arafat would make peace with him. It had been so easy taking over Amman, Arafat thought, why make peace with King Hussein?

With Ambassador Symmes PNGed in the spring and no new ambassador sent out to replace him, I was practically running the embassy. The families and non-essential embassy personnel were all gone. Katherine was in Beirut, where she enrolled our children, Kelly and Sean, in the American Community School and waited for things to calm down in the city that had been our home for seven years. I missed them, but it was good that they were gone. I was told by Jordanian intelligence that I was on the PLO hit list, a threat I took seriously after the assassination of the assistant military attaché. I moved out of my house as soon as an informant told me it was going to be firebombed. It was bombed the next day. Another group broke into the home of my neighbor, an officer in the Political Section of the embassy, who bore a slight physical resemblance to me. They accused him of being me, and interrogated him for two days, despite his protests that they had the wrong man. They ransacked his house, taking everything of value, including his car. He finally convinced his captors to call in the Arab neighbors to testify that he was not me. Only then was he released.

I moved everyone who was still left in Amman to the safest houses we could find, doubling and tripling up as necessary. After my house was firebombed, I rented the new, modern home of Saad Juma'a, the former prime minister who was serving as Jordan's ambassador to London. The few remaining people from the CIA station moved into that house, plus a mix of others. Sometimes an embassy officer would disappear for a day or more and we'd wonder what had happened to him. Either brave or foolish, they would accept dinner invitations in dangerous parts of town, trying to report what was going on. They were at the mercy of whoever wanted to do something to them. But they knew their way around and always seemed to make it back safely.

My temporary quarters were next to the mausoleumlike home of Sharif Nasir, the head of the army. The residence would later serve as home to the Jordanian Prime Ministry. Nasir was a good neighbor, but something of a liability, as it turned out. He was a PLO target. When the fighting started, they shelled his house. They weren't very good marksmen, so a lot of the shells hit the Jumma residence next door. Fortunately, it was made of one-foot blocks of stone. Even after a direct hit, the damage was usually no more than a chipped stone or two. The house was on the edge of town on the road that goes to Hummar, the suburb of Amman five or six miles outside of town where the king and all of the senior members of his government had taken up residence. That's where they spent the war. Every day, the king's trusted aide, Zaid Rifai, would drive from the king's quarters to my house. He often got shot at as he drove. We would exchange whatever we knew, and then away he would go again. I had walkie-talkie communications with the embassy, so I could report (in double talk) what I'd learned.

When I ventured out, I would often get shot at as well. One morning, I picked up the USAID director and started around one of the circles in Amman, on our way to the embassy. There were practically no other cars in sight, when all of a sudden we heard gunfire and felt bullets rake the car. I stepped hard on the gas pedal and speeded home. The army was nowhere in sight, and there were no policemen on the streets, only the fedayeen manning their roadblocks and stopping cars. They were rough-and-tumble guys, all with guns, all high as kites. They thought they owned the town, and they did. It wasn't safe to be on the streets. I told my contacts in Jordanian intelligence that my Chevrolet Sedan with diplomatic plates might as well have a bull's-eye on it and asked if they had something less conspicuous I could drive. They loaned me a Volkswagen. My driver had gone to Beirut with my family, so I drove myself around town.

When I was out in the VW, I would use an Irish passport and an alias. The PLO leaders knew I was the CIA station chief, but the guys at the roadblocks didn't. Needless to say, I had some interesting experiences. One time I was heading down a main road and slowed in traffic waiting to get through a roadblock up ahead. As a Westerner, I attracted somebody's attention. Two or three fedayeen fighters standing by the side of the road came over and asked me in English what my name was and where I was from. I had a bad feeling about them. I pretended I didn't speak English and jabbered at them in what I thought sounded like Russian.

"You don't speak English?" one of them asked.

"Ruskie, Ruskie, Ruskie," I said.

"Do you speak Arabic?"

"No," I said, shaking my head and motioning for them to follow me. I pulled out of the line of traffic and drove a block away down a side street to the Russian Embassy. They followed me in their jeep. I parked in front of the embassy, walked through the iron gate and up the stairs to the front door, where I rang the bell. They parked behind my car and waited. I waved to them. Finally, a clerk opened the door.

"Hi, how are you?" I asked the perplexed Russian.

"There are some people out there that I don't want to have anything to do with, so I came here to the Russian Embassy," I continued, stepping into the foyer and closing the door behind me.

"You don't want anything?" the Russian asked.

"No, but let's open the door a little bit to see if they've gone," I said after a few moments of silence.

The fedayeen had vanished, so I thanked the Russian, walked back down the path, got in my Volkswagen, and took off. If I hadn't made it to the Russian Embassy, I don't know what they would have done to me.

Despite this and other close calls, I was virtually alone in believing that the king and his army would ultimately prevail. The U.S. government was deeply divided. State was pessimistic. The agency was split between my views in Amman and the views of Bob Ames, a rising CIA star who was stationed in Beirut and in liaison with Arafat's intelligence chief, Ali Hassan Salameh. Ames and I were rivals. He was a big guy, dominant, impressive, and very smart. We respected each other and enjoyed exchanging views. We just disagreed about what was going to happen in Jordan. Few, including Ames, would have bet much money on King Hussein's survival in September 1970, an existential moment for him. Ames took the position that the Palestinians would win, but I explained in secret cables to Langley why I thought he was off base. First, he was misinterpreting his own personal experience with urban warfare in Aden, where the Yemeni insurgents had driven British troops from the port city in 1967. This was an example of what an urban militia could do to a regular army by fighting in irregular ways, and Ames thought the Jordanian Army would suffer the same problem as the British. But it was a false analogy. The British weren't from Aden, they were foreigners. For the Jordanian Army, Jordan was home. The second problem with Ames's argument stemmed from bad intelligence: Salameh, the PLO intelligence chief, was feeding him information about how they were winning the battle in Amman. If you were in Amman that summer and drove your car around, as I did, you would think the fedayeen were winning. But all you had to do was go to the edge of town, where the army units were. I had enough contacts to know they were furious with the PLO militias and couldn't wait to get into town and shoot these guys. Was the king going to lose the kingdom or keep it? Big question. How you answered depended on who you voted for. Kissinger ultimately voted for me.

At the CIA, there was a tragic postscript years later: Ames was among seventeen Americans killed in the 1983 terrorist bombing of the U.S. Embassy in Beirut. He had risen to senior status as one of the agency's top experts on the Middle East and was visiting the embassy when the bomb detonated, killing the Beirut station chief and his deputy. In all, seven CIA employees were killed in what was for years the largest single-day loss of life in the CIA's history. Salameh, Ames's secret source, had been assassinated five years earlier by Israeli intelligence for his role in the murder of eleven Israeli athletes at the 1972 Munich Olympics.

Even Jordanian intelligence was hedging its bets as the PLO tightened its grip on Amman at the beginning of September. Mudar Badran had replaced my friend Rasul as head of intelligence. One day, a Jordanian came to my house, said he was from the Mukhabarat— shorthand for Dairat al-Mukhabarat al-Ammah, the formal name of Jordan's intelligence agency—and told me Mr. Badran wanted the Volkswagen back.

"Could you give me the keys?" he said in English.

Badran took the Volkswagen because he knew, as we all did, that there was going to be a blowup, and somebody was going to win and somebody was going to lose. I was told by some of his staffers that he figured he didn't need any visible connection to CIA. Staffers also said Badran started removing files. They didn't know exactly what he was up to, but assumed he was covering tracks. If the opposition took over, he didn't want to be identified as one of the king's men and hanged.

Sharif Nasir, the head of the army, was at the opposite end of the spectrum. I'd met him in 1958 on my first assignment in Jordan, and he was the toughest guy I ever knew. Suffice it to say, he wasn't burning files at home. I'd see him take his morning walk through our neighborhood every day, even as the city fell apart. It was his daily constitutional, and I would always ask him how he thought things were going. A few days before the final attack, I stopped to chat with him outside the iron fence that surrounded my compound. He could see my poodle, Casey, and two offspring that we'd kept from a litter of nine, Clancy and Christy.

"You see those three black dogs in your front yard?" Nasir said. "If you painted gold stripes on them, some people might say they were tigers. But underneath, you and I would know they were only dogs."

He knew how badly his army units wanted to attack, and how heavily they outnumbered, and outgunned, the fedayeen. I sent his analogy to Washington as an intelligence report, figuring it was about as descriptive as anything I could write. At the time, I was virtually alone in predicting that the king and the Jordanian Army would prevail. John Law, the *U.S. News & World Report* representative in Beirut holed up in the Intercontinental, escaped for an hour one day in September to meet me at my home. We had known each other in Beirut. As a matter of practice and principle, I did not talk to the press; Law was an exception. I told him that the crackdown would start the next day. It would probably last two weeks. The king and the army would win and Law should leave immediately for Beirut.

Law said this was contrary to the consensus of the press at the hotel. I said I knew, but to take my advice. He did. He told me later he filed the story I gave him with *U.S. News & World Report* when he returned to Beirut, but the home office refused to publish it because it was so at odds with conventional wisdom. After a few days of heated argument on the phone, his magazine gave in and published his story.

He said it was the only major publication that had predicted the outcome accurately.

The new ambassador, Dean Brown, arrived the same evening, the day before the scheduled attack, on September 16. An embassy driver and the deputy chief of mission (DCM) brought the new ambassador from the Amman airport to the DCM's house. The ambassador's residence was located only a few blocks from the Intercontinental Hotel and was too dangerous to venture near. Since the crackdown would start early the next morning, we recommended the ambassador proceed to the embassy that night and stay there until the city was safe. He needed the embassy communications facilities and a boiled-down staff to keep in touch with Washington and to perform his official duties.

Ambassador Brown accepted our assessment and advice, and together with his baggage moved into the embassy that night. Several rooms had been fitted as bedrooms for the ambassador and the limited staff who were confined to the embassy.

The next morning dawned, and as the morning wore on, there was no army movement, no fighting, only silence. I called a palace contact to find out what was happening. I was told the attack was postponed by one day. I had to tell the ambassador, so I took the back streets to avoid the PLO roadblocks. When I entered the ambassador's office, he was standing behind his desk with a satirical grin on his face, as if to say, "CIA blew another one." Before he could unload, I said as quietly as I could that it had been postponed by a day. I suggested it would give the embassy time to get in more water and provisions and reduce their files. I didn't think he was interested in my suggestions, so I left. I didn't know why the attack had been postponed.

I found out later that the king called it off after his sister-in-law, Princess Firyal, went to a fortune-teller in London frequented by members of the Jordanian royal family. The princess, who had just returned to Amman, reported that the fortune-teller said tomorrow was a very bad day for the Hashemite Kingdom, but the day after would be a very good day. The king was enough of a believer not to take a chance. So he postponed the assault, but nobody knew why, because it was kind of embarrassing that a fortune-teller was a source of decision-making advice.

The next morning, September 17, 1970, the attack began. From my new home on top of one of Amman's seven hills, we had a front row seat to much of the battle. When the Jordanian Army moved in, the militias retreated to their strongholds. The army simply surrounded them and attacked. They knew where all the fedayeen were, they knew the houses they were in, they knew everything—they had a lot of intelligence. We could view army tanks driving down streets within the strongholds, systemically turning their cannons on each building as they passed, destroying all of them and the rebels inside. The militias fought hard. The battle lasted a week longer than predicted, but the outcome was never in doubt, except for two outside threats that could have affected the outcome.

Those threats came from Syria to the north and 25,000 Iraqi troops stationed in northeastern Jordan. Both governments supported the PLO, and if both had engaged fully on the PLO's side at the same time, Jordan would have had a difficult time defeating all three. The Syrians did attack, but as a result of the king's decisions and circumstances in Syria, the Jordanians eventually drove them back. On the other front the Jordanians outmaneuvered the Iraqis in a masterful intelligence operation. In the end, the kingdom survived. But it was through a series of events that were never fully reported.

Throughout the conflict, Henry Kissinger monitored developments at a command center in Washington. Kissinger, in turn, was in touch with Israel and the British. The British chief of station in

Amman had been farsighted enough to establish radio communications with King Hussein and the Jordanians in Hummar, while I was communicating with them via messenger (Zaid Rifai). The main question I received from the Jordanians during the conflict was whether the United States would intervene militarily to help if needed. I forwarded this to the embassy for an answer from Washington. Neither the embassy, nor I, nor the Jordanians, ever received one.

After the Syrians invaded Jordan on the ground with tanks (which had Palestinian Liberation Army labels), Jordan's requests to the United States became more strident. I learned later that Washington did not believe there was any practical way the United States could intervene militarily, which was probably true, and that it would have been against Jordan's political interest for it to do so, which was also probably true. But Washington was not willing to say so.

The Syrians were making serious advances in northern Jordan. The Jordanian commander deserted in the middle of battle. The king asked his friend Zia al Haq, the Pakistani general—who later became president of Pakistan, and who was in Jordan on a military mission— to travel to the Syrian front and telephone an assessment. Zia al Haq introduced the Jordanians to some American slang in his reply, which they did not understand and asked me to decipher. When Rifai asked Zia al Haq how things looked, he said, "I'm shitting green!" Translation: "Things are very bad."

While Nixon and Kissinger ruled out direct U.S. intervention, Kissinger asked the Israelis whether, if requested, they would attack the Syrian forces by air. The Israelis' reply was cagey. They said that an air attack alone would not be sufficient; they would have to invade by ground as well. The United States was alert enough to realize that once Israeli troops occupied that strategic ground, they would probably never leave. In any event, the king would never have approved Israeli ground troops in Jordan. He knew that Dayan, among others, had been very vocal that Israel should have taken the Jordan Heights during the 1967 War, and would not fumble a second opportunity. I asked people later whether the king would have wanted the Israelis to bomb Syria. Many of them said yes, if it would have saved the country. And if it didn't save the country, it would have probably destroyed the country. Fortunately, the Israelis did not intervene by ground or by air.

Instead, King Hussein made a tactical decision, against the analysis of all his advisers.

"I'm going to let the air force loose to stop the tanks," he said. "I don't care if we lose airplanes. Otherwise, we're going to lose the battle." Until then, neither the Syrian nor the Jordanian Air Force had been involved in the conflict. The Syrian Air Force was superior to Jordan's, so Jordan was fortunate that they were not involved. One reason Syria had not used its air force was because it was pretending, halfheartedly, that the forces that invaded Jordan were from the Palestinian Liberation Army, which did not have an air force. Jordan had not gone to the air for fear that Syria would retaliate and knock out all of Jordan's air force. But Jordan was losing the ground battle, so the king decided to go down swinging and ordered an air attack, which turned the tide and drove the Syrian forces back.

"I don't give a damn," the king said. "I'm going to do it."

His airplanes stopped the Syrian tanks, and the Syrians didn't do anything. They didn't come with their air force. The question is, why? The king couldn't have known this. It had been a real gamble on his part. But the reason is that Hafez al Assad, the future president of Syria, was head of the Syrian Air Force at the time. He was opposed to the government in power, under Salih Jadid, and against the invasion of Jordan. He refused to utilize the Syrian Air Force so that the government would fail and hopefully fall. Which is what happened. Assad headed the government that succeeded Jadid. The king's aggressiveness paid off.

The Iraqi troops, meanwhile, were immobilized by one of the cleverest and most complicated intelligence operations I've ever heard of, done by the best intelligence operator I know, General Abud Hassan. He was an Iraqi defector who flew a MiG out of Iraq and went to Jordan, where the king took him under his wing and made him head of the air force. For a brief period before he settled in Jordan, Abud joined a group of Iraqi Ba'ath leaders who escaped Iraq and were granted asylum in Egypt. Abud became Saddam Hussein's roommate and a favored friend for life.

Eventually, he became head of Jordan's Military Intelligence. Abud recruited a European military attaché assigned to Amman whose next assignment was NATO headquarters, he told me years later after we were both out of government service. The attaché provided Abud with the NATO plans for war in the Middle East. Abud doctored those plans to look like they were U.S. military plans for intervening on Jordan's behalf in a Middle East conflict. He then gave these doctored plans to an Iraqi double agent who went to Turkey and sold them to the Iraqi military attaché, who immediately sent them to Baghdad. The Iraqis believed that the plans were authentic. The 25,000 Iraqi troops, who came and went between the two countries so freely and roamed so widely that the Jordanians never knew how many were in Jordan and where all were located, quickly and quietly returned to their base in Zerka, a city situated between Amman and the Iraqi border, so they could make a quick exit if required. Then, with the final PLO-Jordan confrontation looming in Amman, Abud had the commander in chief of the Jordanian armed forces, General Zaid bin Shakir, call the Iraqi military attaché to his office for a meeting. As the attaché waited in a reception area, Abud joined him.

"You know," Abud allowed, "we have some disturbing news—that you have plans and are working with the PLO to get involved in this confrontation that's coming to a head here. We have your plans.

We know what you're planning to do. If you do it, we're going to cut your neck off."

Shaken by what he'd just been told, the Iraqi was ushered by Abud into General bin Shakir's office, only to return a few minutes later to deliver the coup de grâce.

"General," he told bin Shakir, "the advance American team has just landed and they want to come see you."

"Not now," bin Shakir said, silencing him. "We'll talk about that later."

The Iraqi attaché thought the phony American plan that Iraq had received from the double agent was in the process of implementation. He notified Baghdad promptly and ordered the Iraqi troops to move to positions closer to the Iraqi border, so the nonexistent American paratroopers could not cut them off from Iraq. Abud succeeded, through this grand deception, in paralyzing the Iraqis. I don't even think CIA knows about this. But Abud told me the whole story later.

If only the United States had been so clever. The truth of the matter is, the Americans sat on the sidelines during this crisis, talking mostly to themselves. Although President Nixon and Secretary of State Kissinger congratulated each other for saving Jordan, they never answered the king's request for military intervention, if needed, or took significant action. I've asked people around Kissinger what he did to save Jordan, and none of them can say anything. Please, tell me what you did, I would plead. Because we sat out there waiting for you to do something, and you didn't even answer our cables, much less do anything. Fortunately, Kissinger and Nixon didn't involve Israel. Although Nixon was emphatically against Israeli intervention, Kissinger was ambivalent and negotiated with the Israelis on possible involvement, contrary to Nixon's orders. They did move the Sixth Fleet to the eastern Mediterranean to counter moves by the Soviet Fleet. Nixon and Kissinger automatically viewed all Middle East crises through a "cold war" prism, even when it made no sense. Jordan won these 1970 battles all on its own—with assists from Hafez al Assad and an officer at NATO headquarters. As a result, King Hussein earned a boost in admiration and Jordan received an extension of U.S. largesse—until the next crisis.

Although Jordan's victory over the PLO forces was achieved in September 1970, it was not the end of the battles. The PLO, defeated, retreated to the Ajloun Forest in northwest Jordan, where they bivouacked. In the spring of 1971, the Jordan Army drove them out of there, and out of Jordan. They escaped to Lebanon.

In a tragic postscript to the PLO's conflict with Jordan in 1970, history repeated itself—only this time in Lebanon. The Lebanese government was hostile to the influx of militant Palestinians adding to the existing Palestinian population, but there was nothing it could do about it. The PLO took advantage of their new haven to rearm and reinforce their troops. They became a government-within-a-government in Lebanon. They also began mounting cross-border raids against Israel. But this time, Israel did not remain on the sidelines.

On June 6, 1982, Israel took a major military step to wipe out the PLO forces in Lebanon. Using the excuse of a failed assassination attempt against an Israeli diplomat in London as a phony cause célèbre for war, Israel invaded Lebanon. Menachem Begin was prime minister and Ariel Sharon was minister of defense, in charge of the operation. Israel planned a limited engagement; but Sharon exceeded his brief and drove all the way to Beirut, where he hoped to destroy the PLO, expel Syrian forces from Lebanon, and install a friendly Maronite government in Lebanon.

Sharon succeeded, in part. The United States appointed Philip Habib to negotiate a cease-fire and arrange for the evacuation of Arafat and what was left of his group to the faraway confines of Tunis, in August. Syrian troops were defeated but did not leave in toto. Bashir Gemayel, the newly elected Maronite president and Sharon's protégé, was assassinated on September 14 by pro-Syrian elements.

The tragic story ended a few days later when Gemayel's followers, with their Israeli allies standing by, entered the Palestinian refugee camps of Sabra and Shatila and massacred almost 1,000 Palestinian civilians.

Sharon was sanctioned by his own government for exceeding his military mission and for permitting the Sabra and Shatila massacres. Sharon outlived the government sanctions, to become Israel's prime minister, and won a libel suit against *Time* magazine for maligning him in its reporting on the case.

There has long been controversy over Sharon's role in those massacres. Many people believe he had more of a hand than he was willing to admit. Perhaps one day we'll get to the bottom of this, because the truth of what happened is important to Israelis and Palestinians alike.

After the fighting ended in Amman in the fall of 1970 and the PLO were driven into the forest, normalcy returned quickly to the capital. My family returned, and I assumed my role as a covert adviser to the king and members of his cabinet. After eight years in Jordan— far longer than a normal posting—I had almost become part of the government. Yet I sensed it was time for me to go home. My daughter, Kelly, was about to enter high school. I felt my work was done. I'd been through the 1967 War with Egypt and Israel, and the 1970 clash with the PLO. I didn't know what more could happen. I felt that the Hashemite rule had survived. The United States was supporting Jordan. It was time.

Chapter 10

BACK TO WASHINGTON,
BACK TO WAR

Our family barely knew the country we were coming home to in the summer of 1971. We'd missed the sixties, the Beatles, and much of the Vietnam War. Ike was president when we left for Beirut in 1960 with toddlers in tow. Now we were back, post-Kennedy and Johnson, with Nixon soon to fall. Allen Dulles had given way to John McCone, William Raborn, Jr., and, finally, my friend Dick Helms as director of Central Intelligence. I became acting chief of the Near East Division of the Directorate of Plans, soon to be renamed the Directorate of Operations. We bought a white brick house on Searl Terrace in Bethesda from a vice president at the Marriott Corporation who had the distinction of being the highest ranking executive not of the Marriott family. We also enrolled our children in schools as we became reacquainted with the United States and all of the hazards that imposed.

I had no idea what lay ahead. Before leaving Jordan, a doctor told us that Katherine needed to see a cardiologist as soon as we got home. Heart trouble ran in her family, and the doctor could tell there was a problem. I finally got her in to see the specialist, but she died of a heart attack on the couch in our living room in Bethesda, in my arms, a week before the appointment. The autopsy revealed there was nothing that could have been done to save her. I sent for our nanny from

Jordan. Kelly was in high school and Sean in sixth grade. They were a little old for that kind of care, but I needed someone in the house. So Mona Lahoud came over and spent a year and helped me get settled, and my mother moved in with us. That was another stabilizing factor.

I went immediately to see Helms and told him that acting chief of the Near East Division was a 24/7 job that I could no longer handle, with my wife gone and two teenage kids at home in an alien Washington suburb. I told him I was thinking about resigning from the agency and joining my brother's law firm, Connole & O'Connell. He asked me to go on leave of absence without pay instead, so that I could work with my brother until December 1972, when the job of legislative counsel to the CIA would open up.

"You've had operational experience, you're a lawyer, and you'd be an ideal person to represent us with Congress," Helms said. "You could talk to those guys in their own language, and you could educate them on our business. Your office is right there opposite mine, you'll have a car and a driver. Congress is not in session much of the year, so you won't have a lot to do when they're not here, and if Kelly and Sean have to go to the doctor, you'll have time to take them. It will be a good job for you, and for me and the agency, so why don't you do that?"

I agreed, welcoming the security. Connole & O'Connell, as it turned out, was an elite law firm of about twenty lawyers that specialized in oil and gas issues but also represented the National Football League. My brother, Quinn, represented the Alaska Pipeline, which was a huge client. He had also just won a big case between two oil companies and earned a big name in the oil industry for having done so because he wasn't supposed to. His partner, William R. Connole, was an early consumer advocate who served on the Federal Power Commission from 1955 to 1960. He became a legal authority in energy utilization and natural gas. His expertise, and my brother's,

made them and their partners the leading oil and natural gas law firm
in Washington. My first client was Jordan's Prince Hassan bin Talal,
the king's younger brother. As the king's closest adviser, he hired me
to represent Jordan's Office of Economic Planning, which he headed.
I soon got other wealthy clients from the Middle East who understood I was representing Jordan and wanted me to represent them on
their U.S. investments. The next thing you know, I had a number of
clients paying me sizable fees.

At the end of the summer, I went back to see Helms in his seventh-
floor office at headquarters in Langley. His deputy, Bill Colby, who
was both a friend, a neighbor, and the deputy director, happened to
be there. I told them I was quite enjoying practicing law, working
for myself and making more money than I made in the government.
Moreover, my retirement allowance was two thirds of my current
salary.

"Well, if you ever get tired of writing wills and signing contracts,
you've always got a job here," Helms said. Turning to Colby, he added
prophetically, "That is, if we're still here."

Nixon, reelected that fall in a landslide, summoned Helms to Camp
David on November 20 and fired him. Nixon had always distrusted
Helms, and held him responsible for not supporting the cover-up of
Watergate. Nixon appointed Helms ambassador to Iran as an act of
vengeance. The following day, Nixon handed the post of director
of Central Intelligence to James Schlesinger, whose marching orders
were to clean the house of Helms's men. Even had I wanted to return
to the agency as legislative counsel, Helms wouldn't have been there
to appoint me. And if he had, Schlesinger surely would have gotten
rid of me in his purge of Helms's lieutenants. So somebody was looking out for me during that episode.

Soon enough, the king hired me as his Washington attorney. He
wanted me to do a lot of things, beginning with drafting a foreign

investment law, which we did, and they soon enacted it in Jordan. They didn't have an Information Office in Washington and asked us to create one. They sent us a couple of people to work from our offices, with the idea of training them to become information officers. They wanted a lobbyist. We said we didn't do that sort of thing, but we hired a lobbying firm, Dennis Neal & Co., who shared offices with us and started lobbying for Jordan. We also hired a public relations firm, Deramus & Co., which they had us direct. They wanted to promote Jordan's airline and tourism, among other things. Then the king had an American friend, a former State Department protocol officer, whom he wanted to work for him. He had me hire him in my office to do personal things for the king. As a practical matter, I prepared position papers for the king and his aides and wrote the king's speeches in the United States. It was more than just legal work. But we did a lot of legal work, involving Westinghouse and other corporations engaged in major contracts with Jordan's armed forces, that needed both negotiations and litigation.

One of my first tasks for the king in the fall of 1972 was to buy a house in Washington for his wife, Princess Muna, and his two sons, Abdullah and Faisal, and his twin daughters, Aisha and Zein, whom he was moving from England because of concerns about their security. I asked him, "Do you care how big the house is, or where it's located?" He said, no, you decide all that. I found a house in Spring Valley, a nice part of northwest Washington, for $250,000. When the king arrived in Washington for a visit later that fall, he told me to meet him at Blair House one night and he would give me the money. After we greeted each other, I asked him one more time.

"Your Majesty, don't you want to see the house, doesn't somebody want to see this house, before I buy it?"

"No, I trust you. Go and buy it," he said. Before I left, I was handed a suitcase full of hundred-dollar bills.

"How much is in there?" I asked.

"Two hundred and fifty thousand," an aide said.

The next day, I went to the bank so that I could close the deal on the house. They had to take half the people in the bank to sit down and count the money. They hated me. But I eventually got a bank check for $250,000 and went to settlement. A week or two later, my secretary told me that there were two members of the Treasury Department to see me.

"What about?" I asked.

"They won't tell me."

"Okay, send them in."

The two Treasury agents came in and sat down in my office at 1100 Connecticut Avenue NW, a few blocks from the White House.

"Mr. O'Connell, did you buy a house in Spring Valley?" one of them asked.

"Yes, I did," I said.

"Was it for King Hussein's wife?"

"Yes."

"Where did you get the money?"

"I got it from the King."

"You know, it's counterfeit," he said.

"You're kidding me," I said.

Actually, they weren't. After carefully counting all of the money, they had determined that five of the hundred-dollar bills were fakes. I owed them $500, and wrote them a check. The next time I was in Jordan, I told the king and staff that $500 of the money they gave me to buy the house was counterfeit, and I had to pay it. I'm still waiting for my $500.

Around this same time, the king also asked that I find a home for him in the United States. I would send him pictures of homes on the market. Do you want a house in Hawaii? No, the king wanted to be in the Washington area. As with Muna's house, he wasn't interested in looking at pictures. "Just buy it," he said. I eventually paid $1.8 million for a beautiful home out on River Road in Potomac, Maryland. The king then bought a smaller house next door for staff. Queen Noor eventually sold both properties in 2001 to Daniel Snyder, the owner of the Washington Redskins.

When Princess Muna and her sons made the move, they were accompanied by my old secretary, Syble McKenzie. After I left Jordan, she had gone to work for the king. She was a CIA reports officer and had been involved in taking notes between the king and me. She wasn't due to return, and as I was leaving, the king wanted to know if he could have her as his secretary. As far as I was concerned, that was fine. When I asked if she wanted to be the king's secretary, she said yes. We got permission from Langley. Later, when he sent Muna and the children to Washington, he asked Syble to go with them and be a companion for Muna, who had never lived in the United States. So they all came. As it happened, the king divorced Muna at Christmas that year and married Princess Alia, the daughter of a Jordanian diplomat.

Beyond buying the house, my firm served as a conduit for about $800,000 a year that the CIA had agreed to pay for a security firm hired to protect the king's children in the United States a year after they arrived. The U.S. Secret Service initially provided their protection. But after a year, the Secret Service claimed it did not have the personnel or the financial resources to continue providing protection—an unwelcome precedent for other countries' leaders. The White House and the State Department were too embarrassed to tell the king that the United States was unable to protect his children, so they pressured CIA to pick up the tab, since they had unattributed funds they could draw upon. The agency agreed and paid my law firm the money, which I then passed on to local private security companies, one of which, ironically, was owned and operated by President Ford's son-in-law, an ex–Secret Service officer. The king never saw the money. But the payments were listed under the accounting for NOBEEF. That was the code name of the original operation through which the agency began its monthly 5,000 dinar payments to the king—$180,000 annually—back in the mid-1950s to help him pay his own intelligence agents before the Jordanian Intelligence Service was formed. It wouldn't take much for someone to look at the agency's books, see a total of $980,000 for the year ($180,000 plus $800,000), and assume the CIA had been paying the king almost $1 million a year for close to twenty years.

As I was buying the house and beginning a new career in Washington, Eugene W. Trone was also back in town, having just ended a CIA tour in Cairo. Trone was a dapper Princeton man who had done graduate work at the Sorbonne and Georgetown Law School. After Nasser broke diplomatic relations with the United States following Israel's invasion of Egypt in 1967, the Egyptian president told CIA he wanted to remain in contact through a CIA officer, who would remain in Cairo—in touch with the chief of Egyptian intelligence, Hafez Ismael. The agency appointed Trone, who worked out of the American Interests Section of the Spanish Embassy under diplomatic cover. He and Ismael met periodically, and Trone dutifully sent reports on their conversations to CIA headquarters, which forwarded copies to the State Department, the National Security Council, and the Pentagon.

According to Trone, CIA paid little heed to what he described as the Egyptians' growing disillusion with the Soviets, both under Nasser and, following his death in September 1970, his successor, Anwar Sadat. Ismael, who became Sadat's national security adviser, made it clear that Sadat was fed up with the Soviets, wanted to get out from under their thumb, and hoped to improve relations with the United States to help solve Egypt's problems with Israel.

Indeed, when Trone finished his tour in 1972, Kissinger asked Dick Helms if he could temporarily borrow Trone. Helms agreed, and Trone moved to Kissinger's office in the White House. Trone's work for Kissinger is little known, but Dick Helms referenced it in another of the memos he sent me in June 2001, without using Trone's name:

> In mid-1972, Kissinger asked Richard Helms, Director of Central Intelligence (DCI) to arrange a meeting with his Egyptian counterpart, Hafez Ismail, former chief of Egyptian Intelligence. The DCI ordered an agency officer, who knew Ismail, to make arrangements.

According to Trone, Kissinger debriefed him on all his conversations with Ismael and had him write up a report summarizing them. Kissinger believed there was enough of a window of opportunity to jump-start a moribund Middle East peace process. He asked Trone to arrange a meeting for him with Ismael, which took place at a rented mansion in Armonk, New York, on February 25 and 26, 1973. The site was near the White Plains hometown of Kissinger's social friend, Nancy Maginnes, so that he could be with her. They were married a year later. Kissinger was accompanied by two National Security Council colleagues, Peter Rodman and Hal Saunders. It was a get-acquainted meeting. Nothing important transpired except an agreement to meet again in France, where Kissinger was negotiating periodically with the North Vietnamese. Kissinger and Ismael met on May 20 at an old provincial farmhouse between Paris and Chartres. Given what Trone later would come to tell me about this encounter, I carefully read Kissinger's account in his memoir, *Years of Upheaval*. While Kissinger's betrayal of King Hussein is, in my opinion, undeniable, it is hard to argue with his assessment of the Hashemite monarch. Hussein, Kissinger writes, was trapped in the paradox that he was the Arab leader most ready to make peace, yet of all the territories it had conquered Israel was most reluctant to relinquish the Jordanian portion, which it most intimately connected with its own traditions. Israel's fundamental demand for direct negotiations was in fact granted by Hussein, yet it did not speed a settlement. And so Jordan remained suspended between contending forces. It made an enormous sacrifice for Arab nationalism, but it was assailed by the radicals then dominating the nationalist movement. In 1970 it was driven to suppress the Palestinian guerillas creating a state within a state on Jordanian territory, and yet did so while retaining its Arab vocation. It had grievances against Israel but did not want to engulf the area in a new conflict that might destroy those vestiges of moderation that were the essence of Hashemite rule.

Hussein's mastery of this challenge stamped him as a formidable personality. His legendary courtesy, which the uninitiated took for pliability, was a marvelous way to keep all the contending forces at arm's length. He was imperiled by the intransigence of Israel, the embrace of the West, the hegemonic aspirations of Egypt, and the revolutionary fervor of Syria and Iraq. He emerged as his own man. Hussein did not take refuge in blaming America for the humiliation of 1967. He did not break relations with us, as did several other Arab states, but he maintained his insistence on a solution just to the Arab cause—even the cause of those who sought to bring him down. [pp. 217–18]

During his farmhouse meeting with Ismael outside Paris, Kissinger writes, the Egyptian stood by the position he had enunciated earlier in Armonk and in subsequent exchanges—that Israel must agree to a return to its 1967 borders for Egypt to take part in another round of peace talks. "He pretended to take umbrage at my suggestion that

Egypt come up with something new to get the negotiating process started," Kissinger writes, noting that he "walked with Ismael in the garden in the spring sunshine." But by this point in the spring of 1973, Kissinger argues, Sadat had been planning to go to war for nearly a year, having decided that "a war was necessary before he could take the decisive steps to fuel the peace process with some genuine give-and-take." Ismael therefore knew what Sadat was planning, Kissinger adds, and "was enough imbued with the extraordinary humanity of the Egyptian to dread what reason told him was now inevitable. The Middle East was heading toward war. We did not know it. But he did."

How did Kissinger know Sadat had decided nearly a year earlier in 1972 to go to war with Israel? No one else in the U.S. government did. In fact, the attack in October 1973 surprised everyone, including Israel. One must conclude that Kissinger's prediction was self-serving—that the war was Sadat's idea, not Kissinger's. But, in any event, Sadat needed to know how the United States would react to an Egyptian attack before initiating it. After Chartres, via Israel from Kissinger, Sadat knew. Moreover, Kissinger's line that "the U.S. does not have a Middle East policy, it only deals in crisis management. To involve the U.S., you have to create a crisis" was a common rejoinder when the Arabs asked Kissinger to pressure Israel. He made the same statement to both King Hussein and Zaid Rifai on various occasions.

Actually, circumstances support Kissinger's key role. The Egyptian government made the formal decision to attack Israel in a secret high-level meeting in October 1973, five months after Chartres. Moreover, the farmhouse in Chartres was rented, staffed, and stocked for several days on the "assumption" that peace negotiations would last several days. But when Kissinger arrived, he stated he was only staying one day. The reason obviously was that he wasn't there to negotiate peace. He was there to tell the Egyptians they had to create a crisis, which would only take one meeting.

Hafez Ismael's reaction to the meeting—head in hands, crying by the side of a brook (confirmed by Kissinger, Trone, and photos)—was indicative of more than a routine exchange of views, and more like "spill some blood." If, as Kissinger contends, Egypt had decided to attack Israel as early as spring 1972, Hafez Ismael is not going to be traumatized if Kissinger suggests the same thing a year later. And he was traumatized. Logically, there was no 1972 Egyptian decision to go to war.

Although Trone and the State Department's Roy Atherton were present at the French farmhouse, Kissinger never mentions Trone by name in his memoir. But he includes the following anonymous reference to Trone: "The American official who had found the meeting place reported to me that after I left, Ismael, visibly dispirited and glum, had sat alone in the garden for a long time contemplating the waterfall behind the house, head cupped in hands."

What makes Kissinger's account particularly fascinating to me is that Trone's version is completely different. Trone, an Arabist who favored bow ties, collected antiques, and restored Civil War–era homes around Washington as a hobby, retired early because of what he thought was an ill-advised tilt toward Israel in U.S. foreign policy. As I practiced law, he became a Washington-based consultant for several corporations doing business in the Middle East. It was at one of our many meetings around town that he gave me his account of Kissinger's meeting with Ismael. Trone was very reluctant to tell me this story—very concerned over what I was going to do with it. I told him I might include it in a book I planned to write.

Trone told me that during the meeting he remained in the garden outside. When Ismael met him there, he was visibly shaken.

Trone recalled him saying, "Gene, do you know what Kissinger told me? 'If you want us to intervene with Israel, you'll have to create a crisis. We only deal in crisis management. You'll have to "spill some blood." He wants us to start a war with Israel.' " Trone remembered Ismael as more than "dispirited and glum." He was so distraught, Trone said, that he sat by a stream beyond the garden and wept.

I had trouble with Trone's story from the first time I heard it, not because I thought he was prevaricating, but I could not believe Kissinger would make such statements in front of Atherton and Ismael's Egyptian aides. They were outrageous statements, and bound to leak. I focused on this for some time, questioning those who had heard firsthand accounts of the meeting, or read the minutes, which made no mention of spilling blood. But after I gained access to photos taken at the meeting showing Kissinger and Ismael walking together in the garden, my doubts disappeared. Kissinger took Ismael aside, put his arm around his shoulder, and told him things no one else heard. Trone died at seventy-seven in November 2001, after accidentally falling from the roof of his home. Ismael is also dead. We can never have a complete account of what was said at the meeting. But whatever words were spoken, I am convinced the Egyptians came away with the understanding that they had to go to war for the Americans to become involved in making peace.

It is reasonable to assume that Sadat, whenever he may have begun planning a military invasion, was influenced by Kissinger's words to Ismael. Ultimately, he enlisted Syria's president, Hafez al Assad, to join in the attack. But Sadat and Assad were fighting for different ends. For Sadat, this was a war of limited ambition, designed not to recover territory but to reclaim Arab pride and switch patrons, dumping Moscow so that it could pursue redress of its grievances through a new diplomatic process sponsored by Washington. He never made this clear to Assad, who was fighting for more conventional purposes—reclaiming the Golan Heights, lost in the 1967 War. Assad knew nothing of Kissinger's talks earlier in the year with Ismael. Nor did he realize that Sadat's forces, once they advanced across the heavily fortified

Suez Canal, would dig in short of the strategic Mitla Pass, allowing Israel to concentrate its forces against Syria in the Golan, mount a counterattack, and drive deep into Syria. When Sadat stopped shy of the Mitla Pass, Assad was furious about Sadat's blatant betrayal—and never forgave him. As a result of Sadat's refusal to remain on the offensive after his successes during the first three days of the war, Israel was able to turn the battle around.

The Egyptian and Syrian preparations for war were so perfectly camouflaged that no intelligence service in the world, Israeli, U.S., Soviet, or British, was aware of it, except for Jordan—and it wasn't sure. The Egyptians and Syrians were aided by the fact that no one believed they would be foolish enough to initiate a war against vastly superior Israeli forces.

In early 1973, Jordanian Military Intelligence began receiving information from a disaffected senior Syrian Army officer that Syria was preparing to invade Israel, in conjunction with Egypt, but he had no details about Egyptian preparations. The information was volunteered through a Syrian civilian cut-out to the director of Jordan's Military Intelligence, General Abud Hassan, who had so brilliantly used the Iraqi double agent to bluff Baghdad out of intervening in September 1970. The source neither asked for money nor was he offered any by the Jordanians. He was allegedly opposed to the Syrian regime and to the planned war. Jordan had no basis on which to cross-check the source's story. It was either important information affecting Jordan's security or a massive deception operation by Syria, though for what purpose Hassan could not fathom.

Hassan finally smuggled the source into Jordan to debrief him, exhaustively. The source was completely cooperative; he drew maps and wrote down details of the plan. At the end, General Hassan believed that the information he was producing was true. But no one else did, and the king was not persuaded.

However, even for the king, the information so directly affected Jordan's security that he could not disregard it, however preposterous.

In one effort to determine the truth, the king decided to go to Israel on a fishing expedition. Surely, if Egypt and Syria were preparing for war, Israeli intelligence would have some clues. He flew secretly to Israel with a few of his aides. They met with Prime Minister Golda Meir and Israeli intelligence officers but picked up nothing about a planned attack by Egypt and Syria. The Jordanians were relieved. The king was now more persuaded than ever that the Military Intelligence reports were not true. General Hassan, however, was still convinced that the information was valid.

During this period, Jordan's diplomatic relations with Syria and Egypt remained broken over its expulsion of the Palestinian fedayeen in the fall of 1970. Syria and Egypt had wanted Jordan to allow the fedayeen back into the country before normalizing relations, a move Hussein had long resisted. But as a matter of policy and practice, the king did not believe Jordan could afford to be isolated in the event of area hostilities involving Israel. He sent Zaid Rifai, who was his political adviser at the time, on secret missions to Damascus and Cairo to sound out Presidents Hafez al Assad and Anwar Sadat on restoring relations. Assad was noncommittal. Sadat was agreeable and invited the king to join him and Assad, who were about to confer in Cairo on September 10–12, 1973. The king joined them, and was surprised at how convivial they were toward him. Sadat restored relations on the spot. After returning to Damascus, Assad did so as well.

During the course of the three days they spent together, King Hussein did not detect the slightest inkling that either was planning an imminent war. He returned more convinced than ever that General Hassan's war story was not true. General Hassan remained just as convinced that it was.

According to General Hassan, a few weeks before the October

War, Henry Kissinger visited the king in Aqaba. There is no record
or other mention of the visit, so it must have been a secret. During the
meeting the king, almost mockingly, asked Hassan to tell Kissinger
his "Syrian war story." Hassan gave Kissinger an account of the Syrian source's information. According to Hassan, Kissinger was totally
disinterested, asked no questions, and made no comments.

There are a number of mysterious aspects to this episode. Kissinger
had to be interested in a war about which he had intimate knowledge.
His disinterest had to be feigned. Why was Kissinger secretly visiting
Jordan? Hassan does not remember the purpose of the visit. Perhaps,
it was to obscure his real purpose for visiting the region—a secret
meeting with Sadat in Sharm al Sheikh, which is only twenty minutes away by air. It is doubtful Kissinger would have been in the area
without meeting Sadat. When I learned of the meeting in Aqaba after
the war, I asked Hal Saunders, who was assistant secretary for the
Middle East during this period, whether Kissinger had ever reported
the briefing he received from Hassan. Saunders replied that he had
never heard the story before and that Kissinger seemed as surprised
as anyone when war broke out. Saunders added that the only mention
of a possible war was a solitary CIA report which no one believed.

It so happened that on a visit to Washington shortly before the
war, in a meeting with the deputy director of CIA, General Vernon
Walters, Hassan attempted to corroborate his "Syrian war story," but
Walters said the agency had no information. Walters did publish a
report based on Hassan's information, but no one paid any attention
to it, as Saunders mentioned. The only purpose the CIA report served
was, inadvertently, to save the agency's neck when postwar blame for
the intelligence failure was being assigned.

On October 4, 1973, Hassan told King Hussein the war would
commence the next day. When nothing happened, the king was even
more convinced that the "war story" was a hoax. Later, Hassan called

the king to tell him the Syrian attack had been delayed by one day. The following day, October 6, 1973—the Jewish holy day of Yom Kippur, the Day of Atonement—Syria and Egypt attacked Israeli positions in a quest to recapture land lost in the 1967 War, launching a military campaign that raged for twenty days before a cease-fire went into effect. Egypt unleashed a relentless artillery barrage and sent two hundred combat aircraft to bomb Israeli positions on the east side of the Suez Canal. Syria sent 28,000 troops and 800 tanks into the Golan Heights.

During the first days, both the Egyptian and Syrian armies were advancing, and the Israelis, completely surprised, were at real risk of losing the war. They needed an immediate supply of arms and ammunition from the United States. Perhaps Kissinger personally took charge of making sure the Israelis received the arms they needed, overruling the Pentagon, calling U.S. Army supply depots and Pentagon suppliers, commandeering military transport planes, and leasing commercial aircraft. Kissinger's office was essentially the command center, and he was commander in chief. President Nixon was on vacation in Florida, where Kissinger urged him to stay.

After halting a belated Egyptian thrust toward the Giddi and Mitla passes, the Israelis counterattacked on October 16, crossing the Suez Canal and surrounding Egyptian troops on the canal's west bank. King Hussein, having fended off Egyptian and Syrian requests to enter the war against the Israelis after it started, faced even more pressure now to commit his forces. Sensing this, Kissinger wrote to the king on October 19 and told him that a cease-fire was near. He promised that Jordan's interest in the return of the West Bank, "which you so eloquently explained to me," would be fully protected, according to State Department papers. "I give you a formal assurance to this effect."

In the end, Kissinger arranged a cease-fire on October 22 to protect the Egyptians. Israel lost more than 2,600 soldiers, with three times that many wounded. The Israeli Defense Forces lost at least 400 tanks and between 100 and 200 aircraft. Egypt and Syria are estimated to have lost more than 8,000 soldiers, with more than 19,000 wounded. Together, Egypt and Syria lost 1,200 tanks and close to 400 aircraft. Neither Egypt nor Syria recovered the territory they had lost in 1967, but their forces fought harder and performed better than Israel or Western analysts had forecast. Israel remained in control of the Sinai and the Golan Heights, but its air of invincibility was gone, and the military equation in the Middle East was altered, giving Kissinger an opening to orchestrate a peace plan that had eluded Israel, Egypt, Syria, Jordan—and the United States—since 1967.

King Hussein emerged from the war with his forces, and Jordan's relations, intact. Jordan had sent a brigade to engage in the fighting on Syria's behalf, but it purposefully did not become seriously involved to avoid the kind of overcommitment of forces that had been so disastrous in 1967. They shot a few shells, but the Israelis never treated it seriously. Although the Egyptians and Syrians had kept this war secret from the Jordanians, they were asking for Jordan's help in the end. The king and Zaid Rifai played it very skillfully and never got trapped into becoming a major combatant. Given Kissinger's assurance that Jordan's claim to the West Bank would be addressed in peace talks, the Jordanians were optimistic in the war's immediate aftermath.

In his memoir, Kissinger describes a stopover in Amman on November 8 during his first trip to the Middle East after the war. King Hussein raised the West Bank issue as well as his belief that Jordan, not the PLO, should act as the official representative of the Palestinians on the West Bank. Kissinger responded, he writes, that the disengagement of Israeli, Egyptian, and Syrian forces was the top priority, and that Jordan's best move would be serving as a sponsor of the upcoming Geneva Conference, which would make it the representative of the Palestinians. To my knowledge, he did not tell the king, as he would later write in his memoir, that Israel's lack of interest, Nixon's distraction with Watergate, and the "passions fueled by radicals" in the Arab world made dealing with the West Bank completely impractical. "It was a great pity," he writes.

But if you go back to the secret talks at Chartres between Kissinger and his Egyptian counterpart, Hafez Ismael, Kissinger had achieved what he wanted: a crisis he could manage. Soon enough, he convened the Geneva Conference, with an unwitting Soviet co-sponsor, under nominal UN Security Council sponsorship, to implement UNSC Resolution 338, a repeat of UNSC Resolution 242, calling for a comprehensive Middle East peace. Israel, Egypt, Jordan, and Syria, the occupier and the occupied, were invited. Syria stayed home. It turned out the purpose was not a comprehensive peace; it was peace between Israel and Egypt. The only accomplishment of the first meeting of the conference was to establish an Israeli–Egypt–U.S. working group to negotiate Israel's withdrawal from Egypt. The conference never convened again. Jordan was the big loser, betrayed by both Kissinger and Sadat. In negotiating an Israeli withdrawal plan for the West Bank, Kissinger, serving as the middleman, once again offered Jordan the Allon Plan. It placed Israeli troops along the Jordan River, cutting Jordan in half, except for a bottleneck opening to the West Bank, and ceded Jerusalem to Israel. When Jordan accepted this as the first step of an Israeli withdrawal plan, Kissinger countered by saying that it was not a step, it was the final settlement offer, reneging on all the territorial promises the United States had made to Jordan since the 1967 War.

Later in the year, as an Arab conference at Rabat approached, the king told Kissinger during a meeting in Amman that unless he could get some kind of concession from the Israelis—similar to the latest Israeli withdrawal from Egyptian territory—the United States and Israel would soon find themselves negotiating over the West Bank with the PLO, not with Jordan. The king suggested a partial Israeli withdrawal to the West Bank town of Jericho. Kissinger told the king not to worry, the Arabs would be with him at Rabat. The Moroccans and the Saudis are going to lead the march for you, Kissinger said.

" 'I've talked to them,' " the king remembered him saying.

I visited Jordan right after Kissinger left. The Jordanians, including the king, were gathered around Zaid Rifai's swimming pool, celebrating the fact that they would be in Jericho by Christmas. Kissinger had led them to believe he was going to meet with Sadat in Alexandria and clear the withdrawal to Jericho with him. We now know he didn't clear it with Sadat. On the contrary, Sadat didn't want any withdrawals from Jordan to interrupt the withdrawals from Egypt. That was all he was interested in. And Kissinger's reading of the other Arabs was absolutely wrong.

I don't know whether Kissinger talked to the Moroccans and the Saudis or not, or whether they told him they would be supporting Jordan, but that's not what they did. At Rabat, the Moroccans and the Saudis, and all the other Arab countries, voted for the PLO, not Jordan, to be the sole representative of the Palestinian people, even though the king had done far more for the Palestinians than any other Arab leader.

Kissinger comes close to acknowledging this betrayal of King Hussein in his memoir when he explains how, in the summer of 1974, he favored addressing the West Bank issue that Jordan had been pressing with the Israelis since 1967. This would also head off a move by the PLO to represent the Palestinians. But the Israelis were not willing to give up the West Bank, Nixon was about to resign from office, and Sadat deeply distrusted the king and was opposed to bringing Jordan into the peace process. So, Kissinger admits to playing for time: "It is a course I have rarely adopted and usually resist intellectually. Circumstance is neutral; by itself it imprisons more frequently than it helps. A statesman who cannot shape events will soon be engulfed by them; he will be thrown on the defensive, wrestling with tactics instead of advancing his purpose. And that is exactly what happened on the Palestinian question.

"When the PLO was designated the sole representative of the West Bank at Rabat," Kissinger writes, "the Israeli dilemma and the Palestinian negotiating stalemate that I predicted—and did not head off—both became inevitable. They have not been resolved to this day." [p. 1141]

Overall, Kissinger outdid Machiavelli. He took a moribund peace process and turned it into a peace triumph between two major Middle East adversaries, removing the only real Arab threat to Israel. Realistically, it is a price Israel should have been willing to pay. Emotionally, it may not have been.

Chapter 11

FROM WASHINGTON
TO CAMP DAVID

By the end of 1974, I was starting to realize that I'd left CIA just before its most turbulent years were to begin. It all commenced with an article in the *New York Times* by Seymour Hersh in late December that described CIA's involvement in a domestic spying operation aimed at antiwar groups and other dissidents, in direct violation of the agency's charter. Hersh reported that the domestic spying was carried out at the behest of the Nixon White House by Angleton's counterintelligence staff. Hersh's findings led Bill Colby, who had replaced James Schlesinger as director of Central Intelligence in September 1973, to fire Angleton. This would finally end Angleton's long and deeply controversial career at CIA running counterintelligence and handling the Israelis.

Earlier in 1974, my old friend and Notre Dame classmate Jim Burke, who had served with me in Beirut, was brought in to help pass judgment on Angleton, whose paranoia about a Soviet mole inside CIA had careened out of control a year earlier. Angleton had appointed a protégé, Clare Edward Petty, to head a search for the mole. Petty subsequently concluded with 80–85 percent probability that Angleton himself was the mole. Burke, with his background in counterintelligence, was asked to assess Petty's findings. He debriefed Petty, a meticulous researcher, for hours, and summarized his findings for

Colby and other senior officials. Colby rejected Petty's work as utter nonsense. I was busy practicing law by this point and wasn't following any of this very closely. I remember talking to Burke about it a couple of times, but he didn't want to talk too much about the Angleton matter, even to me.

The Hersh article that led to Angleton's firing also helped trigger the formation of the Church Committee in 1975. Headed by Senator Frank Church, an Idaho Democrat, the Senate committee investigated intelligence operations by the CIA and FBI and released fourteen reports in 1975 and 1976, covering covert action, domestic spying, and CIA assassination plots against Patrice Lumumba of the Congo, Cuba's Fidel Castro, the Dominican Republic's Rafael Trujillo, and South Vietnam's Diem brothers. I was curious about all these strange things the committee was digging up. Earlier in my career, of course, I'd seen CIA covert operators who were reckless and without control, most notably Bill Eveland, the man I'd first encountered back in 1958 as he dazzled a ballroom full of diplomats at the Waldorf-Astoria. By this period in the 1970s, Eveland was still gallivanting around the world as a corporate executive, though with him appearances were always deceptive. I remember bumping into him around this time at a hotel, the Phoenicia, in Beirut. We shook hands in the lobby, and I suggested we go to the bar for a drink. I asked him what he was doing, and he told me he had left CIA and was in business, heading for the Far East. He was doing well, he said, everything was fine. The next day, the hotel manager, whom I'd known for a long time, approached me in the lobby.

"May I have a word with you?" he asked discreetly. "I saw you with Mr. Eveland last evening."

"Yes," I said.

"Where was he going, do you know?"

"He said he was going to the Far East. Why?"

"He left this morning without checking out," the manager confided. "His room was empty, his clothes are gone, and he's gone, and he didn't pay his bill."

"It seems strange to me that he wouldn't pay his bill," I said. "I got the impression that he was doing well."

Only recently did I find an article that said he had tangled with heavyweights in international business and ended up penniless in a Singapore hotel in 1976. He'd met his match, apparently. But Eveland was indefatigable. He resurfaced and made headlines in 1980, publishing a controversial memoir, *Ropes of Sand*, after refusing the CIA's demand that he submit to censorship. He died in 1990 after a long bout with cancer, still working on a new book.

The Church Committee, in any event, had a field day exposing the exploits of the agency's early operatives cut from the same cloth. But as much as I'd seen Eveland in action back in the Beirut station, I found the committee's reporting hard to take seriously. Since Beirut, I had headed the Amman station for eight years, visited many others, and spent I don't know how many years at headquarters up and down the halls talking every day to people involved with operations all over the world, and I had never run into anybody who knew anything or held a discussion about any of the things that the Church Committee was talking about. I knew the Bay of Pigs, and was certain that most of the people I knew purposely didn't have anything to do with it, including Dick Helms. The botched invasion of Cuba in April 1961 by a band of Cuban exiles organized by CIA led a bunch of us inside the agency to conclude that the only way you could pursue effective military action was with the U.S. Army and the other military services. They were the only ones with the training, the equipment, and the manpower to conduct such operations. The agency wasn't equipped to do that. We were trying to invade Cuba and topple Fidel Castro covertly, so we couldn't use the Army to do it. If the Army does it, you can't keep it a secret, and if the Army doesn't do it, it can't be done covertly, because nobody else has the resources. So the whole thing is a mistake, and we should not get involved. That's what's wrong with a lot of what we're doing now.

So I didn't take the Church Committee's exposés all that seriously. I thought somebody was out to get the agency by focusing on sensational assassination attempts and failed covert actions that were far from mainstream CIA operations. I didn't disbelieve what the committee was exposing. The committee was just being extremely selective, and exposing only a tiny fraction of what the agency did. And I had a good example. They raised the payments to King Hussein and didn't differentiate between the $15,000 a month we had been paying him since 1957 to support intelligence operations, and the $800,000 we started paying to protect his children beginning in 1972. I assumed, if their facts were that sloppy on everything, this wasn't a very solid investigation. The committee's members were grandstanding and cherry-picking.

I know Dick Helms felt that Bill Colby badly damaged the agency by giving the committee the "family jewels," the 700-page dossier compiled by his predecessor, James Schlesinger, on activities that may have gone beyond the agency's charter. I felt the same as Helms. Once you give that kind of sensitive operational detail to Congress, you've lost the secrecy that's required to operate effectively. We've never operated effectively since. Nobody else in the world has as many people talking about their intelligence service, writing about it, overseeing it, as we do. Until recently, no one even knew who the head of British intelligence was—and that's the way it should be. You shouldn't have oversight committees. CIA should be the president's private, personal organization. There's a trade-off between secrecy and accountability. You have to have some trust somewhere, and the trust here is with the president. Helms felt that Colby made the mistake of thinking that if he did a favor for Congress, then Congress would do a favor for him.

That's not the way Congress works. Colby was naive enough to think that it did, and now they've taken over. It's all about power. Oversight's a nice word, but it's about power and control.

I knew firsthand how powerful—and unpredictable—certain members of the House and Senate could be. Take Senator Stuart Symington, a Missouri Democrat who served in the Senate from 1953 to 1976. I met him in roundabout fashion, as often happens in Washington, through John Horton, a public relations executive who was working to develop a campaign for promoting investments in Jordan, and, specifically, for the Royal Jordanian Airline. John was married to Drucie Snyder, whose father was John W. Snyder, Truman's Treasury secretary and also a Missourian. I was with John Horton and Secretary Snyder one evening and I brought up the problem Jordan was facing with Congress in 1975 in trying to obtain a $350 million air defense system made up of Hawk antiaircraft missiles, which the Jordanians felt were necessary to prevent against incursions by Israel or Syria. Secretary Snyder suggested I brief Symington, who specialized in military affairs and had been the first secretary of the U.S. Air Force from 1947 to 1950. He just happened to be the swing vote on the Senate Foreign Relations Committee, which was deadlocked over the sale of Hawks to Jordan. A few days later, the former Treasury secretary took me up to Capitol Hill for a meeting with his friend Symington.

I briefed the senator, and he told me I made a good case. He called in an aide and asked him how many telegrams the office had received from constituents in Missouri favoring and opposing the Hawk sale to Jordan. Symington knew the answer before he asked the question. The aide returned in a few minutes and said there were five in support and over four hundred opposed. The senator, confirming that he'd known the answer all along, then told me that most of those opposed were Jewish and among his largest campaign donors. Despite this, he said, he was going to vote for Jordan. He said he thought King

Hussein was a good friend of the United States, that he needed our help, and was not a threat to Israel.

"But do you know what this means?" he asked. "It means I am going to have to write over four hundred letters to all those constituents who opposed the sale and explain to them why I voted against their wishes."

Symington, a politician of considerable backbone who had stood up to Senator Joseph McCarthy in the 1950s and become an ardent opponent of the Vietnam War in the 1960s, had developed a reputation as a stickler for constituent service. He believed in answering letters and calls from the Missourians he represented, so he wasn't kidding about writing over four hundred letters to those opposed to Jordan's need for new military hardware.

"You should know, Mr. O'Connell," he said, "there are very few senators in this building who would do that."

Even with Symington's support, Jordan had to accept fewer missile batteries—and they would have to be stationary, not mobile—to overcome opposition by Israel's staunch supporters in Congress. The stationary batteries ensured the missiles could not be used to support Jordanian troop movements against Israel. The king resented the compromise, which underscored for him how Jordan's interests would always be subordinate to Israel's, despite President Ford's assurance in a letter that he had been a symbol of "strength, wisdom and moderation."

Another friend of Jordan on Capitol Hill was U.S. representative Otto Passman, a conservative Democrat from Louisiana who literally controlled foreign aid as chairman of the House Foreign Aid Appropriations Subcommittee. Once, when the U.S. government changed the start of the fiscal year from July to October, costing aid recipients one quarter of their annual appropriation, Israel prevailed upon Congress to exempt it from the deduction, which was quietly done. When I learned of the ploy, I asked a major rice company executive if he could intervene with Passman, whom he knew well. It was a shot in the dark and I hadn't the slightest expectation that anything would come of it. Two weeks later, my friend told me that Passman liked the idea of a balance between Israel and Jordan, admired the king, and was amending the USAID bill to give Jordan $60 million (one fourth of its annual aid package—all cash). It passed, and Jordan received a check.

The State Department was nonplussed. USAID, trying to keep Jordan on a short leash, was apoplectic. Everyone feared Passman, so no one questioned him. I spoke to no one in Washington, where it has remained a mystery until now. The king himself was an important factor in gaining this windfall. Unlike most Arab leaders, who believe that Congress is "Israeli-occupied territory," he made the rounds on Capitol Hill whenever he visited Washington. While the meetings were often taxing and sometimes contentious, he grinned and bore them. With Passman, it paid off.

I was in Jordan in February 1977 when Queen Alia was killed in a helicopter crash near Amman. The king and his third wife had been married for just five years. Beautiful and vivacious, the diplomat's daughter had borne him two children. I didn't know any of the king's wives very well. My time was spent mostly with the men. I met the wives, I had moments with them, attended parties with them, and had dinner with them occasionally, but I didn't see a lot of them, certainly not alone. But the king was deeply saddened by Alia's death.

"You've been through the same thing, you've lost a wife, and it's no fun," he told me.

We commiserated together. The king was in mourning back home nine days after the crash when an article by Bob Woodward appeared on the front page of *The Washington Post*: "The Central Intelligence Agency for 20 years has made secret annual payments totaling millions of dollars to King Hussein of Jordan, The Washington Post has learned." So began a flawed article that left readers with an erroneous sense that the king was on the take, a CIA lackey. Woodward wrote that some CIA officials had reported the payments, which they considered nothing more than "bribes," to a three-member Intelligence Oversight Board created by President Ford in 1976. "Hussein was only 21 when he first became a beneficiary of CIA funds," Woodward wrote. "It was a time when Jordan was virtually a ward of the United States and Hussein had little money to support his lifestyle, which earned him the reputation as a 'playboy prince.' "

The truth is, the king didn't receive money for his personal use, and I never would have felt comfortable saying, "Can we give you some money?" I would have felt that I was insulting him, frankly. From 1957 to the day I left as station chief in 1971, the modest monthly payments were for 5,000 dinars, about $15,000. I know because I would deliver them toward the end of every month by leaving a small, white, letter-sized envelope containing the dinars, in cash, on the table beside my chair, and it was never discussed. This was a poor king when the payments started twenty years earlier. Later, he started getting money from other kings, which tided him over. But nobody in our government wanted to break off the payments, which were modest and legitimate. It became an embarrassment for us to say, well, we're not going to give you any more of this. We don't think you need it any more, because you now have your own intelligence service. He might interpret that as we were backing out on him, and we didn't want him to think that, because there was so little we were actually doing for him. Furthermore, the intelligence we got from the Jordanian service probably surpassed that of any other liaison service in the region, if not the world, including the Israelis'. Only later did the agency start paying about $800,000 a year, through my law firm, to local security firms for the protection of the king's children in the United States.

But this distinction was never made fully clear in Woodward's article. As coincidence would have it, my secretary later shared a cab with Woodward. When she recognized who he was, she chided him for failing to check out the story with our office before publishing it. Woodward said he tried to reach me, but I wasn't in.

"That's no excuse," my secretary remembers saying, explaining to Woodward that she took a call from the *Post* and asked that all questions for me be put in writing. "Your office apparently refused to do so. Although he was out of town, he would have answered the questions, had you put them in writing." Woodward responded that he had a deadline and simply hadn't had time. " 'I'd like to see him, can I get to see him?' " she remembers Woodward asking. Her reply: "He has no interest in seeing you after this story, trust me." " 'Tell Mr. O'Connell I owe him one,' " she recalls Woodward responding.

When the story broke, I was sitting in my hotel in Amman, and I was mortified. There it was in the newspapers: "King Hussein is on the CIA payroll," and in Jordan, many knew who I was. I thought, Oh my God, I'm a marked man in this town. And I can't get out easily. I still have people to see. So I walked out and started meeting people, and I know every one of them was looking at me differently than they did before. They think that I've been the bagman for million-dollar payments to the king, the head of their country. I had no idea how they would react to that. But I didn't notice the slightest change. I kept going through the day, and nobody even raised it. I saw the king and he didn't mention it. I don't know why nobody raised it, and I didn't raise it. I went through almost a week in that town with that news being the lead story, and nobody ever mentioned it. President Carter immediately cut off the payments but said at a Washington news conference five days after Woodward's article was published that he had reviewed the matter and had "not found anything illegal or improper."

Once the payments ended, the king had no choice but to pull his children out of their schools in the United States. Eventually, I sold the house I'd purchased for Muna and the children in Washington. Syble McKenzie, my old secretary, was left without a job. As it happened, the breakup of the household proved fortuitous for both of us. She retired from the agency and we were married in 1977 at St. Matthew's Cathedral in downtown Washington. We tried our best to keep the wedding low-key and simple. The fact that we had shared the agency life, friends, and overseas experiences made our next twelve years before her death even more harmonious.

President Carter would come to write the king a personal letter, saying he regretted the embarrassment caused by Woodward's article and all of the press accounts that followed about the payments he received from CIA. Carter noted that he had publicly stated that he had found nothing improper in the payments, and that he was counting on the king's "wisdom and guidance" as they worked together for peace in the Middle East. Frankly, I never understood the king's relationship with Carter. Carter believed in all the things the king did. He was the one president who thought that the king ought to get the West Bank back, and he was the one president who was willing to stand up to the Israelis. In September 1977, as Israeli forces attacked PLO militia bases in Lebanon, Carter grew annoyed when it became clear that the Israeli Defense Forces were using U.S. military equipment for offensive purposes, which was prohibited. My close friend and colleague Richard N. Viets, who was deputy chief of mission at the U.S. Embassy in Tel Aviv at the time, remembers how American diplomats repeatedly raised the issue with the Israelis, only to encounter a host of denials and excuses.

Finally, Carter had had enough. Viets, a diplomat's diplomat from Vermont who had served in Dar es Salaam, Tokyo, Madras, New Delhi, Bucharest, Tel Aviv, and Amman, remembers a code clerk handing him a telegram from the president one Friday with instructions to deliver it immediately to Prime Minister Menachem Begin.

Carter was demanding that Israel cease its use of U.S. weaponry for cross-border raids or face an immediate cutoff of all U.S. military aid. Viets, serving as chargé d'affaires in the absence of Ambassador Samuel W. Lewis, realized the instant he read the message that this would represent a major U.S.-Israeli collision if the Israelis refused to accede to the president's wishes. Driving to Jerusalem before dawn the following morning, on the Sabbath, he decided to make one last effort to persuade Begin to stop the raids. This was against the president's orders, which were, simply: You will deliver this letter. (Much later, after both men had left office, Viets told Carter what he had attempted, and Carter responded that he had done the right thing.) He was shown into the prime minister's study. Begin was anxious to know why Viets was disturbing him so early on a Saturday morning. Viets began with a familiar litany of American arguments but got nowhere. He was immediately reminded of what a tough, savvy lawyer he was dealing with. Finally, he took the letter from Carter out of his breast pocket and handed it to Begin.

"Once you read this, you'll understand why I hoped I wouldn't have to deliver it," he remembers saying, describing the encounter as though it were yesterday.

Viets saw the color drain from Begin's face as he watched him read the letter. Before he had finished, he looked up and handed the letter back to Viets.

" 'I cannot believe what I'm reading,' " Viets remembers him saying. " 'I cannot believe that any President of the United States would write such a letter to the Prime Minister of Israel. Our countries are just too close for this kind of communication. And this is just no way to conduct policy with your best friend. I can't read any more of this. You must read it to me.' "

Viets, summoning his best John Barrymore voice, finished reading the letter. There was dead silence for half a minute. Begin then got up from where he was sitting, walked over to a cabinet on the wall, opened it, and took out a bottle of scotch and two large glasses. He poured a shot or more into both glasses, handed one to Viets, then raised his own glass in a toast, even though it was only seven o'clock in the morning.

"You win, Mr. Viets," he said.

Congress never would have gone along, but Begin didn't want to take the chance. He told Viets that he wouldn't be able to convene a cabinet meeting until after dark. A half hour past sundown, he rang Viets. "Call your president," he said, "and tell him we will stop."

President Carter had another impact on Israel of which he may not be aware. In 1978, he gave a speech in which he stated that the Palestinian people had "the right of self-determination."

A very astute member of the Israeli Embassy reported the speech to the Israeli government, with the wise admonition that "self-determination" was as American as apple pie and, if it caught on with the American people, Israel could "kiss the West Bank goodbye." He suggested a counteraction, pointing out that "terrorists" didn't enjoy rights, therefore if every reference to the Palestinians, their organizations, and their leaders was prefaced by the word "terrorist," it would nullify the Palestinian right to "rights." The Israeli government henceforth hyphenated everything Palestinian with the "terrorist" label. It worked. In reality, the "war on terrorism" began in 1978 from the seed of "self-determination," not on September 11, 2001, with the al Qaeda attack. To compound the contradictions, the leading Palestinian "terrorist" organization, Hamas, won a free Palestinian election based on the right of self-determination.

As I said earlier, Carter's willingness to stand up to Israeli intransigence should have been the bond for a close relationship with King Hussein. Carter took office strongly favoring a resumption of a comprehensive peace process begun at the Geneva Conference. He believed an Israeli withdrawal from the West Bank and a resolution of the Palestinian problem were central to peace in the Middle East, as did the king. But by the summer of 1978, Carter invited Egypt and Israel to a peace conference at Camp David in September in an attempt to revive Egyptian president Anwar Sadat's failed peace initiative with Israel, which he began the previous fall as the first Arab leader to officially visit the Jewish state. While King Hussein was left on the sideline, he expected to be invited to such a conference once negotiations turned to the issue of the West Bank. Before Sadat went to Camp David, he wrote a letter to King Hussein. I never saw the letter, but the king told me about it. Sadat said he would not make a separate peace at Camp David that did not encompass Jordan and the West Bank, and he proposed meeting with King Hussein in Casablanca afterwards to agree on their next move, speaking as though they were partners in whatever was going to happen. I had come from Jordan, and when the king went to London expecting to get word to come and join everybody at Camp David, I had gone back to the States, expecting the king to get involved. Once the conference began and the parties started grappling with the difficult issues of the West Bank and Palestinian autonomy, I'm told the American working group wanted to bring over the king. It was part of their working papers, they told me. But Sadat said, I don't think we want to do that, because it's only going to complicate things. Begin agreed. Whereupon they established the foundations for a separate Israeli-Egyptian peace.

The Camp David Accords, hammered out after thirteen days of negotiations, consisted of two parts. The first was a framework for an Israeli-Egyptian peace treaty. It required an Israeli withdrawal from the Sinai Peninsula, a UN Peacekeeping Force to make sure the Sinai remained demilitarized, and the normalization of relations between Egypt and Israel. The second part was a framework for a broader peace in the Middle East and referenced UN Security Council

Resolution 242, which was still the seminal statement of principle more than a decade after we'd negotiated it in New York. The issue of when Israel would withdraw from the West Bank would be left until "final status" negotiations after a transition period in which Palestinians would have limited autonomy on the West Bank and Gaza while Israel maintained military control. As part of the framework for the West Bank, Carter thought Begin had agreed to an open-ended termination of all Israeli settlements. Begin claimed he had only agreed to three months. So Begin betrayed Carter on the settlements, and Sadat betrayed King Hussein in negotiating the separate peace he promised he would not agree to. Camp David was, in fact, a betrayal derby.

The king was very bitter about Sadat. He described himself as "absolutely shattered," and I don't think he ever saw Sadat again. After Israel and Egypt signed their formal peace treaty in March 1979, the king had no interest in taking part in negotiations relating to Palestinian autonomy. His refusal badly strained relations with the Carter administration, and particularly with Carter himself, who believed the king, as an Arab peacemaker, should have embraced Camp David. However, America's relationship with Jordan endured and military aid continued. The fall of the Shah of Iran in January 1979, and the Soviet invasion of Afghanistan in December of that year, were both signs that the United States needed a solid relationship with Jordan, particularly after the king condemned the Soviet invasion. By the time of the king's final official visit to Washington during the Carter administration in June 1980, relations were cordial but not particularly close. His snubbing at Camp David, and all the tensions that followed, left the king looking for a new place to begin. He found it that November.

Chapter 12

GIVING UP THE WEST BANK

King Hussein was elated when Ronald Reagan easily defeated Carter and brought a new certainty and confidence to the White House. While he really didn't know Reagan, he considered George H. W. Bush, the vice president–elect, a good friend. The two had worked together when Bush served as director of Central Intelligence for just under a year at the end of the Ford administration, and I remember seeing Bush regularly at functions at the Jordanian Embassy in Washington. Long before the inauguration, the king had me chasing Bush all over the country, trying to find him so the two could speak by telephone, which they did, at length. The king's first meeting with President Reagan in Washington took place in early November 1981, and included a gala White House dinner for the king and his dazzling new bride, Queen Noor, an American of Syrian, British, and Swedish descent whom he'd married in 1979. Among the ninety-six invited guests was Bill Macomber, the first ambassador I served with in Amman, who was then president of the Metropolitan Museum of Art. The Benny Goodman Quintet played on that evening, a performance arranged by none other than Frank Sinatra, who also attended.

The king was ebullient after two days of talks, telling reporters at a press conference on the White House lawn that the meeting "has left me more reassured than any in the past and more confident in the future." Reagan stood beside him and told reporters after the king had left: "We just became friends." The Reagan administration strongly supported the Camp David peace process, which the king still resolutely refused to embrace. But he was happy to see Carter gone, and he made it clear that peace in the Middle East was his prime concern, as long as the framework for negotiations continued to be UN resolutions 242 and 338.

Reagan embraced both when he put forth his own peace plan in September 1982, just as Israel's siege of Beirut was ending. The president expressed renewed interest in finding peace between Israel, the Palestinians, and Jordan after watching the Israeli Defense Forces commanded by Ariel Sharon invade Lebanon, drive Arafat and the PLO out of the country, and push all the way to Beirut. At the end of the campaign, hundreds of Palestinian civilians were killed by Lebanese Christian Phalangist militia at the Sabra and Shatila refugee camps, which at the time were surrounded by Israeli forces. An Israeli investigative commission later found that Israeli civilian and military leaders bore "indirect responsibility" for the deaths and recommended that the general step down, which he ultimately did. I remember Dick Helms telling me that he sent Reagan a message that summer as the Israeli invasion of Lebanon was getting out of hand and told the president, who was in Europe at the time, that he'd better get back to Washington and rein in his secretary of state, Alexander Haig, whom Dick believed was encouraging the Israelis. George Shultz replaced Haig as secretary of state in July.

With his peace initiative, Reagan clearly wanted to regain control of the situation and jump-start the peace process. He proposed an Israeli withdrawal from the occupied territories as envisaged under UN resolutions 242 and 338 and Palestinian self-government on the West Bank in association with Jordan. But he did not support creation of a Palestinian state. The king felt he had to become involved in helping solve the Palestinian problem, given the weakened state of the PLO, but he insisted that Palestinians must be involved as well, and he talked about the necessity of building a bridge to the PLO.

With the Reagan administration urging the king to support its plan on the eve of another visit to the White House in December 1982, I told the king we needed to use the upcoming talks to educate Reagan, still fairly new to Washington, about the realities of the Middle East peace process, which had produced no peace for Israel, Jordan, and the Palestinians since the 1967 War. We had to present our issues, one by one. We'd learned one rule years earlier: Don't come to Washington unless you have something to say. If you're a head of state, you just don't come and ask for things. You must come with an agenda. Very often, people come without one. They just come. But if you want to be received and be invited back, you need to have an agenda, present it in a businesslike manner, and get the attention of the White House and the State Department. How do you do that? You start out with talking points. But with talking points, we found over the years, the king would come, present his talking points, and leave. And once he left, the talking points dissolved, there was no follow-up, and nothing would happen. So we figured out how to build in a follow-up by incorporating our talking points in a paper that required an answer. We set down our position, and we described any differences that may exist, issue by issue. If there weren't any, we said we seem to be in agreement. Where differences existed, we posed a question about how our differences might be resolved. So, this was not a dead letter. It was a paper that required an answer. The idea was to keep the dialogue rolling, and we hadn't done this in the past. This was a new technique, and we finessed them into answering us on issues of our choosing that were critical to us.

I wrote the paper in conjunction with people in the State Department who had views similar to mine but could never get them past their superiors. By virtue of the king's paper, they knew they could vault right over their bosses. But to whom do you give the paper? This was the second lesson the king learned. The secretary of state was the logical recipient. But as we'd seen many times before, if the secretary of state didn't agree with your paper or your talking points, nobody else would ever see them. So, we didn't give our paper to the secretary of state. We gave it directly to Reagan, which is something we rehearsed.

" 'Your Majesty,' George Shultz will want to say, 'Have you got your paper for me?' And you say, 'No, I have one for the President,'" I told the king. " 'And when you go to the White House, you hand it to the President, because he's the one you really want to read it.' "

You can't be sure, if you give it to anybody else, whether the president will ever read it. He might read a summary of it by somebody, or he might be briefed on it orally, but it won't become meaningful. So we put all of our issues down on paper, point by point, position by position, without mincing any words, gave it to the president, and asked him to answer the questions we posed.

When I finished the paper, it was twenty pages long. My stealth collaborators in the State Department told me Reagan would never read twenty pages. They told me I would defeat my purpose. He will give it to somebody else to read; he won't read it; he doesn't read things. But at three o'clock in the afternoon on the day the king gave Reagan his paper, just as we'd planned, I received a call from my friend Marc Grossman in the State Department.

"Jack, you won't believe it," he said.

"What?"

"He read it. Reagan read the paper. And he's calling everybody in town wondering why people have never told him what was going on in the Middle East."

Indeed, Reagan wanted to know why people had not told him all these things the king had written. And then he asked Shultz to answer the letter, which he did, just like we wanted him to, right down the line. The six-page, single-spaced document was entitled "Response by the government of the United States to the 'Talking Paper' presented by the Hashemite Kingdom of Jordan." I still have the paper in one of the thick binders I kept of memos, itineraries, policy papers, and newspaper clippings throughout the seventies, eighties, and nineties. It is highlighted in yellow marker, with certain passages underscored in blue pen and others in red—evidence of just how carefully we pored over this document. "Foundation of the search for peace in the Middle East is United Nations Security Council Resolution 242 in all its parts," the U.S. response reads. "The President is fully committed to that proposition. . . . The President believes, consistent with Resolution 242, that territory should not be acquired by war. He believes as well, however, that Resolution 242 does permit changes in the boundaries which existed prior to June, 1967, but only where such changes are agreed between the parties." I underlined that last clause—which I'd helped negotiate back in 1967—in red ink. "Finally, the U.S. believes that all of the principles of 242—those which hold out the promise of peace and those which hold out the promise of return of territory—must be fulfilled to the maximum extent possible, each basic principle balanced with the others."

This was the ideal answer, precisely what we had been hoping for. And that's how our paper worked out—the Jordanians had a document in return from the U.S. government, saying there would be no changes to the 1967 borders that Jordan didn't agree to. It demonstrated how it is possible to get through to the president and keep him informed, even if he is surrounded by people who try to keep him isolated. This was evidence that Reagan was not fully briefed when it came to foreign affairs in the Middle East. Everybody under-estimated him. So the optimism expressed by the king in December 1982, following his talks with Reagan, proved to be well founded, at least as far as this response was concerned. Indeed, his optimism was boundless and would carry him throughout much of the rest of the decade, through meetings with Arafat and the Israelis and a series of peace initiatives from the Americans—none of which produced peace, or the return of the West Bank and Jerusalem.

Soon enough, the king proposed his own peace initiative—in conjunction with Arafat. He met with the PLO leader in the spring of 1983 in an effort to advance Reagan's proposal for a Jordanian-Palestinian federation along with implementation of UN Resolution 242, but PLO hard-liners objected to the role the resolution con-ferred on the Jordanians. The following year, the king continued his meetings with Arafat as he proposed an international conference that would involve the five permanent members of the UN Security Council plus the parties to the Middle East peace process: Jordan, Israel, Syria, and Egypt. By early 1985, the king and Arafat agreed to a formal Jordanian-Palestinian accord that called for Israel's with-drawal from the occupied territories, Palestinian self-determination in confederation with Jordan, and a resolution of the Palestinian refu-gee issue in accord with the provisions set forth in 242.

But the Reagan administration was lukewarm and the Israelis were flatly opposed to dealing with the PLO or, for that matter, relinquish-ing the West Bank, preferring direct negotiations with Jordan. For the king and Arafat, it was all downhill from there. By early 1986, the king was still trying to sell the PLO on an American compro-mise to back an international conference that included the PLO, as long as the group renounced terrorism and agreed to negotiate with Israel. But when the PLO refused and said it could not accept even the framework put forth in 242 unless the Americans recognized the right to self-determination for the Palestinians, the king's long and troubled relationship with Arafat finally came to an end.

I never trusted Arafat, so it was just as well, as far as I was concerned. I hadn't tried to actively oppose him—I didn't take those positions with the king. But I never have said anything very favorable about Arafat. His record was such that you wouldn't trust him. The king always saw the bright side of someone; maybe he could make a deal with Arafat, he thought, and if he could, that would solve all the problems. That was why he waited so long in 1970 to go to war against the PLO militias in Amman, and that was why he kept trying to negotiate some sort of framework for peace with Arafat. He was always trying to avoid conflict and work out problems with people. I never thought working things out with Arafat was possible, and our intelligence certainly didn't indicate that any kind of deal was possible with him. He didn't want to make a deal. He thought he could win without one.

Even as he was trying to work something out with Arafat, the king resumed his secret meetings with Israeli leaders, beginning in July 1985 with Prime Minister Shimon Peres in London. It was their first meeting in almost a decade. Peres strongly favored dealing with Jordan as an alternative to the PLO. The king's talks with the Israelis only gained momentum when his relationship with Arafat finally collapsed. In early 1986, he met secretly with Yitzhak Rabin, then serving as defense minister, near Strasbourg. The following year, after Peres and Yitzhak Shamir had swapped places, with Shamir becoming prime minister and Peres foreign minister, the king met with Peres in London and hammered out the so-called London agreement. It called for an international conference, formation of a number of bilateral working committees, and resolution of the Palestinian issue based on acceptance of UN resolutions 242 and 338. Shamir never supported the deal for a moment.

The king didn't feel he could ever work with Shamir. They had no relationship. The king had a better relationship with Peres, but never trusted him. Peres talked a good game, but the king didn't think he was sincere. I don't know if there's anything you can put your finger on as to why he didn't trust Peres, but I know he didn't. And he would say so. Rabin was his favorite of all the Israeli leaders. Although Rabin did not have a high opinion of the king in the early days of their relationship, he gradually came around and changed his thinking. In the end, they were very close. If Rabin had lived, I think there would have been peace in the Middle East.

When the London agreement went nowhere, Secretary of State George Shultz and Richard W. Murphy, assistant secretary of state for Near Eastern and South Asian Affairs, met with the king in London in the fall of 1987 to try to convince him to link Middle East peace talks to an upcoming summit between President Reagan and Soviet leader Mikhail Gorbachev. I was in London at the time meeting with the Jordanians, and I remember Shultz and Murphy were on their way to Moscow. They met with the king at his London home, pitched him on their idea for linking the summit and peace talks, and told him they needed an answer the following day before they left. The king promised he would have one for them. After the Americans left, one of the king's aides found a briefing book that the Americans left behind. It was Murphy's. They made a photocopy and put it back where they found it. A few minutes later, two State Department people showed up at the king's house and said somebody left something there. Could they come in and look for it? They found it right where Murphy left it and took it with them as they quickly left. The briefing book not only gave the American position on everything, but gave some tactical suggestions on how to deal with the king. It said the king was stronger when he was around his own people, so it would be better to get him alone for this one. In fact, the book went into great detail about how the king was weaker when alone.

The king was greatly offended when he read this, not by what the Americans wanted to do, but by what they thought of him. So the next day, when Shultz came back, he found the king absolutely against anything that they were suggesting, without any reason, and the Americans never understood why. The next time I visited Jordan, when I went down to Aqaba, Zaid Rifai and the king said they wanted to show me something, and pulled out the copy of Murphy's briefing book. I read it intently, looked up, and said, "By God, they don't really think much of you." We all had a good laugh. There was some truth to the American briefing on Hussein. He was always searching for a way to make peace, and he tried to be accommodating to the Americans, even though they consistently sold him out, from 1967 on, in favor of the Israelis.

So it was that Shultz's meeting with the king in early 1988 followed a familiar script. Shultz was pushing his own plan that called for an "interlock," tying interim talks on Palestinian self-rule with final status negotiations on Middle East peace. The king came in loaded for bear, wanting to start final negotiations with the Israelis and feeling there was no reason left for delay. He met with Shultz before he met with the president, and we weren't sure exactly where the secretary of state was coming from. But wherever it was, we told the king not to buckle, to stand firm. This was when Shultz first introduced the concept of interim talks preceding final status negotiations. He told the king that he agreed talks with the Israelis were necessary, but working through confidence-building measures on an interim basis could pave the way for final status negotiations. This seemed reasonable, and the king, in an effort to be accommodating, agreed to it. This really strung out the process—and ultimately left us where we are now. The king made a mistake by going along with what Shultz wanted, because Shultz wanted to delay final status negotiations in any way that he could, which of course was what the Israelis wanted. When it was over,

Shultz told his advisers that he wasn't sure he was going to be able to sell the king on his plan, but the king was much easier to convince than he thought he would be. Many of those advisers were with me on this, pro-Jordanian, and were upset that the king had bought Shultz's phased approach. I consider that a tactical mistake by the king.

But Shultz's plan went nowhere, and soon the king bowed out. He had become so disillusioned by the treacherous behavior of Egypt since Camp David, the callousness of Iraq and his other Arab neighbors, the betrayals of Israel and the United States, and the ingratitude of the Palestinians, that he finally agreed to transfer legal and administrative authority of the West Bank to the PLO, except for the Arab city of Jerusalem. He had exhausted himself over the years trying to convince Israel to return the West Bank to Jordan and revert to the pre-1967 borders. The outbreak of the Palestinian "intifada" in 1987 seemed to take the PLO and Jordan by surprise. The king was deeply affected when the United National Command, the Palestinian leadership of the uprising, called on thousands of Palestinians in the streets to step up resistance to Israel's occupying forces, its settlers, and "collaborators" and officials of the Jordanian regime. Hussein formally announced that Jordan would "disengage" from the West Bank in July 1988.

The thought of relinquishing the West Bank, after working for so many years for its return, first came from Adnan Abu-Odeh, a loyal Palestinian. In 1967, he served in Jordanian intelligence. He was a thinker, an analyst, with an office next to the head of the service. He subsequently became the information minister and served the king in a variety of roles, most prominently as Jordan's minister of communications. He was very good with the media. He framed the argument well: Israel won't make peace and the Arab world supports the PLO as representative of the Palestinian people, so one way to help them was to relinquish Jordan's control of the West Bank.

It got everyone thinking: Why do we want the West Bank? It's got nothing except problems. It has no resources that amount to anything. The people were ungrateful; they will never thank us for anything. Why do we want to hang on to it? Nobody around the king could think of a good reason. So they all decided to get rid of it. The king finally realized that Israel would never give the West Bank back to Jordan or anyone else.

"It's not there," he told me. "I've talked to them alone, all of them. I've offered them everything they want, in terms of peace, and they still can't bring themselves to withdraw from the West Bank. All they do is talk in circles."

The trouble was, the king did not have the authority to transfer territory of the kingdom to any other state without the authority of the Parliament. And the Jordanian Parliament had never given the king that authority. Therefore, the transfer of the West Bank to Israel in 1988 was illegal. But the world has accepted the transfer, and Jordanians are grateful to be out from under it.

Economic woes in Jordan, roiled by the intifada, worsened after the king let go of the West Bank, further shattering confidence. Jordan was forced to turn to the International Monetary Fund for assistance. But budget cuts insisted upon by the IMF, in addition to a sizable tax increase on gasoline and other staples, triggered bread riots in provincial cities throughout Jordan, most notably Ma'an. I was with the king in Washington when he had to cut short a visit in April 1989 with newly elected President George H. W. Bush, to return home to quell the riots. He fired Zaid Rifai, the prime minister and a convenient scapegoat, even though Zaid was hardly responsible for the tax increase that particularly angered truckers. The king and his aides had imposed the tax hike on the eve of their visit to Washington so they wouldn't be there when it happened. But the civil disturbances far exceeded their calculations. When the riots erupted across the country, it was a real blow to the king, who had no idea people would react that strongly against their ruler.

After returning home, King Hussein quickly moved to reconnect with his subjects. That's what saved him throughout his lifetime—good political antennae. He kept in touch with the countryside. The Bedouins were always behind him, and they were the mainstay of the army. He cultivated them, feeling that they were his main support. It was the city populations that lagged behind, and that was where the Palestinians mainly were located, in the cities. So the vast rural areas were with the king, and everybody knew it. The riots were a sign that the king needed to focus on political liberalization. In the fall of 1989, Jordan held its first parliamentary elections in twenty-two years. The following April, a Royal Commission was appointed to draft the National Charter, a legal framework for political parties. By the summer of 1990, a measure of stability had returned to the country. But Saddam Hussein's invasion of Kuwait in early August changed everything. King Hussein's handling of the crisis led to Jordan's isolation. In the Arab world and internationally, the king would spend much of the rest of his life trying to maneuver out of the mess created by his dealings with Saddam Hussein's Iraq.

For me, personally, this period also brought tragedy and a deep sense of loss. Syble died of cancer in May at Georgetown University Hospital after quietly fighting the disease for months. We were a few weeks shy of our thirteenth anniversary. She was just sixty years old. A few years earlier, we had sold the house on Searl Terrace in Bethesda and moved to a home in Potomac, with a brook and a tennis court surrounded by woods. With Kelly and Sean out of college and on their own, I found my own best therapy was immersion in what I knew best, the Middle East. When Saddam Hussein invaded Kuwait in August, I knew there would be no peace—and there might well be a very big war.

Chapter 13

SADDAM HUSSEIN:
FRIEND OR FOE?

The Palestine problem has been the major source of violence and instability in the Middle East since the 1940s, including six wars (1948, 1956, 1967, 1973, 1982, and 2006) and forty years of hostile military occupation—without a peaceful solution. The second major source of violence and area instability has been the Iraq problem. Although the Iraq problem is not as old and has not lasted as long and only involved three wars (Iran 1981–88, coalition 1991, and United States 2003) and seven years of military occupation, there are many similarities. Egypt and Nasser, and Iraq and Saddam, both posed what Israel perceived as existential threats that needed to be destroyed. The United States secretly acquiesced in Israel's destruction of Nasser's Egypt, and ended up doing the dirty work for Israel against Iraq—even though neither country nor leader threatened the United States. Ironically, both wanted friendly relations with the United States.

It's almost hard to remember a time when the United States was interested in pursuing friendly relations with Iraq. But I tried to help make that happen early in the Reagan administration, when reestablishing diplomatic ties was the State Department's goal. I remember a meeting I had at the State Department in October 1983 with Richard Murphy, to discuss a few Jordanian issues of no historic interest. We had served together in Amman in the 1960s. When we finished discussing Jordan, Murphy leaned back and said the top item on his agenda, which was frustrating him, was the restoration of U.S. relations with Iraq, broken off by Iraq during the 1967 War. He was puzzled that both countries wanted to restore normal diplomatic relations but both were talking past each other and nothing had happened for almost a year. As assistant secretary of state for Near Eastern and South Asian Affairs, he was under White House pressure to provide an answer. I told him I wasn't qualified to help him with that one.

I returned to my office to meet a friend and client from New York. He was an Arab-American businessman, whose company did considerable business in Syria and Iraq. A fluent Arabist, he was well acquainted with the leaders in both countries. He was also very politically well versed on the Middle East, where several of his Arab relatives still resided. At one point he tipped off an aide to Saddam Hussein about a plan to assassinate Saddam on a trip to Syria, when he was in asylum in Egypt before his rise to power. Saddam never forgot what he had done. In Iraq, when the Ba'ath Party was ousted in 1963 and the leaders left the country, one of my client's Ba'athist friends gave him their official files for safekeeping. The Ba'athists returned to power in 1968.

I told my friend about my conversation with Murphy. He said the United States was not handling the matter properly. Restoring relations with the United States could only be Saddam's decision. He was a proud man. To restore relations, the president would have to write Saddam a personal letter asking that relations be restored and it should be delivered by a U.S. official of stature. It so happened that Donald Rumsfeld, President Reagan's special envoy to the Middle East, was scheduled to visit the area the following month, in November, on behalf of the president, but Iraq was not on his schedule. I asked if

Rumsfeld would be appropriate. He said he thought Rumsfeld would be perfect.

I immediately telephoned Dick Murphy and passed on my friend's idea. Murphy said it had merit, but if he recommended this to the president and Saddam refused to see Rumsfeld, Murphy thought he could lose his job. He needed more assurance. My friend said he was going to France on business in two days and would look up the Iraqi ambassador, who was a member of the ruling clique, and ask his advice.

About ten days later, he was back from France and back in my office. The Iraqi ambassador heard my friend's story and immediately, in his presence, called Iraqi foreign minister Tariq Aziz in Baghdad. Aziz said he would be in China during most of Rumsfeld's trip, but if Rumsfeld was coming with a letter from President Reagan to Saddam, Aziz would return from China one day earlier, host a dinner for Rumsfeld that night, and take him to see Saddam the next morning. He said he was sure the outcome would be favorable.

I asked my friend to outline the type of letter the president should sign and took it with me when I visited Murphy the same day. Murphy said the assurance was sufficient. The president signed the letter, Rumsfeld added Baghdad to his schedule, Tariq Aziz returned early, hosted a dinner, and the next day, December 20, 1983, Saddam Hussein famously shook hands with Rumsfeld and all but agreed to restore relations with the United States.

Secret State Department notes of the meeting, declassified in 1994, state that "in his 90-minute meeting with Rumsfeld, Saddam Hussein showed obvious pleasure with the President's letter and Rumsfeld's visit and in his remarks removed whatever obstacles remained in the way of resuming diplomatic relations . . .

"Further expanding his thinking on U.S.-Iraqi relations," the meeting notes continue, "Saddam said Iraq also felt that not being able to conduct relations at a full diplomatic level was unnatural." Interestingly, the president used a direct quote from Rumsfeld's statement to the foreign minister the previous evening when he said that "having a whole generation of Iraqis and Americans grow up without understanding each other had negative implications and could lead to mix-ups."

While U.S. relations were formally restored after the negotiation of terms in November 1984, Rumsfeld's remark about a lack of contact leading to misunderstandings, negative implications, and mix-ups seems like a prophetic understatement of epic proportions.

Rumsfeld stopped in Jordan on his way to Iraq. He had an audience with King Hussein after meeting with my friend Dick Viets, the State Department official who had delivered President Carter's telegram to Menachem Begin as deputy chief of mission in Tel Aviv and was now ambassador to Jordan. In his talks with Viets and the king, Rumsfeld projected more talking points than the restoration of diplomatic relations. The most controversial was his intention to suggest that Saddam build an oil pipeline between Iraq and Jordan's port city of Aqaba, with a spur to Haifa in Israel. Rumsfeld still had presidential ambitions at this point and seemed to relish this trip as an opportunity to burnish his reputation as a heavyweight in foreign policy. Bechtel Corporation was proposing to build the pipeline, which held tremendous promise for the Iraqis, who were concerned about the Iranians interrupting their oil exports through the Gulf, and the Jordanians, who were dependent upon oil handouts from the Saudis. The one great fly in the ointment had always been the Israelis—would they allow the pipeline to be built? Indeed, Saddam, in his talks with Rumsfeld, noted this concern about the Israelis and said he was delighted that the U.S. government was now backing the pipeline proposal. But the Israelis, at this point, were on board too, because of a sweetener that would have helped deal with Israel's own oil insecurities—the spur to Haifa. Key figures in the American Jewish community were lobbying hard in Washington for the pipeline and spur, which was one of the reasons Rumsfeld was so interested.

There was a saying at the time that Baghdad was on the road to Jerusalem, meaning that unless the Iraqis, who cast a long shadow in the region, were involved in the peace process, there wouldn't be one. And, of course, King Hussein, beyond the obvious financial benefits, was interested in the pipeline as a means of helping his ally, Saddam Hussein, end Iraq's isolation and show the West he could be a trustworthy economic partner.

But Dick Viets knew that King Hussein was adamantly opposed to the proposed Haifa spur because he did not feel the Iraqis should be seen as pumping the riches of the Middle East to Israel. He told Rumsfeld that he couldn't support the idea, and was sure the king wouldn't, either. Rumsfeld was none too pleased and told Viets that he soon might be looking for another job. When the king did precisely as Dick predicted, Rumsfeld backed off.

"He had a vile temper," Dick said of Rumsfeld. "There were threats. I just went head to head with him, and he didn't like it. I don't think he ever liked anybody disagreeing with him, least of all probably somebody representing the State Department, which I'm sure he held in some contempt."

A month after Rumsfeld's trip to the Middle East, my Arab friend, who arranged the Rumsfeld visit, received a message from an aide of Saddam's to meet in Geneva. It was apparent from the message that Saddam had been impressed with the fact that my friend had organized the presidential letter and Rumsfeld's trip and, thus, should be a reliable back channel to the president.

Saddam's message to President Reagan was that he wanted to work closely with the United States in the Middle East. He would appreciate an invitation for an official visit to Washington to discuss an alliance. If an official visit was not practical at this time, Saddam was willing to meet President Reagan any place in the world. In addition, Saddam suggested that a covert communication channel be set up between him and the U.S. president. One matter Saddam was particularly interested in discussing was the war he was currently waging against Iran.

My friend relayed all of this to me on his return from Geneva and sought my advice on who should receive Saddam's message. I reasoned that since I had the CIA's trust and the agency was generally aware of my friend's bona fides, we should meet with a senior agency officer I knew well. We would leave it to the agency to advise the president and get back to me and my friend, if needed.

Two weeks later, two CIA officers appeared in my friend's office in New York. The sole purpose of their visit was to find out if my friend would introduce an agency officer to the Iraqi messenger he met in Geneva in the hope of recruiting him. My friend quickly rejected the idea and asked what the reaction was to Saddam's message to the president. They didn't know what he was talking about.

There is no evidence that Saddam's request ever reached the president or even left CIA. By the time we realized that, it was too late to follow up. This was the first of several missed opportunities in the United States' dealings with Iraq. But it provides an insight into the man the United States might have worked with.

King Hussein certainly thought Saddam was trustworthy. His brother, Prince Hassan, didn't agree. He tried for years to convince the king to stay away from the Iraqi leader. One of the king's biographers, Nigel Ashton at the London School of Economics and Political Science, has called the king's "faith in Saddam . . . probably the biggest character misjudgment of his reign, and one for which he was to pay a high political price." I'm not sure it's quite that simple. The king first turned his foreign policy toward Iraq for reasons of regional security in the late 1970s after Israel, Egypt, and the United States dealt Jordan out of the Camp David process. Jordan also depended on Iraq for cheap oil and trade, particularly the opportunity to serve as an arms middleman in the transshipment of weaponry to Iraq through Aqaba during the Iran-Iraq War. There was also no denying that Saddam respected the king, and part of the king's warm feelings toward Iraq may have been dynastic—until the assassination of his cousin Faisal in 1958, Iraq had been part of the Hashemite Kingdom. One little known fact is that when King Hussein visited Baghdad, Saddam Hussein would take him to visit King Faisal's grave. Saddam didn't tear him out of the ground and throw him into the sea. He put flowers on the grave of the king that the military overthrew in 1958. The king would tell me about these solemn visits to his cousin's resting place, and it obviously meant a great deal to him that Saddam allowed this to take place.

"Everybody knew we were going out there, there was a little parade," the king said, "and he let me put flowers on the grave, and say a prayer, and salute the grave."

In the back of Saddam's mind, I think he envied the king his title. They were both heads of state, but the king was a king, and Saddam was just a president. He seemed to think that was rather important, and he looked up to the king. One time when Saddam was going to kill his son, Uday, because he had killed one of the servants, Saddam's wife called the king in Amman and said, "Saddam is going to kill our son, would you please come to Baghdad?" So King Hussein got in a plane, went to Baghdad, and talked Saddam out of killing his son. Nobody knew very much about it. The king just went off by himself, taking nobody with him. And he didn't advertise it. I knew he wasn't in Amman but I didn't know where he was. So they had a relationship that was more than just official. He had influence on Saddam. The wife knew it. The king knew it.

With this ability, and this talent, the king didn't want to go to war with the guy; he thought his role should be trying to bring about peace. He could explain things to him in a way in which few people could, and Saddam listened. He didn't really ever sit down and discuss Saddam with me as a person. I think he saw his weaknesses, and did not consider him a personal friend. He was a public character with whom he had a good relationship. They didn't have that much against each other. The king wasn't trying to overthrow him; he wasn't supporting any of the opposition people in Iraq. But King Hussein needed oil from Iraq, and wanted help from Saddam. It was all about helping each other. They never had a lot in common in terms of personal traits. As I've said, the king's brother, Hassan, disagreed with him. Hassan had the conventional view of Saddam—that he was a murderous tyrant. But the relationship stood as an example of the king's belief that he could achieve something good, no matter how difficult his partner. He showed the same instinct over the years with Arafat. The king was the one, after all, who brought Egypt back into the fold, after the Egyptians had made their separate peace with Israel, even though he was the one who was harmed the most by it. So he did a lot of things which seemed contrary to interest, but they all had the same goal: let's unify the Arabs, let's forget the past, let's make peace.

By the late 1980s, Saddam was a fairly well known commodity for anyone who had an interest. He was ruthless to those Iraqis who opposed him, but he held together, in one functional entity, a multireligious, multiethnic population, something only possible under a strong ruler. Saddam was a secular leader. He opposed a religious state and bloodied Iran in a war against Islamic fundamentalism. He wanted to replace the Shah as America's man in the Middle East and to form partnerships with major U.S. firms.

His meeting with Rumsfeld in 1983 certainly pointed toward that, as did his own follow-up efforts through my Arab friend and client to establish a working relationship with President Reagan. But I had another, impeccable source telling me that Saddam desperately wanted close ties to the United States: General Abud Hassan, the brilliant intelligence operative who had bluffed Iraqi troops out of invading Jordan in 1970 with an Iraqi double agent, a doctored NATO war plan, and some very good acting. Hassan's bona fides were gold-plated. He started out as a pilot in the Iraqi Air Force and was a member of the Ba'ath Party. When President Abdul Karim Kassim, the military officer who staged the bloody coup in 1958 against King Hussein's cousin, Faisal, purged the Ba'ath Party, Saddam and other Ba'ath leaders escaped to Egypt in 1959. They were granted asylum and became guests of the Egyptian government for almost two years. Hassan flew a MiG out of Iraq and escaped to Cairo, where he joined Saddam and the other Ba'athists. Saddam and Hassan were roommates during the entire time. When the exiled Iraqis returned to Iraq after Kassim's demise, there was little Hassan did not know about Saddam. He later went to Jordan, where he began a new career under King Hussein's personal tutelage as chief of Military Intelligence and head of the air force.

General Hassan never lost contact, or favor, with Saddam. Hassan shared his thoughts on the Iraqi leader with me: ruthless, proud, and pragmatic. Saddam practiced primitive justice, executing his enemies without hesitation. But he was an Iraqi patriot, Hassan said, who had no interest whatsoever in Islamic fundamentalism. Most interestingly, Hassan always described Saddam as an admirer of America. Hassan repeatedly told me Saddam would make a deal with the United States any time the United States wanted, and that he could arrange a covert channel of contact with Saddam.

After UN Resolution 598 ended the Iran-Iraq War in August 1988, Saddam thought the United States, the West, and the Sunni Arab states in the Middle East owed him a debt of gratitude for opposing the Shiite Khomeini revolution in Iran, which was intent on spreading its fundamentalist religious revolution throughout the Arab world. The United States did not want the Ayatollah Khomeini's revolution to spread either, so it supported Saddam with satellite intelligence and special weapons during the war. In fact, the United States and the Arab states did owe Saddam a favor. A postwar bone of contention involved the money some Arab states had loaned Iraq to fight the war. Saddam thought the loans should be converted to gifts. The lending countries, including Kuwait, saw things differently.

Once the war ended, it seemed that some in Israel now saw Saddam as an existential threat. This was why, in my opinion, the United States, following Israel's lead, would ignore or rebuff Saddam's entreaties. With the Iran-Iraq War over, articles advancing a consistent line began appearing in the world press in 1988: that Saddam's victory made him the major threat to peace in the area. On a visit to Jordan shortly after the war, Saddam raised the subject with King Hussein. Saddam said he was mystified. He asked the king if the United States could be behind it. The king asked me. I received a negative response from Washington and reported it to the king, who passed it back to Saddam. But the steady media rumblings against Saddam continued. I was told that an office in the Pentagon was aware of the anti-Saddam campaign, had researched it and published an unclassified monograph on the subject, identifying Jewish sources in the United States. Two weeks after publication, the monograph was withdrawn from circulation and never seen again. I attempted to obtain a copy, without success.

By the spring of 1990, Saddam, bellicose and belligerent, engaged in a war of words with both the United States and Israel. He said U.S. Navy ships in the Gulf posed a threat to Iraq, and he threatened Israel with a chemical strike if the Israeli Defense Forces staged any kind of attack. Clearly, he was thinking back to the IDF's bombing raid on his nuclear reactor at Osirak in 1981. But the most serious tension in the region—which, in retrospect, was not taken seriously enough—involved Saddam's grievances against Kuwait, which began with his belief that Kuwait and other Arab states had failed to forgive Iraqi debt incurred during its war against Iran. Saddam also accused the Kuwaitis of exceeding OPEC quotas to drive down the price of oil, stealing Iraqi oil through slant-drilling, and setting up police stations, military installations, and farms on Iraqi territory along the border.

At this point, there was little doubt on anyone's part that Saddam's grievances were, probably, legitimate. The United States finally woke up to the fact that tensions were building dangerously and that it needed to weigh in. The State Department sent a cable, signed by Secretary of State James A. Baker III, providing the U.S. position on the Iraqi-Kuwait flare-up. It was delivered by my friend April Glaspie, whom I mentored in the mid-1960s when she arrived at the embassy in Amman as the first female Foreign Service officer in the Middle East. Now, twenty-five years later, after tours in Kuwait, Stockholm, Beirut, Cairo, London, New York, and Damascus, she was ambassador to Iraq, the first woman to lead an embassy in the region. "While we take no position on the border delineation raised by Iraq with respect to Kuwait, or on other bilateral disputes, Iraqi statements suggest an intention to resolve outstanding disagreements by the use of force, an approach which is contrary to U.N. charter principles," the cable read. Glaspie was then summoned to a meeting with Saddam on July 25. The way she conducted this meeting, the government's last formal interaction with Saddam before he invaded Kuwait on August 2, has been the subject of controversy ever since, probed by Congress, investigated by journalists, and studied by historians.

Glaspie clearly saw Saddam as a "man who lives by the sword," as she told the House Foreign Affairs Committee the following year.

But she also saw him as someone the United States could negotiate with. The message she delivered was ambivalent in the English translation. It could not have been less so in Arabic. In effect, it said the problem is between Iraq and Kuwait, and the United States could deal with the Kuwaitis on a bilateral basis. After receiving Baker's ambivalent cable, Saddam assumed he had a green light to redress his grievances. In secret cables to Washington, later declassified, Glaspie said of Saddam: "His emphasis that he wants peaceful settlement is surely sincere. Iraqis are sick of war." But she added that she had "made clear that we can never excuse settlement of disputes by other than peaceful means." Her critics said she took a weak, conciliatory line with Saddam, a charge she later denied in her congressional testimony. In any event, she shouldn't be blamed for Saddam's miscalculation; and as events unfolded, her contention that Saddam desired a peaceful solution to the crisis was borne out—if only the United States had been willing to negotiate terms through which Saddam could have withdrawn his forces from Kuwait.

In hindsight, there's no doubt that the Bush administration's communications with Saddam were inconsistent, and certainly confusing. Three days after Glaspie's meeting, President Bush sent Saddam a three-paragraph message that some officials in the Defense Department thought was too weak and tried, unsuccessfully, to stop:

> I was pleased to learn of the agreement between Iraq and Kuwait to begin negotiations in Jedda to find a peaceful solution to the current tensions between you. The United States and Iraq both have a strong interest in preserving the peace and stability of the Middle East. For this reason, we believe that differences are best resolved by peaceful means and not by threats involving military force or conflict.
>
> I also welcome your statement that Iraq desires friendship,

rather than confrontation with the United States. Let me reassure you, as my Ambassador, Senator [Robert] Dole, and others have done, that my Administration continues to desire better relations with Iraq. We will also continue to support our other friends in the region with whom we have had longstanding ties. We see no necessary inconsistency between these two objectives.

As you know, we still have fundamental concerns about certain Iraqi policies and activities, and we will continue to raise these concerns with you in a spirit of friendship and candor, as we have in the past, both to gain a better understanding of your interests and intentions and to ensure that you understand our concerns. I completely agree that both our Governments must maintain open channels of communication to avoid misunderstanding and in order to build a more durable foundation for improving our relations.

Days later, Saddam launched the August 2 invasion of Kuwait, sending four Republican Guard divisions across the border. Saddam soon declared that the Kuwaiti state had become Iraq's nineteenth province. Within a matter of weeks, the administration's willingness to negotiate an end to the occupation vanished. Nothing less than forcible, military eviction would suffice. There is also no doubt that April Glaspie became a scapegoat for the administration's failures. She was in London, on her way back to the United States, when Saddam invaded Kuwait; she would never return to the embassy in Baghdad, even though she technically retained the title of ambassador for the better part of a year.

She was privately bitter about the way she was treated, but she didn't show it publicly. She was very noble about it all, a good soldier, and didn't complain. April didn't have any witnesses, it was that simple, and there was no way the Bush administration was ever going to take the blame for failing to adequately warn Saddam, which it clearly did not do. The State Department ultimately made her consul general in Johannesburg, which is where she retired.

I called her when Richard N. Haass's book, *War of Necessity, War of Choice: A Memoir of Two Iraq Wars* was published in the spring of 2009, just to warn her that the events of July and August 1990 were likely to be briefly back in the news again. I sent her the book and told her I wasn't sure whether she even wanted to talk to me about any of this. But none of it seemed to faze her. "There isn't anything I wouldn't tell you, Jack," she said.

Haass's judgment in the book, on April's performance, and that of the Bush administration, which he served as a senior member of the National Security Council staff, seems fair in hindsight:

Both Ambassador Glaspie and the administration were criticized after the fact for not having done more to convince Saddam Hussein not to attack. I do not believe that there was more under the circumstances we could or should have done or, more fundamentally, that anything we might have done would have made a difference. Saddam was a selective reader of history, and it is clear from his July 25 meeting with Glaspie that he viewed the United States as soft. This was the lesson he took from Vietnam and, more recently and closer to home, from the American withdrawal in Lebanon in 1984 following the bombing of the Marine barracks there the previous year. To be sure, statements by various administration officials that we had no formal alliance commitment to Kuwait were unfortunate and may have reinforced these perceptions. And nearly all of us were wrong in discounting the possibility that Saddam might invade Kuwait as he did. Still, on any number of occasions the United States signaled its commitment to its friends, and U.S. forces remained

in the region to underscore the commitment. There was no way
the Ambassador or anyone else could have credibly threatened
Saddam with a response of the scale of what the United States
and the world ultimately did in the Persian Gulf War. It is also
important to keep in mind Saddam's lack of respect for his fellow Arabs. He almost certainly dismissed the possibility that
they would rally around widely disliked Kuwait and stand up
to him. I am also reminded of the small sign that Bob Gates
kept on his desk: "The best way to achieve complete strategic
surprise is to take an action that is either stupid or completely
contrary to your self-interest." [pp. 58–59]

Chapter 14

A WAR THAT NEED NOT HAVE
BEEN WAGED

The machinations that followed Saddam's invasion of Kuwait rivaled the hectic prelude to the Arab-Israeli 1967 War. King Fahd of Saudi Arabia called Saddam, as soon as he received news of Iraq's invasion, to urge him to limit his movement of troops to the disputed border area. He also called King Hussein and asked him to repeat the request to Saddam. The king could not reach Saddam until the afternoon. When he did, Saddam told him to relax. Saddam said he was only interested in teaching the Kuwaitis a lesson, not in taking over their country.

Coincidentally, an Arab League Foreign Ministers Conference was scheduled in Cairo for the following day. King Hussein and Jordan's foreign minister, Marwan Kassim, flew immediately to Alexandria to consult with Egyptian president Hosni Mubarak. They decided Hussein should fly to Baghdad the next day to persuade Saddam to withdraw from Kuwait. They telephoned King Fahd, who approved the trip. Hussein and Mubarak also called President Bush, who gave the king forty-eight hours to accomplish his mission.

Mubarak was afraid the Arab foreign ministers' assembling in Cairo might cause something foolish to happen over the Iraq situation, so he offered Foreign Minister Kassim his plane to fly to Cairo to help keep a lid on that group. King Hussein flew back to Jordan the same day.

The next day, the king flew to Baghdad and met with Saddam. Saddam agreed to begin withdrawing from Kuwait in four days, provided that the Arab foreign ministers gathering in Cairo did not blame him for invading Kuwait and no one threatened to eject him by force. The king returned to Amman elated. He placed several calls to Mubarak before reaching him. He told Mubarak the good news. Mubarak said it was too little and too late. He was under extreme internal and external pressure to condemn Saddam. Nothing short of an unconditional withdrawal would do. The king was dumbfounded.

Marwan Kassim reported to the Egyptian Foreign Office the next morning after his arrival in Cairo and asked to meet with Usama al Bas, Mubarak's top foreign policy adviser. Kassim was told al Bas was out of the country. Kassim found this to be remarkable, with the Arab League foreign ministers convening the same day. Kassim asked if al Bas had gone to the United States. The Foreign Office official said, "No. He left in a small plane." Kassim assumed al Bas had gone to Israel.

That night, a resolution condemning Saddam and demanding Iraq's immediate withdrawal from Kuwait was railroaded through the Foreign Ministers' Conference. Several Arab states, including Jordan, abstained. A copy of the resolution was on each Arab representative's desk when he arrived at the conference. There was no debate. It was an up and down vote. The Arabic text, according to several in attendance, was an obvious translation from English. The next day, when Foreign Minister Kassim was leaving through the Cairo airport, he spotted al Bas returning.

Two days later, President Bush flew back to the White House from Camp David. As he passed the welcoming crowd on the White House lawn, a newspaper reporter yelled out: "What's new on Iraq?"

"A few days ago I gave a friendly Arab leader forty-eight hours to persuade Saddam to withdraw from Kuwait, but he failed," the president said.

Obviously, no one had given Bush a truthful account of King Hussein's meeting with Saddam. Actually, Saddam did withdraw some troops four days after he promised King Hussein he would do so, despite the fact that Saddam's two conditions had not been met; namely, that the Arab League Foreign Ministers' meeting in Cairo not condemn Iraq for punishing Kuwait and not threaten Iraq with the use of force.

The United States proceeded to organize a Western-Arab coalition, and transported troops and equipment to Saudi Arabia and the Gulf in preparation for the eviction of Iraqi troops from Kuwait. But before the buildup began, Thomas Pickering, the Bush administration's UN representative, cornered Abdullah Salah, the Jordanian UN representative, and suggested measures which might be taken to answer Iraq's grievances against Kuwait in exchange for a peaceful Iraqi withdrawal schedule from Kuwait. At this point in mid-August, Pickering believed the United States could still assemble enough organizations and parties to carry out the various measures involved. He cited five ways in which Iraq's grievances could be alleviated: (1) reduce or eliminate Iraq's debt to Kuwait; (2) stop Kuwaiti slant-drilling of Iraqi oil fields and compensate Iraq for lost oil; (3) enforce OPEC quotas on Kuwait; (4) arrange for Iraqi leasing of two islands from Kuwait in Shatt al Arab; and (5) the United States might support a possible change of rulership in Kuwait.

Abdullah Salah called General Zaid bin Shakir in the palace in Amman and relayed the message. General Shakir called Salah back asking him to find out if this was Pickering talking or the U.S. government. Salah raised the question with Pickering in his office. In Salah's presence, Pickering telephoned Secretary of State Baker, who was in

Wyoming, having just returned from a trip to the Soviet Union. Baker told Pickering he would call him back in a few minutes. There was little doubt in Pickering or Salah's minds that Baker was checking it out with President Bush. Baker answered to no one else. Then he called back and told Pickering, "We can live with that." Salah passed the message to General bin Shakir in Amman that it was the U.S. government talking and the United States wanted King Hussein to pass the message to Saddam.

I was in Marbella, Spain, when these UN conversations were taking place. I was to meet Dick Viets in Rome, en route to Amman. Pickering knew of our schedule. At the time, Viets was working for the Jordanians as a diplomatic and political counselor under a contract I had arranged for him, a role he would fill from 1988 through 1994. Pickering called Viets in Washington, told him of the encounter with Ambassador Salah, and asked Viets that we reinforce the request to the king to pass the message to Saddam when we reached Amman. Viets took notes on Pickering's call, which he still has.

When Viets and I arrived in Amman, before we had even unpacked at the hotel we received a summons to the palace. When we arrived, we were ushered into a room in which the king was briefing senior palace and government officials on a visit with Saddam in Baghdad from which he had just returned. As the meeting came to an end, Viets asked the king about the message from Pickering concerning the U.S. proposal to deal with Iraqi grievances against Kuwait as a prelude to Iraq's withdrawal from Kuwait. The king didn't know what Dick was talking about. I glanced around the room; most of the king's advisers were looking at the ceiling, including General bin Shakir. It dawned on Dick and me that no Jordanian had passed the message to the king.

It was hard to know exactly what was going on, but the king and some of his advisers clearly had different agendas. Some of those advisers were managing arms supplies to Iraq, and were betting the United States would not risk the lives it would take to drive Iraq out of Kuwait. They were against a mediated U.S. negotiation. General Ali Shuqri, the king's secretary, who was close to these machinations, did not believe that General Shakir, who was Jordanian ambassador Salah's contact in the palace, made any of the political decisions. He would have passed the question on to Prime Minister Mudar Badran. Badran was the leader of the pro-Saddam group in Jordan, and he was betting on Saddam winning the showdown with the United States. If true, it was another contribution to a war that need not have been waged.

Surrounded by these men, the king broke the awkward silence at the palace meeting by saying we were all going to Washington that afternoon and then on to Kennebunkport, Maine, for a meeting with the president. The king wanted Viets and me to meet them at the airport and join them on the trip. A car would be sent to the hotel to pick us up. The car never arrived. The king and his party left without us.

Viets and I met with Prince Hassan, who was regent in the king's absence, to tell him the story. "They didn't want you on the plane to tell the King your tale," he said. We made other airline reservations, reaching Washington before the king and his party, who spent the night there before they left for Maine. I was able to meet with Foreign Minister Kassim in Washington to ask what was going on. He only said that time had passed the proposal by. The group, joined by Secretary of State Baker, flew to Kennebunkport the next day. Baker conditioned them for what would likely happen at the president's vacation home on August 16. It wasn't pretty. The king was still interested in pursuing strategies for negotiating with Saddam. But by then, whatever interest Bush had in a negotiated settlement had given way to his ultimate hard-line position. He was interested only in an Iraqi withdrawal from Kuwait, without conditions, and restoration of the Kuwaiti regime.

After this, Bush's relationship with the king became badly strained, quite possibly because the two had been so close up to this moment. Bush felt personally betrayed by the king's suggestion that a peaceful resolution with Saddam was possible. The king sensed the president's irritation and in turn felt that he'd been treated shabbily. I wondered whether Bush even knew about Saddam's stated willingness to withdraw, which the king had brought away from his first meeting with the Iraqi leader within the first forty-eight hours after his invasion of Kuwait. Had Bush and the king both fallen victim to aides telling them only what they felt their bosses needed to know? Clearly, some of the king's aides stood to gain from their relationships with Saddam. Just as clearly, some of Bush's more hard-line aides saw Saddam as a tyrant and a threat to Israel and wanted to engage him in battle, not negotiations.

After the meeting, the new U.S. ambassador in Amman, Roger Harrison, handed the king a message which said that "the perception of a de facto Iraqi-Jordanian alliance has already damaged the reputation of Jordan in the United States and elsewhere." While Jordan technically remained neutral during the war, the king paid a heavy price in the United States for his refusal to join the coalition and his willingness to continue dealings with Saddam. At that point, he was the only Arab leader still willing to do so. The coalition, involving thirty-four countries, came together in the fall of 1990 after UN resolutions established January 15, 1991, as a deadline for Iraq to leave Kuwait and authorized all means necessary to deter Iraqi aggression. The Coalition Forces came to number more than 950,000 troops, three quarters of whom were American. Most of the rest came from Saudi Arabia, Egypt, and the United Kingdom. In retrospect, Viets feels the king's support for Saddam and his refusal to join the coalition hurt him far more than I do.

"I think he paid a terrific penalty for doing what he thought was the right way to play that card," Dick told me. "Only toward the end of his life did he get rehabilitated in this country. There was a long period after that war when people wouldn't give him the time of day."

Whatever it may have cost him, the king was right. The United States could have, and should have, negotiated an Iraqi withdrawal from Kuwait. If we had only given Saddam the respect he craved, there's no doubt in my mind that we could have come away with terms that would have made more than a decade of sanctions, no-fly-zone enforcement, escalating hostility, weapons inspections, and, finally, the second Iraq war in 2003 unnecessary.

The king wanted to avoid a war and convince Saddam to withdraw from Kuwait before he was ejected. He was a voice in the wilderness, echoed periodically by a Pickering or a Baker. But Richard N. Perle and the American neocons were having none of negotiation, to say nothing of the Israelis, who handled the Iraqi problem more cleverly than the Palestinian problem. Ironically, the only consistent peacemaker, King Hussein, was castigated by the United States for failing to join the U.S. military coalition. On the eve of the war, Bush told Baker that he was sending him to Baghdad to negotiate with Saddam. A group of hard-liners led by Perle, an assistant secretary of defense during the Reagan administration, talked Bush out of it on the grounds Saddam could hold Baker hostage. We knew from the Rumsfeld trip in 1983 that a high-level Baker visit was the best way to deal with Saddam. Instead, Baker delivered a humiliating letter in a public forum in Paris, to Tariq Aziz, Iraq's foreign minister. It was intended that Aziz would reject it, which he did. Baker then read remarks, already written, assuming the rejection.

Led by the U.S. military, the coalition launched Operation Desert

Storm on January 16, 1991, driving Iraq's forces out of Kuwait and annihilating them on the battlefield in southern Iraq. The war lasted forty-three days, most of it a spectacular air assault featuring squadrons of fighter-bombers, stealth aircraft, laser-guided bombs, and cruise missiles fired from the air and from U.S. Navy ships in the Persian Gulf. Bush wisely decided not to occupy Iraq. Overthrowing Saddam had never been part of the war's mandate. His son would not be so wise. The United States encouraged Iraqi and Kurdish resistance after the fighting ended, but failed to support it, resulting in unnecessary Iraqi sacrifices. Saddam survived to fight another war.

Once the war ended, Dick and I tried to find out what had been going on inside the Bush administration in the aftermath of Saddam's invasion of Kuwait the previous August. Viets took Tom Pickering to lunch and brought out the detailed notes he took of his conversation on the five steps to defuse the crisis peacefully, including a look at supporting new leaders in Kuwait. Pickering said he had no recollection of the conversation. Viets came back from lunch and told me that Pickering denied that he had said the things Dick had written down. Later, I asked Pickering out to lunch. He's an old friend and one of the most competent and honest men I've met in Washington.

"Tom, you must remember what you told Dick," I said. "To say that didn't happen is not you—are you under some vow or oath not to tell anybody anything?"

"No, you're right, I had that conversation with Dick," he replied.

"Well, then, you had two policies, didn't you, one to make peace with Saddam, and the other to overthrow him? Who was behind which policy? And why did one win?"

"There weren't opposing policies," he said. "They were alternative policies. We had one for peace and one for war and we tried them both at the same time."

"Tom, that might have been what you were thinking, but Saddam didn't know which was which at any given moment," I said. "So he didn't know what to do. All you were doing was confusing him. That's no way to make policy."

And that's the way our conversation ended.

It was during the war that I got an angry call from a State Department official who said Queen Noor would never be invited to the White House again after she gave a speech that First Lady Barbara Bush thought was anti-American. Noor makes a reference to this in her own memoir, *Leap of Faith*. "I would continue to speak out after the war started about humanitarian consequences of the war and the suffering of the people of Iraq, which evidently so angered Mrs. Bush that she sent a message through an American official that she considered me a traitor," she writes. "I imagine that the message was intended to stop me from talking about uncomfortable issues for the Bush administration." Noor found this turn of events particularly distressing because Barbara and George Bush were "old friends" and visited with the king and her on many occasions. She notes how Bush, as vice president, "played with our delighted boys in the pool in Aqaba." It was George Bush, after all, who had written across the bottom of an effusive letter to King Hussein shortly after his election in 1988: "P.S. On the personal side, Barbara sends her love to Queen Noor and all the family. I value our friendship—I really do!"

But the Bushes weren't alone in fuming about the outspoken queen. Abu Shaker, then chief of the Royal Hashemite Court, and a group of senior Jordanian officials approached me about the same speech when we were all in Aqaba at one point during the war. They told me to tell the king to have his wife refrain from giving any more public speeches. This was typical of things, sensitive things, that they would ask me to tell the king because they were hesitant to tell him themselves.

"No, I'm not going to tell him to do that," I said. "You tell him."

Chapter 15

COLD PEACE

The old Mossad operative contacted his CIA counterpart through an intermediary. He expressed a desire to have a talk alone. A drawing room was found at Ditchley Park, with a fireplace and a bottle of scotch. The Georgian mansion outside London in Oxfordshire was big enough that no one at the conference would miss them for an hour. The setting for my meeting with David Kimche was straight out of John le Carré.

He was a former senior Mossad officer working, in May 1991, as security adviser to Israeli prime minister Yitzhak Shamir. We knew a good deal about each other but had never actually met before this Middle East conference sponsored by the Ditchley Foundation. Leading Middle East scholars, politicos, and spies, current and former, had gathered to survey the region as the United States brought its forces—at least most of them—home from the Gulf. Saddam regrouped, and a solution to the Israeli-Palestinian standoff seemed as elusive as ever. Kimche asked Dick Viets, whom he knew from Dick's days as deputy chief of mission at the U.S. Embassy in Tel Aviv, to introduce us.

We drank, and I listened. He wanted me to pass a message from Shamir, on behalf of the Likud Party leadership, to King Hussein. In essence, the message was that the Palestinians presented a security problem for both Israel and Jordan, almost three years after the king had formally relinquished control of the West Bank. One way to minimize the problem would be to include the Palestinians in a loose confederation composed of Israel, Jordan, and Palestine. It would also provide economic benefits to each party, which would contribute to everyone's security. I agreed to pass on the message.

On my next trip to Amman, I relayed the message to the king. He listened attentively. I asked if he wanted me to give Kimche an answer. He said no. He never mentioned it to me again. And, as far as I know, it never came up in the secret meetings between the king and the Israelis. Abba Eban espoused the same idea from time to time, but without serious takers on either side. The devil was in the details—like borders.

Perhaps Kimche was just freewheeling. According to a mutual friend, Kimche was in secret contact with top Iraqis under Saddam Hussein. The United States found out, and "his knuckles were rapped." I know from other sources that Labor Party leaders in Israel favored a deal with Saddam and that Kimche was probably not acting on his own. King Hussein was willing to offer the Palestinians a federation if the West Bank was returned, in its entirety.

Back in Washington, Dick and I hired a limousine and attended another function together that proved memorable: the annual Gridiron Dinner, a night of satirical skits by members of the press, as well as remarks by the president and leading members of both parties. We were the guests of Philip L. Geyelin, the former editorial page editor of *The Washington Post*, whom the king and I first engaged to write this book. He had a good table near the head table, befitting his place in the Washington media establishment. He had won the Pulitzer Prize for editorial writing in 1970 after turning the *Post*'s editorial page against the Vietnam War. After stepping down as editorial page editor in 1979, he began to write a foreign affairs column focused on the Middle East. Sitting across from me at his table was a beguiling woman, Evangeline Bruce, the legendary Georgetown hostess and widow of diplomat David K. E. Bruce. The first thing she did was go up to the head table where the president and administration and congressional leaders were seated and walk down from one end to the other, saying hello to everyone. She wasn't showboating in the slightest. She knew them all, and they all knew her, and liked her. She came back to our table. We were introduced.

"Do you know who you remind me of?" I asked.

"Who?" she said.

"Greta Garbo."

Apparently, it was the perfect compliment, and we chatted throughout the evening. When the Gridiron show was over, Evangeline walked out with us. They called for our car, and when she saw the limo, she remarked, "I don't have anything that good. Could I go with you guys?"

So she got in the backseat with us and we took her to her home in Georgetown. As she was saying goodbye, she explained that she had a soirée every Sunday. "Would you like to come to the next one?" Viets was out of the country, but I went, and brought her flowers, which pleased her. Then she took me by the arm and walked me around the room introducing me to everybody. There were very few people that I knew. But one of them was David Ignatius, the brilliant *Washington Post* writer and columnist. He was with Katharine Graham, the *Post*'s publisher, whom I didn't know but recognized. I was obviously the least important person in the room. Nobody knew who I was, and that saved me. People began asking, sotto voce, if I was her new boyfriend. I wasn't her new boyfriend, but I didn't have to answer that. She invited me back, again and again. Once, the Forbes yacht sailed into town on a cruise to someplace, and Evangeline called me and asked if I wanted to be her guest at an elegant party on board. She needed an escort. I spent most of the evening talking to Senator John F. Kerry, who was interested in the fact that I knew Evangeline and Queen Noor. He had met the queen and wanted to exchange notes. Later, I invited Evangeline to dinner at the Georgetown Club. She invited me to some kind of barnyard dance her daughter was hosting on the Potomac, and we danced. Another time, she wanted to know whether I could join her and Pamela Harriman and some of their other friends at a villa they rented in France, but I wasn't able to go.

Our friendship lasted about a year. She had some medical problems. Then she wasn't available. I wasn't aware that she was as sick as she was—it was kind of shocking when someone said she was on her deathbed. She seemed in good health when I was with her. Indeed, she was effervescent, interesting to talk to, smart, well-read, abreast of public events. I learned in hours of conversation that she was the daughter of a diplomat, educated at Radcliffe in the late 1930s, where she studied Chinese history and French literature. During World War II, in London, she had worked for the OSS. We never really discussed anything controversial, but our political views certainly seemed compatible. We became quite close, though it never really got to be a romance. She was a very charming lady whose company I greatly enjoyed. She had all the polishing that you get in this life. She died, at seventy-seven, in 1995.

But my social life in Washington provided only a brief respite from the conflicts in the Middle East, which only grew more Byzantine, and unsolvable. In the aftermath of the Gulf War, with Saddam enormously weakened, President Bush and Secretary of State Baker moved to capitalize on his weakness by seriously addressing the Palestinian problem. They convened a conference in Madrid that October, 1991, inviting all parties to the conflict to negotiate a comprehensive peace agreement. The king was never close to the businesslike Baker, as far as I could tell, but he respected Baker for being willing to take on

Israel. There was never any question about Jordan going to Madrid, even though the secretary of state had gone of out his way to make clear that relations with Jordan were still badly strained over the war. He didn't have to fight with the Jordanians over participating, and they took on a lot of responsibility.

In convening the conference with the Soviet Union as co-sponsor, the Bush administration assured Jordan that the goal was a comprehensive peace based on UN resolutions 242 and 338. But the conference, the first negotiations ever to involve the Israelis, Syrians, Lebanese, Jordan, and the Palestinians, turned into a bigger task than anyone was up to. There were too many missing links. Yitzhak Shamir attended under the duress of U.S. aid cuts, but vowed he would negotiate for nothing, and he didn't. For him, and other right-wing Israelis, peace negotiations were anathema. Negotiations meant concessions, and they weren't ready to make any. The PLO was invited, but Arafat, the PLO chairman, was not, so he spent the week in his hotel room. The PLO representatives who did attend were a tame group, without authority, and attended as part of the Jordanian delegation. Baker had also made it clear to them that the only issue on the table was self-rule in the territories. But for the first time, the Palestinians were treated as equals of the Israelis at the negotiating table.

Although the conference resulted in no significant accomplishments, it put everyone in the same room together for the first time, which was a form of progress. Jordan was the party that adapted several different positions, to accommodate abnormal situations. The Hashemite Kingdom was a prop for the United States to use to bend corners and get everybody inside the door legitimately. In the end, nobody really agreed to anything. But at least the king's relations with President Bush were on the mend. While the aim of the conference was to set the stage for talks between Israel and Lebanon, Syria and a Jordanian-Palestinian delegation, it was not even clear after three days of discussion whether any of those subsequent talks would take place. Shamir began the closing session by calling Syria "one of the most oppressive, tyrannical regimes in the world." He also described Palestinian massacres of Jews before the State of Israel was created. He then left the conference before the Arab delegations spoke.

But if Shamir never had any intention of negotiating on anything close to implementation of UN Resolution 242, the man who defeated him the following June, 1992, Yitzhak Rabin, clearly did. He and the Labor Party decisively beat their Likud rivals, emphasizing security and a commitment to negotiations under the Madrid framework. While Likud remained committed to Israeli settlements on the West Bank and Gaza, Rabin and Shimon Peres, whom Rabin named his foreign minister in July, said they favored completion of an agreement with the Palestinians on self-rule in the territories within a year. The Labor victory took place as Democrat Bill Clinton campaigned against Bush and appeared on his way to victory in November.

The summer's other development, fraught with portent, came in August, when the king checked into the Mayo Clinic in Minnesota for surgery on an obstruction in his urinary tract. Doctors found precancerous cells in the ureter leading from his kidney. They removed the kidney as a precaution, confident they caught the cancer at an early stage. The king returned to Jordan in late September and was greeted in the streets by what some estimated as a third of Jordan's population.

He was back in Washington in June 1993, for his first meeting with Clinton, the ninth president with whom he had conducted the affairs of state. The king's recent public statements in opposition to Saddam Hussein's continued rule in Iraq had gone a long way toward repairing relations with the United States, though a General Accounting Office report concluding that Jordan had shared intelligence and military spare parts with Iraq during the Gulf War showed that he had not yet put the Saddam problem completely behind him. Viets and I met him at his home in Potomac before he went to see Clinton at the White House. We weren't that high on Clinton. We told the king to be careful with him and not assume that he was going to be a friend. He took off in his limousine to see the president, and we waited at his house for him to come back. When he returned, we were taken aback.

"I just met the best president I've ever met," he announced.

We thought, Oh my God, he's bought into the guy. But he saw Clinton at his best—charming, charismatic, and up to speed. Aides could brief Clinton on something, and he got it instantly. He could then go and perform as though he was an expert on the subject. There was no quicker study. The king got a dose of that in his first meeting, and he was impressed by somebody, new to the job, who seemed to be so well informed.

"He's a very knowledgeable guy, a very well oriented guy, and I'm going to have a good time with him," the king said.

By then, secret talks between the Israelis and the PLO in Oslo had been underway for six months. I don't know whether Clinton and the United States had an inkling of what was going on, but the king did not. When word of an agreement between the two became public in August 1993, the king felt lied to and betrayed, though he quickly realized the deal was a good one for the Palestinians, calling for a return of the Gaza Strip and the West Bank town of Jericho. Beyond that, Oslo was more of a framework for further negotiations than an actual peace treaty. There were three things of significance about this development: the negotiations had been conducted in secret; they didn't involve the Americans or other third parties; and Israel was much better prepared for the negotiations than the Palestinians. From those who have talked to the Israeli negotiators, Israel had several fallback positions, but the Israelis did not have to fall back to any of them. By threatening to terminate the negotiations, the Palestinians quickly fell in line.

Rabin and Arafat shook hands on a historic declaration of principles on Palestinian self-government on September 13, 1993, on the South Lawn at the White House. President Clinton lauded their "brave gamble that the future can be better than the past." No agreement on Israeli West Bank settlements was an important omission. The following day, with much less pomp and circumstance, a Jordanian-Israeli common agenda for negotiations was agreed upon during a low-key meeting in the State Department's Jefferson Room. By the following spring, the king had made it clear that he was willing to throw caution to the winds and negotiate a comprehensive peace agreement with Israel. When the king pushed Washington for $700 million in debt forgiveness to help him sell a peace agreement to his countrymen, a majority of whom opposed a deal with Israel, President Clinton personally intervened. He told the king that a public meeting to sign a peace agreement in Washington, which he would host, would go a long way toward convincing Congress to forgive the debt.

The signing ceremony for the Washington Declaration took place at the White House on July 25, 1994. It officially ended a state of war between the two nations. I watched King Hussein and Yitzhak Rabin with great pride. They sat on either side of President Clinton at a desk on a stage on the South Lawn of the White House—the same desk used by Rabin and Arafat to initial their declaration ten months earlier. But unlike Rabin and Arafat, Rabin and Hussein shared the stage as friends, even though Rabin, almost thirty years earlier, had been the one who commanded the Israeli forces that captured the West Bank during the 1967 War. I found the king's oratory emotionally overwhelming.

"We will meet as often as we are able to and as required with pleasure to shepherd this process on in the times ahead," the king said. "At this moment, I would like to share with you all the pride I have in my people, the people of Jordan, and their maturity and their courage, and, in what I have been blessed with, their trust and confidence, and I believe the commitment of the overwhelming majority to the cause of peace."

The declaration read, in part:

In their meeting, His Majesty King Hussein and Prime Minister Yitzhak Rabin have jointly reaffirmed the five underlying principles of their understanding on an Agreed Common Agenda designed to reach the goal of a just, lasting and comprehensive peace between the Arab States and the Palestinians, with Israel.

1. Jordan and Israel aim at the achievement of just, lasting and comprehensive peace between Israel and its neighbors and at the conclusion of a Treaty of Peace between both countries.

2. The two countries will vigorously continue their negotiations to arrive at a state of peace, based on Security Council Resolutions 242 and 338 in all their aspects, and founded on freedom, equality and justice.

3. Israel respects the present special role of the Hashemite Kingdom of Jordan in Muslim Holy shrines in Jerusalem. When negotiations on the permanent status will take place, Israel will give high priority to the Jordanian historic role in these shrines. In addition the two sides have agreed to act together to promote interfaith relations among the three monotheistic religions.

4. The two countries recognize their right and obligation to live in peace with each other as well as with all states within secure and recognized boundaries. The two states affirmed

their respect for and acknowledgment of the sovereignty, territorial integrity and political independence of every state in the area.

5. The two countries desire to develop good neighborly relations of co-operation between them to insure lasting security and to avoid threats and the use of force between them.

The final peace accord was signed on October 26 under a blazing sun at the Arava Crossing along the desert border between Israel and Jordan, with President Clinton and 4,500 other guests present, including foreign ministers from a dozen nations. Once again, I found the king's remarks stirring, given how long he had worked and how much he had sacrificed for this moment:

It is with a sense of enormous pride, a sense of fulfillment that I stand here before you today—together with President Clinton, Prime Minister Yitzhak Rabin, President Weizman, and all our distinguished colleagues and friends. An unusual day. A day like no other in terms of the hopes, in terms of the promise, and in terms of the determination. . . .

We will always cherish the memory and honor all those who have fallen over the years from amongst all of our peoples. I believe they are with us on this occasion and at this time, as we come together to insure—God willing—that there will be no more death, no more misery, no more suspicion, no more fear, no more uncertainty of what each day might bring, as has been the case in the past.

Prime Minister Yitzhak Rabin and I had the honor of signing the Washington Declaration with President Clinton—our partner and our friend. And we took it upon us—Prime Minister Yitzhak Rabin and myself—to shepherd the process of negotiations to a successful conclusion. I believe that both of us share in this moment of achievement and pride and relief—for, hopefully, we have contributed towards a better future of our peoples for all times to come. This is peace with dignity. This is peace with commitment. This is our gift to our peoples and the generations to come. It will herald the change in the quality of life of people. It will not be simply a piece of paper ratified by those responsible, blessed by the world. It will be real, as we open our hearts and minds to each other, as we discover a human face to everything that has happened and to each other—for all of us have suffered for far too long. . . .

But as moving as these words were, and as great as my sense of satisfaction was at that moment in the glare of the desert sun, I knew this was, at best, a partial peace. They made peace over land for which there was no issue between them. They didn't resolve any of the issues, including Jerusalem, including refugees, including the West Bank and the other occupied territories, the three big issues. They skipped all those in their treaty. I think the king panicked. He was looking out at the world. Egypt had made peace with Israel—a full peace. The Palestinians had just signed the Oslo Accords; it looked as if they were on the way to making peace. And there were rumors that the Syrians and the Israelis were talking about peace, which the Israelis promoted. The king's fear was that Israel might end up at peace with Syria, Egypt, and the PLO. Jordan would be sitting on the sidelines, the truest peacemaker of them all, without peace. I think he figured he had to get into the act.

As it turned out, the fears were false. Oslo did not turn into peace, and the Syrians did not make peace with Israel. Jordan was the only one that made peace, or more accurately, a partial peace. The king and his advisers seemed rushed into it, and I was afraid there would be loose ends, although I don't think there are any great ones. But it was the right thing for them to do, because it got them out of the war business. For the past sixteen years, they haven't been in confrontation with Israel. That's been a good thing, and I don't think any reasonable Jordanian would disagree.

Chapter 16

MISSED OPPORTUNITIES,
MISCALCULATIONS,
AND MISTAKES

I f the Oslo Accords and the Israeli-Jordanian peace plan created at least a semblance of momentum on Palestinian self-
governance, the West Bank, and Jerusalem, the other great issue
roiling the Middle East remained unsolved: Saddam. Despite his military defeat and tight international sanctions that enabled him to sell
oil only for food and medicines, the Iraqi president was still considered a menace by Israeli hard-liners and U.S. neocons. They wanted
him deposed. But there were important exceptions to this view in
Israel, expressed by Prime Minister Rabin and President Ezer Weizman. In the United States, former President Jimmy Carter shared the
same ideological space and was intrigued by the notion of reengaging
with Saddam.

After shaking hands with Arafat and making peace with King
Hussein, Rabin reached the intellectual conclusion that it would be in
Israel's strategic interest to make a deal with Saddam. He thought Iraq
would be a buffer against Iran, which was a much greater potential
threat to Israel than Iraq. He was also aware that Iraq was the economic plum of the Eastern Arab world, with water, oil, and an educated workforce. As economic partners, both Israel and Iraq would
prosper. Finally, if Israel and Iraq made peace, Rabin believed that

Syria would be compelled to follow on acceptable terms. I don't know whether he shared these views with many Israelis, but he shared them with King Hussein, and asked the king to pass the message to Saddam. Rabin told the king that if Saddam was agreeable, he would travel to Baghdad and raise Saddam's hand in the public square, extolling the partnership between the two countries.

While Rabin and Hussein were plotting, Viets and I were also considering how we could break the ice jam between Saddam and the United States, assuming Saddam would be willing to make a deal that would be in the interests of both countries. Former President Jimmy Carter naturally came to mind. He had broken the ice with North Korea and Haiti. Once broken, a reluctant U.S. administration had no excuse not to follow up. We wondered if Carter would be interested in opening the door to Iraq. Viets knew one of Carter's principal advisers at the Carter Center in Atlanta and sounded him out. He was interested, and soon, so was Carter, whose only condition was that if he met with Saddam, he come away with something.

We put Carter's principal adviser in touch with Nizar Hamdun, the Iraqi UN representative. As a former Iraqi ambassador to the United States, he was Iraq's senior diplomat and a member of Saddam's inner circle. Carter's staff chief and Hamdun met several times to work out the logistics and substance of a meeting between Saddam and Carter in Baghdad. Hamdun was interested. So was Saddam.

As the prospects of a meeting neared fruition, I felt obliged to inform King Hussein of what Viets and I had done. The king was surprised and completely negative. He said the timing was awful. He then told me about Rabin's desire to make a deal with Saddam. He said he feared a Carter visit would complicate the picture and hoped we could call it off or delay it.

The Rabin proposal was so out of line with the official Israeli position and so out of sync with Israeli hard-liners that we questioned whether Rabin's desire was accurately understood by the king. While we were still in Jordan, Viets crossed the Israeli border to sound out President Ezer Weizman, whom Dick had known when stationed in Israel.

They met in Weizman's office in Jerusalem. After an exchange of general views, and Viets's comments on the situation in Jordan, he said to the president, "I think Israel ought to make a deal with Saddam Hussein." Weizman arose from his chair and moved toward Dick, who feared he might be going to slap him. Instead, Weizman put his hands on Dick's shoulders and said, "You're absolutely right, and there are several in the government who feel the same way." Weizman expressed some of the same reasons Rabin had mentioned to the king. Viets questioned whether the United States would go along with it.

"No," Weizman said, the United States had already stopped two Israeli attempts to make a deal with Saddam. Israel would have to take a strong lead and the United States would, as usual, eventually follow. Viets made no mention of his knowledge of Rabin's approach to the king, but he left assured that Rabin's approach was for real—and history was, possibly, in the making.

Unfortunately, Rabin's proposition and Carter's friendly intervention failed. While Viets and I were pondering how to call off, or delay, Carter's meeting with Saddam, Carter took steps which unintentionally had the same effect. As for Rabin's proposal, it was never accurately conveyed to the Iraqi leader.

A wealthy Lebanese businessman, who was a friend of Carter's, found out that the former president intended to meet Saddam. The businessman then contacted an Iraqi Ba'athist close to Saddam, who had moved to Paris to pursue a business career. He was still connected to Saddam through his brother, an official in the Iraqi regime. Together, the Lebanese and the Iraqi represented an American oil company. They felt that if they could facilitate Carter's meeting with Saddam, they might receive some favors for the oil company in Iraq.

Thus, the Lebanese businessman offered to help Carter. Without knowledge of his ulterior motive, Carter accepted, and the businessman and his Iraqi contact took over negotiations in Baghdad to arrange for the visit. Viets and I gratefully backed out.

Shortly thereafter, Ambassador Hamdun called Carter's chief of staff with a message for Carter from Saddam. Saddam said he knew that Carter was an honorable man and that his request for a meeting was intended to be in the interests of both Iraq and the United States. But Saddam said he thought Carter was dealing through the wrong people. For that reason, he said, it was in the interests of both countries to cancel the meeting. End of message. End of meeting. End of another opportunity.

King Hussein decided not to deliver Rabin's offer himself. He did not want to be the messenger for such an offer, yet he wanted Saddam to know what Rabin might be thinking. He delegated the messaging to a senior Jordanian official. As I learned later, the official, privately, did not believe in the mission, so he garbled the message. He did not tell Saddam the offer was from Rabin, but from some prominent American Jews from Detroit, who were close to Rabin and acting on his behalf.

Saddam heard him out, then replied by reminding the envoy that when Jordan made peace with Israel in 1994, Saddam had said nothing because Jordan was acting in what it considered its best interest, which it had every right to do. In the same spirit, Saddam did not want Jordan telling him how he should act toward Israel.

The king and his communications chief, General Ali Shuqri, had suspicions that the Jordanian official had not delivered the offer accurately. Shuqri asked for my opinion. At the time I thought that it had gone as planned, and told him so.

It seemed to Dick and me that the Jordanians were taking a big gamble that Saddam would involve Jordan in such a sensitive secret negotiation, because Saddam could have been so easily blackmailed by adversaries if they had discovered he was engaged in secret bilateral talks with Israel.

Whether Saddam would have given the envoy a different answer if he knew the message came from Rabin is a good question. We will never know. Rabin was assassinated on November 4, 1995, by a right-wing Jewish militant, Yigal Amir, as he left a huge peace rally in Tel Aviv. Later, the king asked me if I thought Rabin had been assassinated because he was prepared to make a deal with Saddam. Did the Americans do it? he asked. I said it was incredible to think the U.S. government would assassinate an Israeli prime minister. It would be suicidal. The king explained that he didn't mean the U.S. government, but the followers of the Brooklyn-born Rabbi Meir Kahane, an ultranationalist who served in the Israeli Knesset in the mid-1980s. He advocated annexation of the West Bank and Gaza before he was killed in 1990 by an Egyptian-born American extremist now serving a life sentence. The king said Jordan had information that Rabin's assassin had secretly traveled to New York and met with followers of Kahane before the assassination. But subsequent investigations in Israel and the United States found no such evidence. Amir was convicted and sentenced to life imprisonment after Israeli officials concluded he acted alone on the night he murdered Rabin. Amir's brother and a third religious nationalist were later convicted of conspiring with him to kill the prime minister and attack Palestinian Arabs.

One meeting with Saddam that did take place as planned in July 1995 involved Bill Richardson, the Democratic congressman from New Mexico who, by virtue of his seniority on the House Permanent Select Committee on Intelligence, was developing quite a reputation as a pinch-hitting envoy for the Clinton administration. His experience suggests that Saddam had not lost his desire to deal with the United States, even after the Gulf War and UN sanctions. Richardson's mission was to meet with Saddam and convince him to pardon two U.S. military contractors, William Barloon and David Daliberti, who were stationed in Kuwait, got lost on a hike, and ended up in Iraq by mistake. They were tried, convicted, and jailed for illegally entering the country. The Iraqis suspected they were spies, but could find no proof. Their detention was an embarrassment for President Clinton. Richardson had spent three months talking about a possible release with Nizar Hamdun, Iraq's UN representative, before being told that if Richardson brought a letter from President Clinton, Saddam would be lenient.

Richardson arrived with three people from his office and the White House. They were ushered into Saddam's palatial office with a small group of Iraqi aides. Saddam entered, greeted the guests, then sat behind his desk. After a few minutes of strained silence, Saddam, red-faced, rose from his desk and left the room. Richardson asked the Iraqis what went wrong. They told him he had crossed his legs, sitting opposite Saddam, and ended up with the sole of his shoe in Saddam's face: in the Arab world, this was a major insult. After many apologies and much scurrying, Saddam returned and the session resumed.

Richardson told Saddam what his official position was, that he was a close friend of President Clinton, and that he was bearing a personal message from the president seeking the pardon and release of the two Americans. Saddam asked Richardson if he had a letter from President Clinton. Richardson replied that he had not, that President Clinton thought Richardson's presence was more significant than a letter.

Saddam leaned forward and said that the two Americans had been convicted in a fair, public trial. The only person in the country with the authority to pardon them was the president of Iraq. Saddam said that in his opinion if the president of the United States wanted the president of Iraq to pardon two Americans, the least he could do was write a letter requesting it.

Saddam went on, asking Richardson, rhetorically, what President Clinton thought Saddam was going to do with the letter, wave it before the Iraqis and the world, bragging that he had extracted a letter from the American president asking for a favor? Saddam said the opposite was true. Many Iraqis wanted pardons that I have not granted, he said, so if I get a letter from the American president and automatically pardon the Americans, it would make me look like an American stooge.

Saddam told Richardson that if he had brought a letter from Clinton he would have put it in his desk drawer and not advertised it. But satisfied that Clinton had been courteous enough to write a letter, he would have quietly released the prisoners. Richardson apologized, making the best of a bad situation. Saddam bid him farewell, then surprised his guest by adding that the prisoners were in the next room and Richardson could take them with him on his way out!

A member of Richardson's party briefed me on the meeting with Saddam, who had lectured Richardson on Clinton's bad form—and then gave the Americans what they wanted anyway. Later, Viets and I met with Richardson in his office. He repeated the account. When he finished, I asked him if, after his experience, he thought Saddam was someone the United States could work with. Without hesitation, he said yes. I asked him if he planned to share his assessment with President Clinton. No, he said, it would be presumptuous. Those around him weren't ready for it.

A month after Richardson's meeting with Saddam, two of Saddam's sons-in-law, their wives, and a group of Iraqi military officers drove to Amman in a convoy of Mercedes-Benzes and defected. While

King Hussein had been distancing himself from Saddam since the end of the Gulf War and saying the country needed to be democratized, he kept lines of communication open, if only to keep from angering a Jordanian elite that was getting rich off business ties to the Iraqis. The king immediately granted asylum to the Iraqis, who were led by Lieutenant General Hussein Kamel, the head of Iraq's missile development, chemical and biological weapons program, and its nuclear research. He was married to Saddam's eldest daughter, Raghad. His brother, Colonel Saddam Kamel, oversaw Iraqi special forces and was married to another of Saddam's daughters, Rana. The king put the entire Iraqi entourage up at Hashimiyah Palace and allowed Hussein Kamel to hold a press conference shortly after his arrival, at which he vowed to work for Saddam's overthrow. At one point during the press conference, I remember, Kamel pointed to a man in attendance and said, "Get him out of here, he's an Iraqi spy!"

Middle Eastern and Western analysts took the defections as a sign of growing weakness in Saddam's inner circle. The defections also served to energize exiled Iraqi opposition leaders such as Ahmed Chalabi of the Iraqi National Congress and Ayad Allawi of the Iraqi National Accord, both of whom were actively organizing opposition groups and plotting to overthrow Saddam. Less than a week after the Kamel brothers showed up at his doorstep, the king signaled that he was finally ready to break with Baghdad and throw his support to the opposition groups, telling an Israeli newspaper that he hoped the defections would begin a "new era" in Iraq.

I remember friends in the CIA telling me in the summer of 1995 about a half-baked covert operation the agency was involved in to overthrow Saddam. It was a lousy plan built around Allawi, a neurologist by training who was living in exile in London, and his opposition group, the Iraqi National Accord (INA). Allawi would ultimately become interim prime minister of Iraq in 2005 after the second American invasion. Anybody in the agency who had any background or experience in the Middle East was steering away from this operation, even though President Clinton himself was actively pushing the CIA to develop a plan to topple Saddam. The INA had apparently convinced the agency that it had contacts inside Saddam's elite Republican Guard who could spark a coup.

The king arrived in Washington in late September for a briefing on the operation at CIA headquarters in Langley. I met him and Abdul Karim Kabariti, Jordan's prime minister, at the Four Seasons Hotel and immediately began warning them away from the plot.

"Listen to what they have to say," I said. "They're going to show you charts, and they're going to substitute charts for facts, and the charts will depict the army, and the religious groups and the tribes, and they're going to describe how a small number of coup plotters will become an army and then overthrow Saddam; but it's childishness. Ask them who heads these military units. They won't know. You know this better than they do."

The American ambassador to Jordan, Wesley W. Egan, Jr., was with them at the hotel. I told him what I was trying to do, and he said, "Thank God!" He went off to the meeting with them, having muscled his way in somehow. He wanted to know what the CIA was going to do in his country. They came back from the meeting a couple of hours later and we met again at the Four Seasons.

"It was everything you said," the king told me. "It's a plan without a plan. It's just a lot of nonsense. Nothing is for sure."

"It was embarrassing," Egan said.

I thought I'd won the battle. They've seen the plan, and they won't agree to take part in it. But the next day, when they met President Clinton at the White House, things changed. The president got the king aside, with his arm around him, and told him they had a plan to overthrow Saddam, but they wouldn't be able to carry it out unless the king was part of the project. So it was up to the king: either we do it or we don't do it, and you're the key. Well, knowing the king, the people who brief the president had it right. The king didn't want to be the spoiler, so he agreed to go along with it.

Jordanian intelligence worked directly with operatives from an Iraqi National Accord field office established in Amman, as did officers from the CIA. Amazingly, there was nothing secret about the INA's office, or its mission. Allawi showed up in February 1996, held a press conference, and talked about both. This was right around the time Hussein Kamel and his brother took their wives back to Baghdad after it became clear that neither King Hussein nor any of the Iraqi opposition leaders saw them as viable opposition figures. Upon arriving in Baghdad, they were instantly divorced by their wives and executed in a family shoot-out at Saddam's behest. Operational security around the INA coup plot was so lax that an article appeared on the front page of *The Washington Post* on June 23, 1996, with the headline: "With CIA's help, Group in Jordan Targets Saddam; U.S. Funds Support Campaign to Topple Iraqi Leader from Afar." I can only imagine what senior CIA officials thought when they started reading: "In an office suite on a quiet street in Amman, Jordan, an exile group called the Iraqi National Accord is working feverishly to implement the latest CIA-backed plan to topple Iraqi President Saddam Hussein." Operational security was not a part of the plot. The article went on to say that President Clinton had signed a "finding" in January 1996 authorizing $6 million for the operation and quoted Allawi as saying, "We believe the end is near. We have entered the final chapter in salvaging Iraq."

But by then the coup attempt had been thoroughly penetrated by Iraqi intelligence. In July, Saddam rounded up several dozen Iraqis working with the INA and CIA and executed them. At some point during the blown operation, Iraqi operatives captured satellite communications equipment that INA operatives in Iraq had apparently been using to communicate with CIA officers in Amman. They learned that the coup plot had been penetrated when the Iraqis called them on their own equipment and told them so.

Another miscalculation by the king that also may have had dire consequences came in May 1996, during the Israeli parliamentary election. Peres, who had replaced the slain Rabin as prime minister, was leading the Labor Party against Binyamin Netanyahu and Likud. The king was so popular in Israel, thanks to the 1994 peace treaty, that many analysts believed he had the power to influence the election, which was extremely close. His decision to invite Netanyahu to Amman during the campaign—while snubbing Peres—helped the Likud leader create the impression that he was committed to the peace process. Some analysts have argued that Netanyahu's visit could have tipped the election in his favor. I don't know whether that's true or not. But I wasn't surprised that the king remained cool to Peres. Why the king didn't like Peres, I don't know. He didn't think Peres could be trusted as a person, and I don't think he liked being with him or having to deal with him, because of this feeling of untrustworthiness. It was evident throughout all the years they dealt with one another, and I don't think the king ever got over it. The king's sense of people was hard to fault, but his preference for Netanyahu over Peres was perplexing, to say the least, especially because Peres was one of the nicest guys you'd ever want to meet, perhaps too nice a guy.

I think the king's support for Netanyahu had mostly to do with his dislike of Peres. I had real reservations about how close he seemed to be getting to Netanyahu. Personally, I liked Peres and I didn't like Netanyahu, but I kept this to myself. I didn't suggest to the king whom to invite to Amman. I saw Netanyahu for what he was—a hard-liner who didn't want to make peace and only bended when he was forced to. I kept waiting for the king to see that. Occasional comments would indicate my feelings, but mostly, I stayed out of the election. Ultimately, he realized his miscalculation. Instead of experiencing the benefits of peace with Israel, the king watched Jordan's relationship with Israel deteriorate under Netanyahu.

First came Netanyahu's decision in late September, in the dead of night under heavily armed guard, to open a new tourist entrance to an ancient archeological tunnel that runs under the holiest sites in Jerusalem, including the al Aqsa Mosque. The opening of the tunnel entrance had been opposed for years by the Palestinians, who thought it threatened the Islamic religious sites. Thus, it came as no surprise when Netanyahu's provocation triggered violent clashes for days across the West Bank and Gaza Strip. The king was outraged, particularly because the Jordanian-Israeli peace treaty stipulated that Jordan would maintain custodianship over Muslim religious sites. Then, Netanyahu's government tarried in redeploying forces from Hebron in February 1997, the last West Bank city that had not been transferred to Palestinian control under the Oslo Accords, and announced that it would build a settlement at Har Homa, encircling Arab East Jerusalem. Finally, in September 1997, the Mossad tried to assassinate Khaled Meshal, a Hamas leader, on the streets of Amman. The king was furious. I wondered why he was so furious. I didn't consider Meshal a friend of Jordan's, and he certainly wasn't a great supporter of the king. Quite the contrary. Hamas was not pro-Jordanian. I think it was just a matter of principle as far as the king was concerned. Having made peace with Israel, he thought Israel's intelligence people coming into Jordan and poisoning a Hamas leader, waging their own little private war on Jordan's soil, was outrageous. And the whole episode made King Hussein look bad. He'd made peace with these people, and here they were in front of the entire Arab world acting as though Jordan wasn't a country.

The only thing he could do was ask them to send an antidote for the poison. The king's fury made the Israelis realize they had made a mistake. They immediately sent the antidote and, as a result, saved Meshal's life.

But soon, the king was left fighting a far more ominous problem than even this cold, partial peace.

Chapter 17

"A PLACE BEYOND OURSELVES"

The king left Amman for the Mayo Clinic in November 1997, complaining of fever, a loss of appetite, and swollen lymph glands. When the decision was made to go back to the hospital, his doctors in Jordan wanted him to go to Memorial Sloan-Kettering Cancer Center in New York, because of the possibility that cancer had been lingering since his first trip to the Mayo Clinic for surgery back in 1992. I talked to them, and they felt strongly that Sloan-Kettering was the best hospital for him. But the king didn't want to go there. He wanted to go to the Mayo Clinic because he felt comfortable there. He knew the nurses, he'd given them gifts, and he'd bonded with them and the doctors as individuals. It was a personal choice, and it says a lot about the king, though it was the wrong way to choose your cancer doctors. According to Jordanian doctors, they misdiagnosed him at Mayo, at least initially in the fall of 1997, concluding he had some kind of virus. What they could have done differently, I don't know. But to those around him who were worried about cancer and what was going on medically, this was the beginning of the tragedy.

He was released after undergoing tests and headed for Washington, where he met with President Clinton and discussed the faltering Middle East peace process. The king was back in Washington for another meeting with the president, same topic, in March 1998. Prior to the king's arrival in Washington, I put together, as was our custom, some briefing papers for his use. One of them involved a thought I had been entertaining for some time. The total lack of progress on peace between Israel and the Palestinians for several years was a puzzler for everyone. It finally crossed my mind that as far as Israel was concerned, the Palestinians had nothing to offer that would compensate for the West Bank and Jerusalem. All the Palestinians could offer was "peace"—and maybe that wouldn't hold.

I began to expand the thought and ended up with a proposal that all twenty-two Arab states offer to make peace with Israel, if it returned the West Bank to the Palestinians. I took the idea to Tom Pickering, who was under secretary of state for political affairs. He was a former U.S. ambassador to Jordan and Israel as well as to the United Nations, and the wisest diplomat I knew. His reaction was positive. I remember him saying, "It's the only act in town; you might as well go with it."

He suggested we draft it in the form of a resolution to be presented to the Arab states. This we did. But, he warned, if the Arabs went ahead with this and convened a summit, President Clinton should not be surprised. Before the summit, King Hussein should have his ambassador in Washington hand-carry a letter to the president explaining the plan. Pickering said I could let him know, so he could monitor it from inside.

I gave His Majesty the proposed resolution with a covering note, together with a batch of other papers. He made no comments on it during his visit. I assumed he did not find it practical. Two weeks after the visit, his private secretary, General Ali Shuqri, telephoned from Amman saying the king wanted to know what I was doing about the Arab peace resolution. I said I wasn't doing anything. I didn't know if there was any interest. In any event, what was needed was an Arab summit, and I knew I couldn't make that happen.

A couple of weeks later, I went on a routine visit to Amman. The king told me he had been in Cairo and tried the Arab peace resolution idea on President Mubarak. He liked it and volunteered to host an Arab summit conference to attempt to adopt the idea. The king said Mubarak was a better sponsor than he and thought he could carry it off. Whereupon Mubarak announced the Summit Conference and issued invitations.

When Secretary of State Madeleine Albright heard about the Arab conference, she immediately telephoned Mubarak and told him to call it off. She explained she was in the middle of a shuttle diplomacy exercise in the area and an Arab conference would be a major distraction from her efforts. Mubarak obligingly postponed the conference. The king became ill and nothing further was done under his regime. He checked back into the Mayo Clinic in mid-July. The palace made a public announcement about his condition on July 28, telling the people of Jordan that he was undergoing treatment for lymphatic cancer. The Mayo Clinic said in a statement of its own the same day that the king's non-Hodgkin's lymphoma was "highly treatable with chemotherapy," and that, having undergone his first treatment, his blood tests showed signs of significant improvement. He would remain in the hospital, undergoing chemotherapy every three weeks, for the rest of 1998.

He left the hospital only for a few days in late October, when President Clinton summoned him to the Wye Plantation on Maryland's Eastern Shore, where Israeli and Palestinian delegations had for days been struggling to conclude their latest round of negotiations. Clinton believed the king could help convince Netanyahu and Arafat that they had to make tough choices to achieve a lasting peace. The king delivered an emotional appeal at the start of a final, all-night round of talks that negotiators on both sides said were critical in making the final deal possible.

When the parties appeared at the White House the following day to sign a further agreement committing Israel and the Palestinians to the Oslo process they'd begun in 1993, President Clinton credited King Hussein's "courage, commitment, wisdom and frankly, stern instruction at appropriate times" for making the agreement a reality. The document established a timetable for Israeli withdrawals from an additional 13 percent of the West Bank, bringing the total of occupied land relinquished to 40 percent. In return, the Palestinians agreed to take specific steps to fight terrorism and remove language from their charter calling for the destruction of Israel.

"If I had an ounce of strength, I would have done my utmost to be there and to help in any way I can," the king said, standing beside Clinton, with Netanyahu on one side and Arafat on the other.

"We quarrel, we agree, we are friendly, we are not friendly, but we have no right to dictate through irresponsible action or narrow-mindedness the future of our children or their children's children," the king went on.

> There has been enough destruction, enough death, enough waste, and it's time that together we occupy a place beyond ourselves, our peoples, that is worthy of them under the sun, the descendants of the children of Abraham—Palestinians and Israelis coming together. . . . I think that such a step as is concluded today will inevitably trigger those who want to destroy life, destroy hope, create fear in the hearts and minds of people, trigger in them their worst instincts. Let's hope that the overwhelming majority of us, those who are committed to the future, those who know what responsibilities they now hold, will be able, through steady progress and a determined joint combined effort, be able to thwart their aims.

It wasn't easy for him to come to Wye. He made it look easy, but his head was still bald as a result of his chemotherapy regimen and he was much sicker than people realized. He appeared to be in good spirits, though, especially at the White House. He was the most relaxed person there. It was one of his finest hours, indeed. He was very informal, very relaxed. He was almost like the godfather to the others, telling them how to behave.

Back at the Mayo Clinic, where the king immediately resumed his chemotherapy treatments, doctors announced in November that his cancer was in remission. When he finally left the hospital on December 29 after six rounds of chemotherapy and a bone marrow transplant, his brother, Prince Hassan, said that he had been cured. He went from the hospital to his home in Potomac. I went out to see him, and he asked me to go home with him on his plane with Noor and all the children and other family. I was touched, but I thought that disembarking from the airplane with the royal family as all of Jordan watched would not be a good thing for him or me.

"I think I'd rather be there when you arrive to greet you," I said.

So I flew on ahead and watched him land his own plane in Amman on January 19, 1999—a cold and rainy day. He knelt and kissed the ground as he disembarked from his Gulfstream jet and walked the short distance to a hangar that had been set up for a welcoming ceremony. I was sitting in a second row of seats, right behind Prince Abdullah, his eldest son and successor, though the king had yet to unveil his succession plan. He gave a short speech and pronounced himself fully recovered. But he looked weak, his frail body showing the ravages of cancer and chemotherapy. I went up and said hello to him, and he gave me a big hug. The king took a long time with me there, holding on to me. He thanked me for all I'd done for him. I thanked him, overcome with emotion. I went back to my seat, and he ducked inside the royal family's limousine with Queen Noor for the ride out to his home. Hundreds of thousands of Jordanians lined the streets. Fireworks filled the sky. Banners and dancers adorned the city.

But a week later, after his fever returned and doctors discovered abnormalities in his blood count, he flew back to the Mayo Clinic on January 26 for further treatment. Hours before he left, he designated Prince Abdullah, thirty-six years old, as his heir, replacing his brother Hassan, who had been crown prince for thirty-four years. Prior to his departure, the palace released a personal and highly critical letter from the king to Prince Hassan in which he explained why he had anointed Abdullah as his successor. The following day, his doctors confirmed he had suffered a relapse and was gravely ill. A week later, on February 4, after a second bone marrow transplant failed, the king flew back to Jordan for the final time. He was not piloting the plane. It landed on another cold, rainy morning. I was there once again to greet him, having stayed in Jordan since his first return. This time, the king, clinging to life and unconscious, was taken straight to the King Hussein Medical Center. He died two days later, at 11:43 a.m. on February 7, 1999.

At the funeral the following day, the palace had created staging areas for the many countries that sent delegations. Viets and I were private citizens and not part of the U.S. delegation that included President Clinton and former Presidents Bush, Carter, and Ford. So we were assigned to a holding area in Queen Noor's office, a small detached building on the palace grounds, with the Israeli delegation. Viets knew Ezer Weizman, the Israeli president, very well from his time in Israel. He went over and sat next to him, and I trailed along. He introduced me. I didn't have anything to say to Weizman, but I listened to Dick's conversation. Every single important Israeli was there—Weizman, Prime Minister Netanyahu, former Prime Ministers Shimon Peres and Yitzhak Shamir, and Foreign Minister Ariel

Sharon—and they had never been together in the same room before, ever, according to Weizman. Sharon actually didn't come into the room. He sat on the steps outside chain-smoking.

In the course of the conversation, Weizman started calling Netanyahu the foulest of names in a loud voice as he talked to Viets—"that son of a bitch over there . . ." Netanyahu wasn't very far away, well within earshot. Netanyahu totally ignored it, he didn't answer, he didn't look up. He acted as though Weizman didn't exist. If you didn't know better, and you were told these facts, you'd think you were in a crazy house—they'd all been confined, and here's how they behaved. It was embarrassing. This was an awful thing, watching and listening to the Israeli leaders who could not get along, even at the king's funeral.

One member of the Israeli delegation whom I met and whose behavior was dignified was Efraim Halevy, a lawyer who was then head of the Mossad. The king had liked and trusted him. From what I knew, he was an honest broker. His main contact was Ali Shuqri, who was very high on him. Shuqri gave Halevy credit for solving some of the thorniest issues in the Israeli-Jordanian peace accord.

"I wanted to say hello, since we both had the same job, in a way," Halevy said to me. "From what I know of your work it was good. Congratulations."

"I would like to say the same thing to you," I replied, "but I was with the King for forty years, and all he wanted to do was make peace with Israel, that's all he really wanted to do, and he spent most of his time trying. I just happened to be at his side while he was trying. You could have made peace with him, in a real sense, any time along the line, and you never did. And I hold you responsible for that. You could have saved the whole area a lot of trouble if you had just not been so selfish and made peace with Jordan. You had a leader here with his hand out, and so I can't say the same thing to you that you said to me—I think you blew it."

I was probably too rude to him. He was trying to be nice, and I wasn't. I was bitter. "Not you personally, I know you personally did an awful lot of good," I hastened to add, mid-tirade. "But I think your country blew it, and it's too bad you couldn't have had enough influence with them to change that."

"That's not true," he said. "We really did want to make peace with him."

"No," I interrupted, "you didn't want to make peace with him. If you had wanted to make peace, you could have—and you may never have a similar chance. He spent his whole life—and got nothing."

Aside from the Israelis, the other funeral guests who were with us in Queen Noor's office were the king's doctors from the Mayo Clinic. "Tell me, doctors," I asked, "was this a medical release or a political release—did you let him out of the hospital because you thought he was well, or because he wanted to come home to die?" They said, "No, we thought he was well." How they could be that wrong about a patient they'd had that long, I don't know. Fortunately, few seemed to be aware of this. It would only have deepened the tragedy.

The king's body lay in state in the throne room at Raghadan Palace, where Clinton, Bush, Carter, and Ford slowly filed by to pay their respects. They were joined by hundreds of other world leaders. The most emotional moment for me was looking at the king in his coffin, seeing him for the last time. He was such a larger-than-life figure, and always will be for me. Following the viewing, palace officials took the casket to a royal cemetery nearby. From the palace, a thick knot of guests and dignitaries began to move there, en masse, as King Abdullah, Prince Hassan, and other members of the royal family assembled by the grave to receive them. Because so many people at the palace knew me—guards, Foreign Office workers, members of the military—they helped me quickly navigate my way to the graveside.

"Come this way, Mr. O'Connell."

"Please, Jack, follow me."

Before I knew it, I was at the front of the line—ahead of four presidents, who were coming up behind me. I knew this was wrong and stepped back. Bush was leading the way. "Please, Mr. President," I said, allowing him and the others to pass. They didn't know how I'd gotten there, but they thanked me for letting them through.

Later, I waited to see King Abdullah, who was greeting those who knew his father in a sitting room at the palace. I'd known him since he was a little boy in Amman. When I bought the house for his mother, Princess Muna, in Washington, and the king transferred him and his brother to schools in the United States in 1972, they would come over to my house in Bethesda and play with Sean and Kelly, and my kids would go over to their house, which was nearby. They didn't have any other friends at first. Before we were married in 1977, Syble McKenzie, who came back to the United States to work for the princess, helped raise Abdullah. So I knew him very well, and still feel very close to him today.

"I was the lawyer for your father, and now he's gone, so you have the right to pick somebody you know, someone from your generation, you'd like to have as your lawyer," I told him. "Lawyers are close to their clients. You shouldn't have me imposed on you."

I don't think he expected that, but it was the proper thing to do.

"Jack, I don't want you to resign, so let's keep it the way it is for now," the new king said.

"Whatever you want, Your Majesty," I said, "but just know that I'm not trying to hang on here. I've had a long run. You deserve your own team."

Chapter 18

MOST OF OUR ENEMIES,
WE MADE

y idea for an Arab peace initiative had been dormant for months at the time of King Hussein's death. But it was still hard to resist the notion that all twenty-two Arab states could offer Israel peace in return for full implementation of UN Resolution 242, meaning Israel would return the occupied territories, withdraw to the borders that existed before the 1967 War, and agree to some kind of resolution to the Palestinian refugee issue. After the funeral, I gave King Abdullah a copy of Tom Pickering's draft resolution and a brief. He liked the idea, but didn't say whether he would try to advance the peace plan with other Arab leaders. Later, he gave a speech in London in which he alluded to the multiple peace offers as a solution. Then he discussed the idea with Crown Prince Abdullah bin Abdul Aziz al-Saud of Saudi Arabia, leaving a copy of the resolution with him. King Abdullah told me that the Saudi crown prince, who later became king, had remarked that it wasn't a bad idea, but Saudi Arabia would be the last to sign on to it.

Meanwhile, as the Clinton administration moved to jump-start the Israel-Palestinian peace process in the spring of 1999, the issue of Palestinian refugees was among those still to be resolved. It arose during negotiations between the State Department's Dennis B. Ross and Yasser Arafat, chairman of the PLO. They were talking as though

Arafat was representing all Palestinians, worldwide. It was a power play by Arafat. For Ross, the administration's Middle East coordinator, it simplified the U.S. negotiating role.

Ross was pro-Israeli, and clever about it. He was bureaucratically very skillful at easing people out of the picture and letting others in, all the while getting his views accepted. He saw me as someone who had undermined his tactics in trying to get a deal with Arafat for all the Palestinians. After he'd served as the chief deputy to Secretary of State Jim Baker in the Bush administration, I couldn't believe he was back as Clinton's top Middle East adviser. Everything he had been involved in over the years had been a failure, and yet he kept coming back. Presidents changed, but Ross didn't. What was his secret, and who were his backers? Apparently, the secret to his success was not a powerful backer but bureaucratic efficiency. He was—and still is—a very efficient civil servant. His policy judgments were suspect. He was so pro-Israeli that he would not give the Jordanians the benefit of the doubt on anything, and he knew the issues so well that he was able to outmaneuver everybody else.

When I reported Ross's negotiating strategy to King Abdullah, he reiterated that Jordan, not Arafat, would represent those Palestinians who were Jordanian citizens. In order to enforce his decision, the king had to notify the relevant parties immediately. He sent letters to the United States, Israel, and Arafat advising them of Jordan's position. The responses were somewhat surprising. Israel didn't seem to care. Arafat was more stoic than irate. But Ross went through the roof. He felt Jordan had undermined his negotiating strategy and spoiled any hope for progress. He wanted to know who was responsible for this and settled on me. He immediately notified all the pertinent offices in the State Department that a member of his staff had to attend any meetings with me. While Ross's watchdogs showed up a couple of times, most of those I visited at State were old friends, who fortunately ignored Ross's notice. I think Ross was afraid to take on U.S. Ambassador to Jordan Bill Burns, who also supported the king's decision. Ross didn't know that I knew a lot of these people better than he did, and they were on my side of the issue.

The refugee problem is not going to go away. Who will represent the Palestinians when they are citizens of another state? Jordan has answered the questions for its citizens, but it could still be challenged. The more important question is, how many refugees would want to go back and how many would Israel accept? Israel's justifiable concern is that if too many returned, Israel would lose its character as a Jewish state. Twenty percent of Israel's citizens are Arabs, not Jews, so the "democratic Jewish state" concept is already something of a fiction. Most of the Arab residents consider themselves second-class citizens, with some justification.

While few Palestinians might opt to return, Israel is not prepared to take the risk. In particular, Israel is not willing even to entertain the suggestion that returning to their old homes is a Palestinian "right." The deadlock has not changed for sixty years. I'm not surprised that Ross has now returned as a special assistant to President Obama and senior adviser on the National Security Council staff. Why anybody would want him, after all those losing efforts, is beyond me. But he's done it again.

Around this time, I read the minutes of a mock court proceeding from McGill University in Canada between leading Jewish and Palestinian lawyers on the rights of Palestinian refugees. The Jewish lawyers presented such a superior case it was startling. It should have been a "heads-up" for the Palestinians, but there was no indication that it was. The next time I saw King Abdullah in Jordan I mentioned this to him, since about half of Jordan's citizens are Palestinian. That being the case, the king put together a team composed of the best international lawyers available and the top world specialists on the Palestinian refugees to prepare a case on behalf of Jordan's Palestinian citizens.

Sir Arthur Watts led the endeavor. He was one of England's best known and most popular international lawyers, moving back and forth between service in the Foreign Office and his own high-profile private practice. (He died in November 2007 at age seventy-six.) He was joined by Charles Brower, a Washington lawyer and former president of the American International Law Society who is currently serving as a judge on the Iranian Claims Tribunal at The Hague. The team drafted a lengthy brief in support of the rights of the Palestinian refugees for use by Jordan at the negotiating table, whenever the time came. Meanwhile, Jordan accelerated a program it had undertaken to computerize all the data on the properties of Jordan's Palestinian citizens which had been confiscated by the Israeli government. Both projects concluded about the same time in 2002.

Beyond the refugee issue, I had long been concerned with the Israeli settlements on the West Bank. They were such an unchallenged violation of the Geneva Conventions and all other international law that, as a lawyer representing Jordan, I could not resist sending a proposed UN resolution to the Jordan UN representative, Prince Zeid bin Raad, calling for the World Court to rule on the issue. I had asked Watts and Pickering to help me draft the document. I was told that drafting UN resolutions is an art. If you don't know what you are doing, you are very unlikely to get what you wanted. Sir Arthur had a good sense of how the World Court would rule on the issue and was confident that we would win.

I suggested to Prince Zeid that he pass the proposed resolution on to the Palestinian UN representative, Nasser Kidwah. Prince Zeid got back to me later, saying Kidwah did not want to rock the boat. There were several UN resolutions favorable to the Palestinians on the settlements and Kidwah did not want to risk these in case the World Court ruled against the Palestinians. So I closed the file, at least for the time being.

Then the world changed in ways we're still trying to understand: al Qaeda terrorists hijacked four airliners on September 11, 2001, and flew two of them like missiles into the twin towers of the World Trade Center in New York and one into the Pentagon in Washington. The fourth, probably headed for the U.S. Capitol, crashed in a field in western Pennsylvania after passengers overpowered the hijackers. I could see the airplane sticking out of the Pentagon from the balcony of my seventeenth-floor condominium in Arlington, Virginia. As horrific as the al Qaeda attacks were, they were misunderstood by most Americans. Had we insisted upon full implementation of UN Resolution 242 after the 1967 War, and had we not sought a war with Saddam Hussein in 1991 and then left our forces in the Gulf throughout the 1990s, I believe those attacks would not have been carried out. I'm not an expert on al Qaeda, but this small group of several hundred Islamic fanatics was reacting to us and our behavior in the Middle East over a quarter century. Out of ignorance, we had made a lot of people hostile to us in the Arab world. Most of our enemies, we made. And in our response to 9/11, we've made a lot more by invading Iraq, sanctioning torture, and holding Muslims without charge at such infamous places as Abu Ghraib and Guantánamo Bay.

The Bush administration's decision to quickly dispatch CIA officers and special forces to Afghanistan to attack al Qaeda base camps and the Taliban in Afghanistan was appropriate and in concert with international law. But the military action should have been directed against al Qaeda and its Taliban supporters. Once you start a war in Afghanistan, you are really fighting the tribes. Afghanistan was never a country; it is a collection of tribes. They had a king, but he wasn't really the king. He was just ruling over a bunch of warlords. Ask the British and the Russians whether you can defeat Afghanistan with guns. You can't. You defeat them with money. You can buy everybody in Afghanistan, and that's what you should do, even today. You can never control Afghanistan unless you control all the tribes. Period.

Then we spread the war to Iraq, where al Qaeda was never a presence. We tried to link Saddam Hussein to the 9/11 attacks and claimed he was producing weapons of mass destruction. Argue it any way you like, but there was no evidence of either at the time of the U.S. invasion in March 2003. Saddam was opposed to al Qaeda, and his WMD programs had been shut down. The rush to war in Iraq began immediately after the Taliban's swift fall in Afghanistan in late 2001—if not before. The momentum for the invasion gathered throughout 2002.

Early in 2002, without warning, my idea for an Arab peace initiative resurfaced in dramatic fashion. Thomas L. Friedman, the influential *New York Times* columnist and Middle East authority, suggested in an interview with Crown Prince Abdullah of Saudi Arabia that all twenty-two Arab nations make peace with Israel in return for full implementation of UN 242. I believe Friedman raised the subject after being briefed either by Jordan's ambassador to the United States, Marwan Muashir, or after hearing a similar idea from a Jewish adviser to the king of Morocco. I've heard both versions. They both may be true. Friedman described the conversation in his column on February 17, 2002: "After I laid out this idea, the Saudi Crown Prince looked at me with mock astonishment and said, 'Have you broken into my desk? . . . The reason I ask is that this is exactly the idea I had in mind—full withdrawal from all the occupied territories, in accord with U.N. resolutions, including in Jerusalem, for full normalization of relations,' he said. 'I have drafted a speech along those lines. My thinking was to deliver it before the Arab summit and try to mobilize the entire Arab world behind it. . . .' "

The following month, in late March, Saudi Arabia sponsored the idea at an Arab Summit Conference in Beirut, where the peace initiative was adopted by all twenty-two Arab states in a historic act of unity. It included a provision for the "right" of return of Palestinian refugees. The Arab post-summit Follow-Up Committee acknowledged that the number of refugee returnees would be a subject of negotiations. Negotiations imply agreement, so in effect Israel would have a veto over the number of returnees, which was the answer to its concern.

But by the time the Arab League adopted the peace initiative, the world's attention was fixated on the war raging in Israel and the occupied territories. Arafat had proven incapable of halting a wave of Palestinian suicide bombings in Israel, which made March 2002 one of the bloodiest months in Israel's history. Prime Minister Sharon had responded by unleashing what the UN secretary-general called "all-out conventional warfare." The day before the initiative was approved, thirty Israelis had been killed by a suicide bomber who attacked a Passover seder. The Bush administration changed course as the month progressed, chiding Sharon at first for his military action, but, by month's end, strongly supporting his hard-line stance against Palestinian terrorists. George W. Bush's global war on terrorism and his management of the Middle East Peace process, if one could really call it that, had become one. He and Sharon were partners fighting terror, and his administration soon focused ever more intently on taking the fight to Iraq.

For the second Iraq war, the neocons were finally in key positions of power. They could not only dictate policy, they could put their own ideological wrappings on it. For them the objective in Iraq was not only to get rid of Saddam, although that was a prerequisite, but to turn Iraq into a democratic base, under U.S. hegemony, which would dispense democracy throughout the area. I never believed Paul Wolfowitz, the deputy defense secretary and a leading neocon, when he talked before the war about spreading democracy in the Middle East. He and the other neocons didn't know what they were talking about. The only contact they had with the Middle East was with Israel. None of them ever had any real and meaningful contact with the Arab world.

Bush and Cheney were not neocons. Their political life blood, obvious in their dealings with Sharon, was the so-called war on terror, which they exploited to expand the president's authority and extend his tenure. But both the Bush-Cheney prosecution of the war on terror and the neocons' desire to spread democracy in the Middle East involved the extermination of Saddam. And the solution for both was provided by an Iraqi exile named Ahmed Chalabi, without whose participation the second Gulf War may never have occurred. He is the son of a wealthy Shiite business family in Iraq that left the country after the Hashemite regime was dethroned. He graduated from MIT with honors, and founded the Petra Bank in Jordan in the late 1970s. His bank was generous in its loans to influential people but would not do business with those dealing with Iraq, owing to his hatred for Saddam Hussein. In mid-1989, Chalabi was indicted for embezzlement after auditors determined that deposits at Petra, the country's third largest bank, were missing. To avoid arrest, Chalabi escaped from Jordan and fled to England. Soon, he was splitting his time between homes in London and Washington. He was tried and convicted in 1992 by a Jordanian military court, in absentia, and sentenced to twenty-two years in prison.

I'd heard of Chalabi in Jordan, but I really got to know him in Washington through Dick Viets, who was well acquainted with him from his years as ambassador in Amman and considered him a good friend. When we first met in the late 1990s, Chalabi said he knew I was a former CIA station chief and wanted to know whether I could help him patch up his relations with the agency, which had fired him. The split came in March 1995. Chalabi, chairman of the London-based Iraqi National Congress (INC), was behind a plot to attack the Iraqi military from a base in Kurdish-controlled northern Iraq. On the eve of the invasion, with CIA personnel helping plan the assault, CIA officials at headquarters backed away and told Chalabi they were withdrawing agency support.

The following September, the Iraqi military attacked the INC base and wiped it out, sending CIA officers and thousands of other opposition supporters fleeing into Turkey. I got in touch with my contacts at CIA's Near East Division to see how bad their relationship was with Chalabi, but quickly realized things were even worse than I'd imagined. They told me Chalabi was blacklisted, burned. They thought he was dishonest. He was so bad, involved in so many lies, that they couldn't trust him. And he didn't fight it. I think that was his last gasp at the agency. Then he asked for another favor. He was receiving payments from the State Department under the Iraq Liberation Act, which Congress had passed in September 1998 with support from the Clinton administration. It appropriated $97 million in basic support subsidies to Chalabi's INC and a half dozen other Iraqi opposition groups. But Chalabi said State consistently held up the payments without reason. Could I help expedite the payments? I said I doubted it—and it turned out I couldn't.

When I told him, he said he guessed he would have to go over the heads of the State Department and the CIA. I found this rather amazing. A foreigner, on his own, without special credentials, taking on State and CIA. The only person over their heads was the president. I said, "You're going to the President?" He said, "No, to Congress." The Iraq Liberation Act had enthusiastic bipartisan support, with

Senate majority leader Trent Lott, the Mississippi Republican, lead-ing the charge. Wolfowitz, awaiting his return to government in the new Republican administration, strongly supported the notion that an Iraqi insurgency could topple Saddam with some support from the U.S. military. Wolfowitz and the neocons fell in love with Chalabi. He told them everything they wanted to hear. Overthrowing Saddam would be a cakewalk. The Iraqis would welcome the American troops with open arms and flowers. Chalabi plied the neocons with favorable intelligence and introduced intelligence sources who provided infor-mation that later proved to be false.

Chalabi's contacts within the administration were not limited to the neocons. One time when I was having lunch with him on Capi-tol Hill, near his Washington office, he had to cut it short because Vice President Cheney was picking him up to see the president at the White House. Whatever Dick Cheney's agenda was, Chalabi had his own—the Prime Ministry of Iraq. Again, the common denomi-nator for both was the elimination of Saddam. Of course, Chalabi did not have enough of a political base in Iraq to successfully con-test an election and become prime minister. And the neocons could not establish a democratic hub in Iraq unless Chalabi or some other like-minded politician they found acceptable could win an elec-tion. But these were mere details that could be ironed out later in Baghdad.

Before, during, and after the war, I saw Chalabi several times in Washington and London. On most of these meetings I was accom-panied by Dick Viets. Chalabi seemed to relish them. He was very open in discussing his plans and activities. He seemed to want to con-vince us of the virtue of what he was doing, and to seek our approval. While I certainly had my doubts about his honesty, I never doubted his charm, or his powers of persuasion. Almost everything he said he planned came to fruition. His predictions were astoundingly accurate.

Although he was never elected to high office, he was unrivaled in his machinations behind the scenes.

To pave the way for him to head the Iraqi government, he said he had to destroy the existing Iraqi power structure, which consisted of Saddam, the Iraqi Army, and the Ba'ath Party. He was instrumental in eliminating all three. At a meeting in London, on his way back to Iraq, he told us he was going back to ensure the army would be disbanded. Our question was whether this would eliminate the only force capable of maintaining law and order. He explained that the army had already disbanded itself. The soldiers had all gone home and their barracks had been looted. In fact, the envoy directing U.S. government activities in Baghdad immediately after the Iraq invasion in March 2003, L. Paul Bremer, informed President Bush in May of a plan to dissolve the Iraqi Army. Disbanding the army was, later, generally recognized as a major blunder, but there were no apologies from Chalabi. It was part of his agenda.

Chalabi said he had supporters in Israel and Iran. He told us one of his first acts when he took over would be to recognize Israel. He said he wanted to visit Iran, but the United States was opposed. He was going to go anyway. At one point in 2004, U.S. intelligence officials said that Chalabi had informed Iranian intelligence that the Americans had broken Iran's code and was able to read messages Iran sent around the world. Chalabi denied the charge and hired lawyers in Washington who asked the Justice Department to find out who leaked the allegations aimed at him. A possible Chalabi link to Iran surfaced again in early 2010, when General Raymond Odierno, the U.S. military commander in Iraq, said in an appearance at a Washington think tank that Chalabi was "clearly" influenced by Iran, and the United States had the intelligence to prove it.

At another point in our discussions, I challenged Chalabi on a couple of issues. I suggested he was being used by the pro-Israeli neocons to serve their purposes. He suggested, smilingly wryly, that the opposite was the case. He was using them. In his view, the U.S. Jewish neocons he was working with were "good guys." To prove he was not an Israeli agent, he asserted that Mossad, the Israeli Intelligence Service, was against him, without further explanation. The truth of the matter is that Chalabi was much smarter than any of the Americans he was dealing with. The relationship worked because they were serving each other's purposes. One thing is certain: Chalabi took orders from only one person—himself. He was his own man, with his own agendas, regardless of the outcome.

My second challenge was why Saddam had permitted Chalabi to wage a war against him from London, and Kurdistan, without liquidating him. I pointed out that his deputy, Tamara Daghestani, had been forced to resign from the INC under threats from Saddam, yet Chalabi had been spared.

Tamara Daghestani was the daughter of a legendary Iraqi general, under the Iraq Hashemite regime. He was so popular that when Kassim murdered King Faisal in 1958, he did not dare touch the Daghestanis. Tamara was the person who smuggled Chalabi out of Jordan in the trunk of her car years later, when Chalabi was about to be arrested in the bank fraud case in 1989. She ended up as Chalabi's deputy in his anti-Saddam organization, based in London.

Tamara told me that one day she was contacted by officials from the Iraq Intelligence Service with a message from Saddam, asking why someone from such a prestigious Iraqi family would be working against the country. Saddam offered to pay her any amount of money, deposited in any bank, anywhere in the world, if she would leave Chalabi and return to her home in Amman. She turned it down, declaring that she did not consider Saddam the legitimate ruler of Iraq.

Months later, the Iraqi intelligence officials contacted Tamara again in London with a different message; she had children, who might suffer fatal accidents if she did not quit her job and return to her family in Jordan. But instead of returning to Jordan, she moved to Madrid, where her brother, Taymur, was serving as Jordan's ambassador. Shortly thereafter, the Iraqi intelligence officials revisited her in Madrid to tell her Spain was not Jordan and to move on. This time she did return to Jordan, where she has remained, devoting her time to serving Iraq: aiding refugees who have sought asylum in Jordan.

I was astounded to run into Chalabi and Tamara later at a secluded country restaurant in England. We agreed to lunch in London the next day. We met in a hotel lobby. Chalabi drove part of the way to his favorite restaurant. Then we walked the rest of the way without bodyguards. We were seated at his established table, with his back to the wall and my back to the restaurant. It was this combination of circumstances that prompted me to raise the question of his immaculate survival. I first asked how Tamara dared return to London after the many threats. They explained she had not returned to work, only for a brief visit. I then asked the more obvious questions. Why was Saddam more concerned about Chalabi's deputy than about Chalabi, who was leading the opposition group? Chalabi appeared to take no protective measures, followed a well-known pattern of life, and, although a sitting duck for anyone who wanted to assassinate him, took no precautions to prevent it. "Why hasn't Saddam assassinated you? I feel uncomfortable sitting at this open table with you. Doesn't Saddam consider your opposition efforts worthy of concern?" These were serious questions, because the situation defied logic—without further explanations.

Chalabi replied by saying Saddam *had* tried to kill him, when Chalabi was in Kurdistan, plotting the invasion of Iraq. Chalabi had a girlfriend with him in Kurdistan who, on a trip to Baghdad, was ostensibly recruited by Iraqi intelligence to poison Chalabi. The intelligence officers gave her a poison to slip into Chalabi's drink. When the girlfriend returned to Kurdistan, she confessed her recruitment to Chalabi and handed him the poison. Chalabi said he sent the stuff to a lab, which reported back that it was the most potent poison in the world and would have killed him instantly. Tamara nodded continuously, indicating she had heard the story before.

The explanation for Chalabi's survival isn't clear to me and may never be. Maybe Saddam miscalculated and didn't take him as seriously as he should have. Events have certainly confirmed that Chalabi's "hatred" of Saddam was for real, and his ability to manipulate the American government unerring. If Saddam had silenced this pompous little man, with poison or a bullet, as he held forth at his favorite restaurant in London, the odds that the United States would invade Iraq and overthrow Saddam would have been much lower.

Chapter 19

MANY DRUMS TO POUND

A few weeks before the United States invaded Iraq in March 2003, I got a call from Bill Rogers, a senior partner at Arnold & Porter in Washington. A friend from Germany, he told me, had just called saying he was in touch with the leader of one of the largest Sunni tribes in Iraq, who was in Berlin for medical treatment, and wanted a CIA contact. Rogers had advised Kennedy and Johnson on Latin America and held senior State Department posts in the Ford administration. I replied that I did not want to get involved, but a former general counsel of the CIA, Jeff Smith, was a partner of his firm. He could contact the agency and pass the message. That is what happened, but I do not know what else transpired.

I only mention this because the Sunni tribes are the most natural allies of the United States in Iraq. They are the natural enemies of al Qaeda and the Shiite extremists, the two biggest enemies of the United States. The fact that the leader of the largest Sunni tribe was looking for a CIA contact means that he realized the importance of a connection and did not have one, which seems inexcusable. In fact, it took four years for the United States to connect with the Sunni tribes, eventually achieving enormous success against mutual enemies. They should have sought each other out before the war.

On the eve of the invasion, I visited Amman on business and met an old friend, Abdul Hadi Majali, former deputy chief of staff of the Jordanian Armed Forces, who was at the time speaker of the Jordanian Parliament. He told me that a few weeks earlier he had met in Amman with two visiting generals from the Iraqi Army, who were old friends of his. They told him that Iraq had concluded that the United States was going to invade, no matter what Iraq did, and that the United States would win a conventional war with Iraq. Therefore, Saddam had decided to avoid a direct confrontation with U.S. forces. The plan was for the Iraqi troops to retreat to Baghdad, put up only a token defense there, then disappear, dispersing to their hometowns and villages where weapons were to be prepositioned. The strategy was to avoid a conventional war, and wage irregular warfare later against the occupation forces. That, of course, is what happened.

I said nothing about it to anyone at the time, since I assumed if I knew it from coffee talk, the U.S. government would certainly have this information. When I mentioned it to U.S. officials after the fact, they strenuously denied the Iraqis voluntarily left Baghdad, insisting that they had been driven out. In fact, the Iraqis did not put up a fight in Baghdad. *The Washington Post* published a brief article stating that U.S. occupation forces had recovered a message in the Basra office of Iraqi intelligence ordering its personnel to preposition weapons and return to their homes. I followed up on the story with the *Post* and with sources in the Pentagon, but learned nothing more. I believe the story is true, but that the U.S. administration was too proud, or too vulnerable, to admit it may have been set up by Saddam.

By November 2003, as attacks on U.S. forces by Iraqi insurgents gathered in intensity, some U.S. commanders feared that this may have been the war Saddam had prepared for. "I believe Saddam Hussein always intended to fight an insurgency should Iraq fall," said Major General Charles H. Swannack, Jr., who was commanding the 82nd Airborne in the Sunni Triangle west of Baghdad. "That's why you see so many of these arms caches out there in significant numbers all over the country. They were planning to go ahead and fight an insurgency."

The following month, as conditions in Iraq continued to deteriorate rapidly, the UN General Assembly voted to ask the World Court to rule on the legality of Israel's proposed 450-mile security fence on the West Bank. American hypocrisy in the Middle East was hard to look past. We invaded Iraq on grounds that Saddam had failed to comply with UN resolutions for arms inspections, yet we stood four-square behind Israel as it violated something like thirty different UN resolutions, going all the way back to 1967 and UN 242.

Earlier in 2003, Nasser Kidwah, the Palestinians' UN representative, had called me out of the blue. He didn't know me from Adam, and I didn't know him.

"Mr. O'Connell," he said, "you sent me, through the Jordanian ambassador, a resolution, a brief, that you drew up against the Israeli government for its settlements, and I responded at the time that I didn't think we should pursue the matter."

"Yes," I said. "I think you made a mistake."

"Well, I'm calling to correct the mistake," he said.

"What do you have in mind?"

"They're putting up a fence now, and we can't afford that," Kidwah said. "So I would like to get a copy of the resolution you sent me. I can't find my old copy. Because I want to submit a new resolution along the same lines to halt the fence—and the settlements."

"I have a copy," I said, "and I'll send it to you through the Jordanian UN representative."

He then asked if I knew a lawyer I would recommend to represent the Palestinians in the case. I recommended the lawyers Jordan had used in the past, Sir Arthur Watts and Charles Brower. He then asked whether I thought they would be willing to represent the Palestinians. I said I didn't know but would find out. He then asked what I thought of Professor James Crawford, a British lawyer both Jordan and the Palestinians had employed in the past. I said I shouldn't be the final word on this, but his talent was in the same zone as Watts and Brower. But I noted that he was head of the Cambridge Law School and the question would be whether he would have the time to devote his talent. I told him either I or Prince Zeid bin Raad, his Jordanian counterpart, would get back to him.

I called Prince Zeid and told him I was sending him a copy of the old UN resolution draft to Kidwah, but added that this was moving very fast. It was too important an issue for Jordan to duck, so Jordan should be involved. It had the best lawyers and it should not let the PLO take them over. After contacting Amman, Prince Zeid called back to say that King Abdullah wanted Jordan involved and to contact Sir Arthur in London and get to work. The Palestinians engaged Professor Crawford. Egypt and a few other states elected to file briefs. Sir Arthur led Jordan's legal team.

After the UN General Assembly approved the resolution in December 2003 asking for the World Court to issue an advisory opinion on the Israeli fence, representatives of the Arab principals and their lawyers met, in preparation, in London, Geneva, and The Hague. Sir Arthur, during preparation and at the trial, was the star. At one point during one of Sir Arthur's preparatory presentations, Ambassador Kidwah said, "Now I know why the British Empire lasted so long."

The case was heard by the World Court in February 2004. Israel and the United States did not take part. Since Israel did not submit to the jurisdiction of the court, its opinion would only be advisory in nature, not binding. The Palestinians described the fence as an illegal barrier erected to annex their land and oppress their people. The Israelis said it was the only way to stop Palestinian terrorists from attacking Israel.

The World Court found in favor of the Palestinians in July 2004, calling on Israel to dismantle all sections of the fence on Palestinian land in the West Bank and compensate the landowners. The vote by the judges was 15–1, with the only no vote coming from an American, Thomas Buergenthal. The majority held that the fence, most of which is inside the West Bank, violated international human rights law and was a de facto annexation of Palestinian land. The United States repeated its position that the court was dealing with issues that could only be resolved through diplomatic negotiation.

Later in July, the UN General Assembly voted 150–6 in favor of a resolution calling for Israel to abide by the court ruling, dismantle the fence, and pay compensation to Palestinian landowners whose property had been taken. The United States again voted no, saying the issue of the fence could only be solved at the negotiating table. Kidwah, the Palestinians' UN representative, said he would lobby for a binding resolution by the fifteen-member Security Council, even though the United States would surely use its veto power and kill the measure.

Israel has ignored the World Court's rulings and, in defiance, escalated the construction of the illegal fence/wall and the illegal settlements. The Arabs have done nothing to follow up on their legal victory. One might argue, if the Arabs don't care, why should anyone else. The Arabs must realize that they have many drums to pound: the illegal wall; the illegal settlements; the illegal 1967 War; the illegal occupation; the Arab peace initiative—among others.

It is no coincidence that most issues between Israel and the Arabs are legal ones, for which the law provides explicit answers. Most of the answers favor the Arabs. They should be knocking on courthouse doors as well as pounding the drums. Since a solution serves all the parties, the Arabs would be doing Israel and the United States a favor they are politically unwilling to do for themselves. That is one reason King Hussein wanted to publicize the facts that are obstructing peace.

At the end of March 2004, national security adviser Stephen Hadley, Elliot Abrams from the National Security Council, and Bill Burns, assistant secretary of state for the Middle East, visited Amman bearing what appeared to be devastating news for the Jordanians. Prime Minister Sharon had asked President Bush for a letter undoing UN 242. He wanted the letter to state that the Israeli settlements in the West Bank and Jerusalem had made changes in the demography that would have to be taken into account in any final settlement, and that Palestinian refugees had a right to return to a Palestinian state, but not to Israel. Bush planned to affirm Sharon's request in a letter to be given Sharon when he visited the White House on April 14, 2004.

I have an interesting story to tell about Abrams, whom I saw as another pro-Israeli American. A couple of years earlier, I had asked the White House whether I could meet with national security adviser Condoleezza Rice to discuss a paper I had written on the Middle East peace process and, specifically, the Arab peace initiative. She said her schedule didn't permit it at that time, but she suggested I meet with her chief Middle East aide, Bruce Riedel, a CIA officer on loan to the NSC whom she'd inherited from the Clinton administration and was in the process of replacing. I knew Riedel by name and reputation, but I had never met him before. Since we both had CIA credentials, we got off to a fast start.

"Did she read my paper?" I asked of his boss.

"No, but I read it," he said, "and I briefed her on it, and she knows what's in it."

"Well, this is something that requires somebody to take some action, and I'm afraid she's the only one who could," I said. "You certainly can't take the action without her approval."

"No," he agreed, "but I told her, and can follow up."

"Do you agree with the paper?" I asked.

"I agree with everything in the paper," he said.

He then told me he'd soon be leaving the NSC and going back to CIA.

"Who's going to take your place?" I asked.

"I don't know," Riedel said. "But do you know what she's doing? She's taking every serious applicant for the job and sending their résumés over to the Israeli Embassy for their approval."

"Really?"

"Yes," he said. "I said to her, 'That's not a smart thing to do.' And she said, 'Well, if I don't have the Israelis' approval of whoever is in this office, I won't be able to do any business with Israel. So I might as well face the facts.' That's not the way I would do it."

To make a long story short, Abrams got the job. Now, here he was with Hadley, Rice's successor, and Burns, asking for a letter nullifying UN 242. Viets and I happened to arrive in Amman at midnight on April 5, 2004, after the three had left. We met Foreign Minister Marwan Muashir in his office the next day, April 6. The discussion focused on Marwan's conversation with Hadley and company and the catastrophic letter Bush was going to give Sharon. Viets and I reaffirmed that international borders could only be changed by agreement of the parties and that Bush's letter would have no legal weight or bearing. We suggested King Abdullah immediately write a letter to Bush reminding him of this and to request his own letter from Bush, stating that the terms of any settlement could only be determined by negotiations between the parties, and could not be prejudiced or predetermined by others—a long-standing U.S. position.

Marwan thought that Samir Rifai, chief of the Royal Court and son of the former prime minister, Zaid Rifai, would be reluctant to take on the president on the issue, arguing that it would be too risky, exposing Jordan to further embarrassment if Bush turned down the king's request for a letter. I told Marwan that I was meeting Samir Rifai and some other senior government officials that evening, and would sound them out and let him know the next morning.

I'd known Samir since he was a toddler. When he was a little boy, maybe five years old, I went to visit his father at his home and decided to wait in his study. Samir then pranced in and said hello before he pulled the door shut, turned the key, and ran out into the garden. When his father came downstairs to see me, he tried the doorknob and then said, "Jack, unlock the door."

"I didn't lock the door, your son did," I said. "So get Samir and get the key from him."

Zaid went out to find Samir and then returned a few minutes later. "He threw the key in the bushes outside the house," he said, "I have no way of knowing where it is."

So there I was, CIA station chief in Amman, locked inside a room by a five-year-old for an hour before somebody found a replacement key. And now, here I was, over forty years later, drafting a one-page royal letter for him to preserve the essence of UN 242 and make the fundamental point that the boundaries between Israel and the West Bank could only be changed through negotiations. When I met with Rifai and other senior Jordanians that evening, I raised the subject and passed the draft letter around, asking for their comments. Muashir was right; most thought it was too risky. It might end up as a double loss for Jordan: no letter and an angry Bush. But young Rifai was an exception. He thought it was the thing to do, and his voice was the most important, because of his position as chief of the Royal Court.

The next morning, April 17, I telephoned Muashir to tell him that Rifai was in favor of sending the letter. The two of them got together and presented their point of view to the king. He had sent the draft letter to the president on April 8. I didn't see Muashir again until he and Rifai arrived in Washington on April 17 as the advance team for the king's visit later in the month. Viets and I had returned to Washington on April 13. Sharon met the president April 14 and departed thereafter, with his presidential letter.

After their arrival, Muasher and Rifai worked feverishly with administration officials on the text of the presidential letter. King Abdullah was waiting in California for the letter and his visit to be cleared. The administration could find no valid reason for refusing to give the king the letter he asked for, since his points were legal and consistent with past U.S. policy. Just as Muashir and Rifai got a letter they felt was acceptable, the king canceled his Washington visit and returned to Jordan.

The king's visit was rescheduled for May 2004. The president gave him a letter then that was not as generous as the April draft, but it served the purpose. Israel still waves the president's letter to Sharon as proof that it is entitled to the settled areas of the West Bank and Jerusalem. But it draws no crowds. Bush's letter to Sharon was an act of ignorance, which the Bush administration prudently started walking away from almost immediately, with the president's letter to the king.

The Arab peace initiative, meanwhile, was reenacted in March 2007, at the annual Arab Summit Conference in Riyadh, Saudi Arabia, in precisely the same form that it first passed in 2002. It was a remarkable display of continuing Arab unity on one of the most divisive issues in Middle East history. Together with the Arab Follow-Up Committee's elaborations, it covered all bases, including a negotiated solution to the difficult refugee problem. Touring the region prior to the summit, Ban Ki-moon, the UN secretary-general, called the initiative a "pillar" of the peace process and asked the Israelis to give it a fair hearing. But Israel reacted coolly to the measure's adoption, saying only that it hoped the Arabs' action would contribute to the peace process. A two-state solution, Israel said, could only come from direct negotiations between the Israelis and the Palestinians. Israel will not get a better offer. In fact, the initiative may erode, if it continues to be rejected by Israel and ignored by the United States. Their negative attitudes toward the Arab peace initiative defy rational explanation to everyone except Israeli leaders, who, as a matter of policy, believe force trumps negotiations and peace is hostage to the definition and realization of security. The only excuse for the United States is ignorance.

Chapter 20

IRREPRESSIBLE OPTIMISM

Every morning I sit on the balcony of my condominium over-looking the Marine Corps War Memorial, next to Arlington National Cemetery, and the National Mall, across the Potomac River in Washington. I read the press clippings from the Middle East religiously. The articles are well written, as far as they go. And you read, and you read, and you read, and everything is analyzed every way it can be. After a while, you begin to wonder, where is all this leading? If you've been involved in this, as I have, for more than fifty years, you've got to finally ask yourself, what if you wanted to stop talking and writing articles and start thinking of things to do? How do we move from talk, and violence, to peace? I think the Jordanians, the Palestinians, and the Americans have to start talking the law, talking the facts—talking about the truth.

There really are no more legal issues. They aren't in dispute. Read the World Court opinion. If this were a domestic situation, people would simply say, follow the law. If you break into your neighbor's house, that's against the law. It's clearly unlawful what Israel is doing. I didn't say it. The World Court said it. The world knows it. And yet the United States and Israel don't pay any attention to that, but that's the law. I tell the Jordanians, there are three ways you can deal with Israel: militarily, but that's a mistake, because you can't win; diplomatically, but you're no good at it, you're going to lose there as well; or legally, because that's where you have the advantage, the law is on your side, and that's what you start talking about. King Hussein agreed with this trilogy of options and the analysis. Don't act as though what the Israelis are doing is all right. It isn't all right. They're violating every single provision of the Geneva Conventions to which they're signatories, and over thirty UN resolutions, including 242 and 338. Say that every day on big placards, march through the streets, stage sit-ins, pretend you're Gandhi. "They're violating the law!" That is what should come roaring out of every country in the Middle East. Tell everybody what the law is, and spread this in the United States. The law is Resolution 242. I helped negotiate it. The record is clear. You don't have to fabricate. The Israelis are having to fabricate, they're breaking every law there is, and they're getting away with it.

One of the laws they're breaking is the one against genocide, wherein the World Court has jurisdiction over all of the signatories, and all the key parties are signatories. If you can prove a case of genocide against Israel—or Egypt or Syria or any nation—they would be subject to penalty. Those are things the Jordanians should do now but aren't doing. Clients who are timid and let people walk all over them are almost like President Obama. They don't know how to get tough.

And yet Obama—Obama, the constitutional law professor; Obama, the Christian son of a Kenyan Muslim—is the ideal guy to bring about real change in the Middle East. Everybody would believe him if he talked about the law, and the Israelis would then know he was serious. The minute he started talking that way, they wouldn't have an answer. I found so much to like in his historic speech to the Muslim world in Cairo in June 2009:

America's strong bonds with Israel are well known. This bond is unbreakable. It is based upon cultural and historical ties, and the recognition that the aspiration for a Jewish homeland is rooted in a tragic history that cannot be denied.

Around the world, the Jewish people were persecuted for centuries, and anti-Semitism in Europe culminated in an unprecedented Holocaust. Tomorrow, I will visit Buchenwald, which was part of a network of camps where Jews were enslaved, tortured, shot and gassed to death by the Third Reich. Six million Jews were killed—more than the entire Jewish population of Israel today. Denying that fact is baseless, ignorant, and hateful. Threatening Israel with destruction—or repeating vile stereotypes about Jews—is deeply wrong, and only serves to evoke in the minds of Israelis this most painful of memories while preventing the peace that the people of this region deserve.

On the other hand, it is also undeniable that the Palestinian people—Muslims and Christians—have suffered in pursuit of a homeland. For more than sixty years they have endured the pain of dislocation. Many wait in refugee camps in the West Bank, Gaza, and neighboring lands for a life of peace and security that they have never been able to lead. They endure the daily humiliations—large and small—that come with occupation. So let there be no doubt: the situation for the Palestinian people is intolerable. America will not turn our backs on the legitimate Palestinian aspiration for dignity, opportunity, and a state of their own.

For decades, there has been a stalemate: two peoples with legitimate aspirations, each with a painful history that makes compromise elusive. It is easy to point fingers—for Palestinians to point to the displacement brought by Israel's founding, and for Israelis to point to the constant hostility and attacks throughout its history from within its borders as well as beyond. But if we see this conflict only from one side or the other, then we will be blind to the truth: the only resolution is for the aspirations of both sides to be met through two states, where Israelis and Palestinians each live in peace and security.

That is in Israel's interest, Palestine's interest, America's interest, and the world's interest. That is why I intend to personally pursue this outcome with all the patience that the task requires. The obligations that the parties have agreed to under the Road Map are clear. For peace to come, it is time for them—and all of us—to live up to our responsibilities.

Given that soaring performance, I was disappointed when Obama, moments before his first State of the Union address in February 2010, said he had overestimated the ability of his government to restart the Middle East peace process. But then, just days later, Secretary of State Hillary Clinton touched off a minor firestorm in diplomatic circles when she had the temerity to suggest that the Obama administration wanted to revive negotiations between the Palestinians and the Israelis based on UN 242. "Of course, we believe that the 1967 borders, with swaps, should be the focus of the negotiations over borders," she said. The very fact that her remark caused a stir shows how far we've come, or regressed. If you want to look through the fog that shrouds the process, the Israelis have succeeded in covering up the truth, and mixing up the facts so much that nobody can really understand what's happening.

The settlements are so extensive now. The wall is part of the landscape. The refugee issue only becomes more complex. And the violence on both sides has caused so much hatred that it's easy to despair of ever finding a solution. And yet I think, with American leadership and determination, all of those issues could be resolved. The average American doesn't know what the facts are. But those of us who favor full implementation of UN 242 and a true two-state solution—in other words, those of us who favor peace—we have the truth on our side. And if you can't sell the truth, then hire someone who can. Spend your money on that, overwhelm your adversaries with facts, and declare the start of the war of truth.

I'm encouraged that people, including Obama, are still talking about the promise expressed by the Arab peace initiative. The idea of all twenty-two Arab nations making peace with Israel and recognizing its right to exist in return for full implementation of 242 remains an irresistible notion. Were that to be implemented, I'd still favor some sort of confederation involving Israel, Palestine, and Jordan. Then Israel wouldn't have an interest in taking over anything, neither would the Palestinians, and the Jordanians would be able to fully represent Jordanians of Palestinian descent. The lawyer in me also believes that the West Bank, legally, still belongs to Jordan unless and until the Jordanian Parliament votes to give it to the Palestinians, which it almost certainly would, with or without a confederation.

The refugee problem can also be dealt with. How do you solve it? You don't. There are no longer refugees. There are now three generations since Palestinians were displaced from what is now Israel and the territories in 1948. I looked into this at one point. The Palestinians are not only talking about refugees—the people who came out—they're talking about their great-great-grandchildren. I don't know how long you can string that out and claim they're refugees. All right, negotiators representing Israel and the Palestinians can say, all those who were refugees in 1948 can come back. There wouldn't be that many. And while they were refugees, their grandchildren aren't refugees. So there are other ways you can skin this cat, if you really wanted to do it. But if you don't want to do it, you can always find reasons not to do it.

Nothing has changed between the Israelis, the Palestinians, and the Jordanians since the 1967 War. But we're kidding ourselves if we start to see this status as permanent. Every single ruler in the Middle East is in danger of losing his job, and if he loses his job, somebody from the opposite end of the spectrum will take over. Fifty years from now, everybody who wants nuclear weapons will probably have them, unless somebody stops talking and writing learned articles and does something about it. Once Iran has nuclear weapons, Saudi Arabia would have to get them, and so would Egypt, and maybe Syria. Then everybody's got nuclear weapons and somebody's going to fire one.

Iran with a nuclear weapon would become a game-changer for Israel, because Iran is a big country and Israel is a little country. You make one bomb and that would be the end of Israel, probably, and one bomb wouldn't be the end of Iran. So the people who should be negotiating are Israel and Iran. Israel might just have to live with an adversary having the bomb. We did. We lived with the USSR for more than four decades. It would change their behavior, and they would need some friends, because everybody else in the area would feel the same way: that they were threatened. I wonder if Iran is going to welcome this new position in which everyone is their enemy. But I can certainly see why they would want a nuclear weapon. Then there's the situation in Iraq and the very real possibility that the country could descend into civil war, pitting Shiites against Sunnis, or Arabs against Kurds, or both. Or it could become the locus of a regional war involving Iran, Turkey, and the Sunni states.

So the picture in the Middle East is not pretty right now, certainly not as pretty as when I first went there. It's only gotten worse, and worse for the United States. We're bogged down and likely to have tens of thousands of troops in an unstable Iraq for years, regardless of Obama's latest timetable for withdrawal. We're not having much success stopping Iran's nuclear ambitions. We seem incapable of coaxing Israel back to the negotiating table with the Palestinians. And we're intensely disliked throughout the Muslim world for the way we have prosecuted the war on terror. Presiding over renewed peace talks would do us a world of good.

As I said earlier, most of our enemies, we made, and as much as it hurts me to say it, CIA has made far more than it should have in recent years. Some of those who leave CIA turn out to be hostile toward the agency. It's a tough business, and they quit with a grudge. I have no grudge. I was a cheerleader for the agency, as were many of the people I served with, during the years I was there.

CIA, in my whole time and my whole memory, did not engage in hostilely interrogating criminals, people who were arrested. We used polygraphs to test our foreign agents and our own officers. That's the experience the agency had—we never had experience in hostile interrogations. So I can only think that the people who've engaged in water-boarding and other forms of torture in recent years were not career agency employees. I think they must have brought these people who practiced violence from outside. The agency never should have become involved in this type of thing, in my opinion. And now they've made it very difficult for us to recruit spies, which is our main job. Who wants to work for somebody who believes in water-boarding, and naked interrogations in freezing cold rooms after ninety-six hours without sleep? If I were an agency officer trying to recruit an Arab Muslim in Jordan, I would think that the man is going to look at me, he's going to remember the shame of Abu Ghraib, he's going to see the pictures of nude Muslim men, and he's going to realize I represent that organization. To interrogate someone and tell them, "If you don't tell us what we want, we're going to torture you," isn't what we did. A lot of people may not believe this, but CIA used to be a house on the top of the hill, in terms of principle and discipline.

I'm big on recruitment. I spent a lot of time thinking about it, and a lot of time recruiting foreign agents. But recruitment can't be done by blackmail. There are those in some intelligence services who believe in a kind of hard leverage—if you don't do what we want, we're going to shoot your brother, or we'll burn down your house. But I don't think the United States can act that way. At least when I was with CIA, we didn't say, "We're going to blow up your house or shoot your brother." There were other ways to recruit spies and get information. You could even turn paying somebody's debts into a nice gesture, rather than blackmail. It's how you do it, in my mind. I always wanted the foreign agent I was paying for secrets to see me as a partner. And I wanted to find some basis for that in our relationship. Whether it was money, or relationship, or ideology, you name it, but you've got to find something. It can't just be based on fear. If it's based on fear, agents will constantly be trying to find a way out of the relationship. And if they can give you the worst information to screw you, they'll do it. You're really setting yourself up. When a guy comes to you and asks for help to pay a $200,000 gambling debt because he's worried about what might happen to his family if he doesn't pay, there's a way to help him that's healthy, that sets up a relationship that will endure. So, yes, it is possible to be a moral intelligence officer, and you're better off if you are one.

When I go back to the Middle East, I see a lot of people I knew, some of whom I recruited. They're no longer recruited, either because some successor dropped them, or they decided they didn't want to be involved any more, or they've retired. But there's still a bond, just like the guy I recruited in Beirut and met years later at the Georgetown graduation party. There was something in that relationship that went beyond what we were doing. We both respected each other, and we both thought we were engaged at the time in a noble endeavor. If you can find that kind of bond with somebody, you can turn a terrorist into somebody doing something more profitable than terrorism. But if you treat them as evil, hopeless, despicable cases, you're not going to get them to help you.

The Arabs aren't going to get weaker. They haven't played their hands very well. They haven't been united. But they certainly are going to get more numerous. They're certainly going to become stronger militarily, and they're going to get richer, as long as oil is plentiful. Our industrial complex is addicted to oil, so they've got allies in this country, who are now able to spend all the money they want on politics, thanks to the recent U.S. Supreme Court decision. And as fractious as the Arabs have been, they have come together, twice, and adopted the peace initiative, which I still think is the best deal the Israelis are going to get. If you really wanted to work on it, the initiative has something powerful to offer—peace for everybody in the area. Having lived in the Middle East as long as I did, I can state that the Arabs all wanted peace, whatever they might have said. I mean, when they went to Khartoum in 1967, they were ready for peace—even though they had to lie about that, because they didn't want to admit their weaknesses. So you could have made peace back then. Actually, Israel offered peace to Egypt and Syria. They were ready intellectually to make peace with both countries within two weeks of the war and give back the territory, to make peace, and it would have been a good deal. But they just didn't want to give up the West Bank. Full stop.

The Israelis are much worse off today than they were when I first arrived in the region. They weren't threatened by anybody back then. The Palestinians weren't organized. The PLO didn't even come into existence until 1964. And I don't think the neocons in the Bush administration did them any favors by invading Iraq and toppling Saddam Hussein. Israel's real threat, Iran, remains—stronger than ever.

There is a question the Israelis have to ask themselves, and it's been my thought the whole time I was involved with this, and it was King Hussein's thought: What do they want? Don't they want to have peace with anybody? Do they think they will exist in any happy condition if they don't make peace with any of their neighbors? They're afraid to take the step, because they have come to the conclusion that the Arabs really don't want to make peace with them, so why try. The king was always mystified by this. He would keep going back to them, saying, "What is it that you want?" And they would never tell him.

He wanted to make peace with the Israelis. He had no problem with them. There were no territorial problems before the Six Day War. But they constantly treated him as an enemy, and seemed to be looking for some reason to take over the West Bank if they ever got the opportunity, which they did in 1967. The king realized early on, long before 1967, that they wanted the West Bank. Now, some of them weren't that secretive about it: they wanted the West Bank because God gave it to them and they made no bones about it. There were even religious groups stating this. So he knew that Jerusalem and the West Bank were controversial issues with the Israelis. They had a deed to this that dates back two thousand years, and he had a hard time fighting that. And when he gave them the opportunity, they took over the West Bank. They took over Jerusalem. They took over all the things he thought they had their eyes on the first chance they got.

The Israelis were willing to give Egypt, their main enemy, its territory back. They even said they were willing to give back the Golan Heights to Syria, but they were not willing to make peace with Jordan on the same basis, because they had historic and nationalist interests in the Jordanian territory that would have to be negotiated. This was their answer to the United States. So they made a distinction with Jordan, and it was based on the land. And it just confirmed the king's suspicions all along—they wanted this land, they thought it was theirs. And all of his efforts to talk them out of it on practical grounds got nowhere. The king exhausted himself. He, on his own, without anybody knowing it, met with them. Then, with U.S. backing, he met with them some more, trying to talk them into making peace. The United States seemed to support him in making peace, agreed with him on everything, but never did anything. And in refusing to make peace with King Hussein, the Israelis were harming themselves as much as they were him and his country. They were ensuring that we don't have peace, and one day that will not be in the Israelis' interest. When will that day come?

Finally, what of Jordan? I would say Jordan is better off today. When I first arrived in the summer of 1958, and even when I returned five years later as station chief, people in Washington didn't know whether Jordan was going to last another year. The country had nothing. In 1958, it was a cow town. They were herding sheep where the British Embassy is today. They had a teenage king who probably wasn't going to make it because Jordan wasn't really a country. They had all these Palestinian refugees, who outnumbered the rest of the population. The Israelis wanted half of the country, and they could probably have taken it any day they had a good enough excuse. Nasser of Egypt was trying to overthrow the king and the Syrians were trying to overthrow the king, and the Saudis were a rival monarchy that had kicked the Hashemites out. The country had no natural resources, and people were living on the dole. It was a British colony, for all intents and purposes, and when King Hussein kicked the British out in the mid-fifties, had the United States not stepped in, the country probably would have collapsed. Jordan probably would have been broken up, and everybody would have taken a piece of it. Today, it's a modern state, one of the most pleasant places in the Middle East to live. It's also one of the safest places to live, and it's one of the most liberal places to live. People like to visit Jordan. If I go there, I have all the rights I have in the United States. Nobody bothers me. It's not a police state. They don't just arbitrarily put people in jail.

The odds on that one were very long, and it came to a test several times. They were in a war that took half the country, and they still survived, and they had a civil war in 1970 with the PLO, and they survived. They've had several coup attempts, and they've survived. And the United States was at Las Vegas on this, betting on them, but not betting a lot. We'd bet a little bit, and every time the Jordanians would prevail, we'd bet a little more. And what we got for those meager bets was a steadfast, stable ally in the Middle East.

How did Jordan pull it off? I knew King Hussein was special the first time I met him as a twenty-two-year-old, and his star never waned. It wasn't that he was a brilliant guy—though he had a certain genius. His political instincts were very good, and he was very determined. Persistence was probably his best virtue. By just continuing to bang his head against the wall, sometimes the wall fell down. And just by showing up, he often won. He made some tragic mistakes. The biggest, of course, was getting involved in the 1967 War. A lot of people thought his support for Saddam Hussein was another, but I'm not so sure. He got free oil and other benefits from the relationship, and he didn't lose any soldiers, and he didn't join the United States in a war against another Arab state. And, in any event, his relations with the United States and the West recovered completely.

I was at the State Department once when the king was up at the UN. He had just been in Washington three months earlier, and he asked for permission to come down again and see the secretary of state. Of course, if he came, he would have to see President Reagan. I remember George Shultz saying, "The King was just here, and now he wants to come back? What the hell is he coming for this time? I've never seen people like this. They keep swarming like bees, they never stop." He was irritated, but impressed. The king just had an irrepressible optimism and energy. Looking back on it over all these years, that is the one thing that really stands out: he never gave up.

ACKNOWLEDGMENTS

I would like to thank the many close friends to whom I owe so much and who were essential but whom I cannot name out of concern for their safety. I would like to credit His Late Majesty King Hussein, who wanted the truth written, and His Majesty King Abdullah, who encouraged me to do so. I thank my parents, who gave me my foundation; my brother Quinn, who was my best friend; my law partner Earl Glock, who supported my efforts for more than thirty years; my secretary and friend Cathy; Richard Helms, for whom I worked and deeply respected; the late Gene Trone, who confided in me, and his wife June and daughter Genie, who were kind enough to sit with me for a long interview in 2010; Jeffrey H. Smith, my counsel, who helped guide me through the review process; Andrew Wylie, my agent, without whose interest and support this book would not have been published; Scott Moyers of the Wiley Agency, whose guidance was invaluable in bringing the book forward; Vernon Loeb, who via countless hours of interviews with me at my home helped shape the book and craft the manuscript; my dear friend Mary Saxton, who acted as my sounding board; my daughter Kelly, who typed the manuscript and assisted in its editing; my son Sean, who saw this project to completion; and, finally, my grandson Daniel, who inspired me to make the road on which he is traveling perhaps a bit more clear.

INDEX

Abdul Ilah, Crown Prince of Iraq, 9
Abdullah, Radi, 6–7
    Kennedy's Jordan visit and, 40–41
Abdullah bin Abdul Aziz al-Saud, Crown
    Prince of Saudi Arabia, 214, 219–20
Abdullah I, King of Jordan, 2, 36
Abdullah II, King of Jordan (Prince
    Abdullah), 113, 209, 210, 212–13
    Arab peace resolution and, 214
    G. W. Bush letter to, 234–36
    Israeli security wall issue and, 231
    Palestinian citizens of Jordan and, 215,
    216–17
    West Bank settlements issue and, 234,
    235–36
Abrams, Elliot, 232, 233, 234
Abud Hassan, 106–7, 122–25, 164
Abu Ghraib prison scandal, 243
Abu-Odeh, Adnan, 153
Abu Shaker, 179
Aden, Yemen, 99
Afghanistan, xii, 143
    influence of money in, 219
    tribal influence in, 218–19
    U.S. invasion of, 218–19
Agency for International Development, U.S.
    (USAID), 38–39, 97, 136
Air Force, Egyptian, Israeli destruction of,
    52
Air Force, Iraqi, 164
Air Force, Israeli, 52–53, 55
Air Force, Royal Jordanian, 54, 77, 105, 106
Air Force, Syrian, 105
Air Force, U.S., 134

Aisha, Princess of Jordan, 113
Ajax, Operation, 18–19
Alaska Pipeline, 111
Albright, Madeleine, 207
Alia, Queen of Jordan, 115, 136
Allawi, Ayad, 199–202
Allon, Yigal, 90
Allon Plan, 88, 89, 127
al Qaeda, 141, 218, 219, 228
American International Law Society, 217
Ames, Bob, 99, 100
Amir, Yigal, 196
Amit, Meir, 47–50, 53, 59
Amman, Jordan:
    author's chief-of-station posting to, xvii,
    31, 35, 137, 247
    CIA station in, xvii, 2–3, 5, 7, 11, 27, 31,
    35, 66–67, 96–97, 132, 137, 235, 247
    CIA wiretapping in, 33–35, 80–82
    description of, 31
    Hummar suburb of, 97, 104
    Hussein coup plot in, xiv–xv, 1–14, 27, 28
    Intercontinental Hotel in, 95, 101, 102
    Israeli bombing of airport and king's
        palace in, 52–53
    Jebel Amman in, 31, 35, 46
    PLO attempted takeover in, 95–109, 150
    U.S. embassy in, 51, 102, 104, 166
Andronovich, Nick, 3, 13
Angleton, James J., 25, 26, 56, 57, 65, 66, 67
    firing of, 130
    Jordanian-Israeli talks and, 85–87
    personality of, 85, 86, 130
    Petty's report on, 130–31

Applewhite, Ed, 26
Aqaba, Jordan, 58, 63–64, 87, 89–91, 124,
    152, 162, 179
Arab-Israeli War, 3
Arab League, 171
    annual summits of, 64–66, 127–28, 129,
        220, 236, 245
    Kuwait invasion condemned by, 172, 173
Arab Legion, 4
Arab Mutual Defense Pact, 45, 57, 62
Arab peace initiative:
    Egypt and, 207
    Israel and, 236, 241, 245
    Jordan and, 206–7, 214, 241
    Palestinians and, 206–7, 214–16, 219–20,
        230–31, 236, 241
    UN and, 236
    U.S. and, 206–7, 214–16, 219, 236, 241,
        245
Arafat, Yasser, 99, 145, 220
    exile from Lebanon to Tunisia of, 108–9,
        145
    first Jordan-based raid on Israel by, 39
    Hussein and, 47, 95–96, 149–50, 163
    Madrid Conference and, 184
    Oslo accords and, 187, 192
    Palestinian right of return issue and,
        214–15
    Rabin and, 187, 192
    Wye agreement and, 207, 208
    see also Jordan; Palestine Liberation
    Organization (PLO)
Arif, Abd al-Salam, 8–9
A'rif, Rafiq, 8
Army, Iraqi:
    post-invasion insurgency plan of, 229–30
    U.S. dismantling of, 224
Army, Jordanian, xv, 77–80, 97, 155
    PLO and, 99–100, 101, 103, 108
Army, U.S., Jordan Valley study of, 88–89
Arnold & Porter, 238
Ashton, Nigel, 161
Assad, Hafez al, 105, 108
    Yom Kippur War and, 122, 123
Aswan Dam, 20
Atherton, Roy, 61–62, 120, 121
atomic bomb, x, 3, 29, 242
    see also nuclear energy and weapons
Ayalon Valley, 72
Aziz, Tariq, 158, 177

Ba'ath Party, xix–xx, 25, 106, 157, 164, 194,
    224
Badran, Mudar, 100, 175
Baghdad, Iraq:
    Faisal II's murder in, 9
    U.S. invasion and, 229
Baker, James A., III:
    Iraq-Kuwait dispute and, 166, 167
    Iraq's Kuwait aggression and, 173–74,
        175, 177
    Madrid Conference and, 183–84
    Ross and, 215
Ban Ki-moon, 236
Barbour, Walworth, 41–42
Barloon, William, 197
Barnes, Bob, 36, 37, 40
Bas, Usama al, 172
Bay of Pigs Invasion (1961), 20, 132
Beatles, 110
Bedouins, xv, 155
Begin, Menachem, 108
    Camp David Accords and, 142–43
    Lebanon invasion and, 139–41
Beirut, Lebanon, xi, 15–27, 98, 108
    American Community School in, 96
    Arab League Summit in, 220
    CIA and, 15–27, 99, 100, 132
    Excelsior Hotel in, 23, 24, 26
    Hotel St. George in, 17
    Israeli siege of, 145
    Phoenicia Hotel in, 131–32
    U.S. embassy bombing in, 100
Benny Goodman Quintet, 144
Bethesda, Md., 110, 155, 213
bin Shakir, Zaid, 106–7, 173–74, 175
Bremer, L. Paul, 224
Brower, Charles, 217, 230
Brown, Dean, 102
Bruce, Evangeline, 182–83
Buchenwald concentration camp, 239
Buffum, William B., 69, 70, 71, 73
Bundy, McGeorge, 56, 87
Burgess, Guy, 26
Burke, Jim, 130–31
Burns, Findley, Jr., 40, 78
Burns, William, 216, 232, 234
Bush, Barbara, 179
Bush, George H. W., 144, 154, 185, 215
    Iraq and, 166–70, 171–74, 175–76, 177,
        179

Iraq invasion and occupation and, 221
King Hussein and, 144, 154, 176, 179,
    183–84
King Hussein's funeral and, 210, 212, 213
Madrid Conference and, 183–84
message to Saddam Hussein from,
    167–68
Persian Gulf War and, 177–78
Bush, George W., 178
    Afghanistan and, 218–19
    Chalabi and, 223
    Iraqi Army dismantling and, 224
    Saddam Hussein and, 218, 219, 245
    West Bank settlements letters of, 233–36

Cairo, Egypt, xi, 3
    International Airport of, xiii–xiv
    Obama's speech in, 238–40
Calcutta, India, 3
Cambridge Law School, 231
Camp David Accords (1978), xvii, xix, 142–
    43, 145, 153, 162
Carter, Jimmy, 75
    Iraq and, 192, 193–95
    Israel and, 139–43
    King Hussein and, 138–39, 141–43, 144,
        145
    King Hussein's funeral and, 210, 212
    Palestinian self-determination speech of,
        141
Castro, Fidel, 20, 131, 132
Central Intelligence Agency (CIA), 115
    agent recruitment by, xiii, 243–44
    Amman station of, xvii, 2–3, 5, 7, 11, 27,
        31, 35, 66–67, 96–97, 132, 137, 235, 247
    Arab-Israeli War and, 3
    assassination plots of, 131
    author's joining of, ix
    Beirut embassy bombing and, 100
    Beirut station of, 15–27, 132
    censorship of former agents' writings by,
        132
    Chalabi and, 222
    Congress and, 17–18, 131–34
    counterintelligence group in, 25–26, 85,
        86, 130
    Cuba and, 20, 131, 132
    death of first agent of, 3
    diplomatic immunity and, 15
    Directorate of Operations of, 110

Directorate of Plans of, 110
domestic spying by, 130–31
FBI and, 1, 7–8
G. H. W. Bush as director of, 144
Helms and, see Helms, Richard
Hersh's Times article on, 130, 131
hostile interrogation and, 243
intelligence gathering as mission of, 21
Iran and, 18–19, 21
Iraq and, 20
Iraqi Sunnis and, 228
Israeli misinformation to, 66–67
Jordanian-Israeli secret peace talks and,
    85–91
King Hussein coup plot and, 1–14, 27, 28
King Hussein funded by, 4, 115–16, 133,
    136–39
King Hussein's use of, xvi–xvii, 4–5, 35
Middle East Division of, xiv, 55
Mosaddeq overthrow and, 18–19, 21
Near East Division of, 2–3, 5, 19–20, 21,
    22, 56, 86, 110, 111
Nixon and, 130
Nkruma coup and, 20
non-official cover officers of, 15
Operations Division of, ix, 16–17
Pakistan desk of, 2
"Peter" as interrogator for, 10–13
PLO-Jordanian conflict and, 96–99, 100,
    107
Political Action staff of, 16–21
principal agents and, 22–23
Saddam Hussein and, 20, 161, 199–202
Schlesinger dossier on activities of, 133
Six Day War and, 51–52, 53, 54, 55, 56,
    57
Six Day War run-up and, 47–50
U.S.-Egyptian peace talks and, 116
wiretapping by, 8, 33–35, 80–82
Yom Kippur War and, 124
Chalabi, Ahmed, 199, 221–27
    bank fraud conviction of, 221, 225
    British and U.S. exile of, 221, 222–25
    Cheney and, 223
    CIA and, 222
    Congress and, 222–23
    Daghestani and, 225–27
    G. W. Bush and, 223
    Iran and, 224
    Israel and, 224–25

Chalabi, Ahmed (*continued*)
  neocons and, 223
  Saddam Hussein and, 199, 221–27
  State Department and, 222
  Viets and, 221–22, 223
Chamoun, Camille, 18
Cheney, Dick, 221, 223
China, x, 3, 29
Christian, Linda, 63–64
Church, Frank, 131
Church Committee, 131–33
Churchill, Winston S., 19–20
Clinton, Bill, xi, 185–89
  Arab peace resolution and, 214–16
  Chalabi and, 222
  Jordan-Israel peace treaty and, 189
  King Hussein and, 185–89, 200–201,
    205–6, 207–8
  King Hussein's funeral and, 210, 212
  Oslo accords and, 186, 187, 208
  Saddam Hussein and, 197–98, 200, 201
  Washington Declaration and, 187, 189
  Wye agreement and, 207–9
Clinton, Hillary, 240
Cloak and Gown (Winks), 26
Colby, William E., 112
  Angleton and, 130–31
  Church Committee and, 133–34
Cold War, 108, 242
Communists, 8, 30, 32, 33
Congo, Republic of, 131
Congress, U.S., 111
  Chalabi and, 222–23
  CIA funding and, 17–18
  CIA oversight by, 131–34
  Iraqi National Congress and, 199, 222
  Israel and, 37, 134–36
  Jordan and, 134–36
  see also House of Representatives, U.S.;
    Senate, U.S.
Connole, William R., 111–12
Connole & O'Connell, xvii, 111–12
Constantine, King of Greece, 58, 59
Copeland, Miles, 18, 20
Crawford, James, 231
Critchfield, James, 22, 56
Cuba, 20, 131, 132

Daghestani, Tamara, 225–27
Daghestani, Taymur, 226

Dairat al-Mukhabarat al-Ammah (Jordanian
    intelligence service), 4, 5, 32–35, 67, 96,
    100, 106–7, 116, 137, 153, 201
Daliberti, David, 197
Damascus, Syria, 23
Dayan, Moshe, 47, 49, 56, 57, 86, 104–5
Defense Department, U.S.:
  Iraqi insurgency and, 229
  Iraq-Kuwait dispute and, 167
  Iraq monograph by, 165
  Jordanian rearmament and, 80
  Mosaddeq overthrow and, 19
  September 11, 2001, terrorist attack on,
    218
  Six Day War and, 49, 55
  U.S.-Egyptian peace talks and, 116
  Yom Kippur War and, 125
Democratic National Convention, xi
Democratic Party, 38
Dennis Neal & Co., 113
Deramus & Co., 113
Desert Storm, Operation (1991), 37, 177–78
Diem, Ngo Dinh, 131
diplomatic immunity, 15
Ditchley Foundation, 180
Dole, Robert, 168
Dominican Republic, 131
Dulles, Allen, 110
  CIA PA staff and, 17–18
  King Hussein coup plot and, 8
  Mosaddeq overthrow and, 21
  Nasser and, 20
Dulles, John Foster, 11–12, 13, 14, 18, 20, 27

Eban, Abba, 44, 61–62
  Israeli-Jordanian secret talks and, 87, 90
  UN Resolution 242 and, 69, 75
Egan, Wesley W., Jr., 200
Egypt, xii, xv, xviii, 20, 156
  Arab peace initiative and, 207
  Aswan Dam project in, 20
  author's trips to, xiii–xiv, 3
  Ba'ath Party and, 106, 157
  Israeli peace overture to, 61, 245
  Israeli peace treaty with, xix, 127, 142–
    43, 163, 190, 246
  Israeli security wall issue and, 231
  Jordan and, 33–34, 37, 43, 44–46, 47, 48,
    50, 62, 123, 153
  King Hussein coup plot and, 1, 7, 8, 12

Kuwait invasion and, 171–72
nuclear weapons and, 242
Obama's speech in, 238–40
Persian Gulf War and, 176
Saddam Hussein's exile in, 106, 157, 164
security service of, xiv
Sinai Peninsula of, xvii, 43–44, 48, 55,
    60, 122, 125, 142
in Six Day War, xvii, xix, 51–59, 109, 116
in Six Day War aftermath, 60, 62
in Six Day War run-up, 36, 37, 40, 43–50
Soviet Union and, 37, 48, 53, 55, 116, 121
Strait of Tiran and, 44, 48
UAR and, 7
UN Resolution 242 and, 69, 72, 142–43
U.S. secret peace talks with, 116–21, 127
World War II and, xi
in Yom Kippur War, xvii, xix, 119–26
Eisenhower, Dwight D., 19
Eisenhower Doctrine, 4
Elliott, Nicholas, 26
Eshkol, Levi, 47, 50, 53
espionage:
    moral and legal aspects of, xiii
    World War II and, xi, xiv
Eveland, Wilbur Crane, 5, 13–14, 18, 131–32

Fahd, King of Saudi Arabia, 171
Faisal, Prince of Jordan, 113
Faisal I, King of Iraq, 2
Faisal II, King of Iraq, 2
    overthrow and murder of, xv, 8–9, 20,
        162, 164, 225
fedayeen, 92, 95, 97–99, 101, 103
    see also Palestine Liberation Organization
        (PLO)
Federal Bureau of Investigation (FBI):
    Congressional oversight of, 131
    King Hussein coup plot and, 1, 7–8
Federal Deposit Insurance Corporation
        (FDIC), ix
Federal Power Commission, U.S., 111
Firyal, Princess of Jordan, 102–3
Ford, Gerald R., 135, 137, 144, 210, 212, 228
Foreign Service, U.S., 36–37
    see also State Department, U.S.
Formosa (Taiwan), x, 29
France, intelligence service of, 24
Friedman, Thomas L., 219
Fulbright Fellowships, ix, xii

Gaza Strip, 55, 143, 186, 196, 203
Gemayel, Bashir, 109
General Accounting Office (GAO), U.S.,
    185
Geneva Conference (1970), 127, 141
Geneva Conventions, 75, 217, 238
genocide, 238
Georgetown Club, 183
Georgetown Foreign Service School, x–xi, 3
Georgetown Institute of Languages and
        Linguistics, xi, 25
Georgetown University, ix
    Clinton and, xi
    Helms papers at, 49
Georgetown University Hospital, 155
George Washington University, National
        Security Archive at, 49
Geyelin, Philip L., xviii, xx, 181
Ghana, 20
Glaspie, April C., 36–37
    Iraq and, 37, 166–70
Glubb, John Bagot, 4
Goiran, Roger, xiv, 21–22
Golan Heights, xvii, xix, 46, 55, 60, 91, 121,
    122, 125, 126, 246
Goldberg, Arthur J., 69–76, 88
Graham, Katharine, 182
Great Britain, 14, 247
    Aden and, 99
    Chalabi and, 221
    Faisal II's overthrow and, 9
    Jordan-PLO conflict and, 103–4
    Jordan's backing by, 4, 9
    Jordan's establishment and, 1–2
    Persian Gulf War and, 176
    Six Day War aftermath and, 65
    UN Resolution 242 and, 68
    World War I and, 2
    World War II and, xi
Grey, Gordon, 8
Gromyko, Andrei, 14
Grossman, Marc, 147

Haass, Richard N., 169–70
Habib, Philip, 108
Hadley, Stephen, 232, 234
Hague, The, Iranian Claims Tribunal at, 217
Haifa, Israel, 72, 159, 160
Haig, Alexander, 145
Haiti, 193

Halevy, Efraim, 211–12
Hamas, 141, 203
Hamdun, Nizar, 193, 195, 197
Harriman, Pamela, 183
Harrison, Roger, 176
Hashem, 2
Hashemites, xv, 2, 109, 118, 119, 184, 188,
    221, 225, 247
Hassan bin Talal, Prince of Jordan, 36, 112,
    161, 163, 175, 209
Hawk antiaircraft missiles, 134–35
Helms, Richard, xvi–xvii, 110, 111, 112
    Allen Dulles and, 17–18
    Amit's meeting with, 47–50, 53, 59
    Church Committee and, 133
    Colby and, 133
    death of, xix
    Hussein memoir and, xviii–xix, xx, 48
    Israeli invasion of Lebanon and, 145
    Jordanian-Israeli secret talks and, 88,
        90–91
    Kissinger and, 117
    Nixon's firing of, 112
    Reagan and, 145
    Six Day War and, 55, 56, 59
    Symmes controversy and, 93
    UN Resolution 242 and, 70
    yacht given to Hussein by, 91
Henderson, Loy, 19
Hersh, Seymour, 130, 131
Herzog, Yaacov, 40, 63, 87
Heyworth-Dunne, James, xi, xii, 25
Hijaz, Saudi Arabia, 2
Holocaust, 239
Hoover, J. Edgar, 8
Horton, John, 134
House of Representatives, U.S., 134
    Foreign Affairs Committee of, 166
    Foreign Aid Appropriations
        Subcommittee of, 135–36
    Permanent Select Committee on
        Intelligence of, 196
    see also Congress, U.S.; Senate, U.S.
Hummar, Jordan, 97
Hussein, King of Jordan:
    accession to throne by, 2
    Arab peace resolution and, 206–7
    Arafat and, 95–96, 149–50, 163
    army support of, xv, 77–80
    assassination attempt by Israel on, 52–53

author's first meeting with, xiv–xv
author's relationship with, xv–xvii, 33,
    35–36, 70, 71, 81, 112, 209–10, 212–13
Bedouins and, xv
Cairo prewar trip of, 44–46, 47
Camp David Accords and, 142–43, 145,
    162
Carter and, 138–39, 141–43, 144, 145
CIA as channel for, xvi–xvii, 4–5, 35
CIA funding to, 4, 115–16, 133, 136–39
Clinton and, 185–89, 200–201, 205–6,
    207–8
coup plot against, xiv–xv, 1–14, 27, 28
death of, xix, 210
emotional and mental state of, 62, 63–64,
    68–69
Faisal II and, 2
funeral of, 210–13
G. H. W. Bush and, 144, 154, 176, 179,
    183–84
Hamas and, 203
Helms and, xviii, xx, 91
illness of, xix, 185, 205, 207, 209, 210
Iraq and, 155, 171–79, 193–96
Iraq-Jordan pipeline and, 160
Israel and, 39–40, 41, 42, 52–53, 60–61,
    65–66, 85–91, 150–51, 180–81, 183–91,
    203–4, 238, 245–47
Johnson's meeting with, 63
Jordanian economic and political crisis
    and, 154–55
Jordanian international airline secured
    by, 38–39
Kissinger and, 117–18, 119, 124, 126–29
Kuwait invasion and, 171–72, 173, 174–77
London agreement and, 150–51
Macomber and, 27–28
Madrid Conference and, 183–85
Meshal assassination attempt and, 203–4
Nasser and, 12, 53, 57–59, 64, 65, 247
Netanyahu and, 202–4
peace efforts of, xvii–xx, 60–67, 85–91,
    118, 126–29, 146–54, 180–81, 183–91,
    206–7, 232, 245–48
Peres and, 150–51, 202
persistence of, xvi, 248
personality of, 89
planned memoir of, xviii–xix, xx, 48
PLO and, xv, xvii, 33, 36, 39, 43, 45–46,
    47, 95–109, 118, 123, 146, 149–50, 248

postwar rearmament issue and, 77–85
presence of, 3–4
Rabin and, 193–96
Reagan and, 144–45, 147–48, 149, 248
royal yacht of, 90–91
Sadat and, 127, 128, 143
Saddam Hussein and, 160, 161–63, 165, 171–72, 173, 174, 176, 177, 185–86, 199–202, 248
Shultz and, xvi, 147, 151–53, 248
Six Day War and, 51–59
Six Day War aftermath and, 60–67
Six Day War run-up and, 43–50
Symington and, 134–35
Symmes and, 78–79, 91–94
UN peace address of, 63
UN Resolution 242 and, 68–76, 143, 149, 150, 188
U.S. homes of, 113–15, 139, 186, 209, 213
Washington Declaration and, 187–89
West Bank transferred to PLO by, 153–54, 181
wives of, xvi, 58, 113, 115, 136, 144, 179, 183, 209, 210, 213
Wye agreement and, 207–9
Yom Kippur War and, 122–26
Hussein, Raghad, 199
Hussein, Rana, 199
Hussein, Saddam, xx, 156–70
Abud Hassan and, 106, 164
al Qaeda and, 219
Arab League condemnation of, 172, 173
Carter and, 192, 193–95
Chalabi and, 199, 221–27
CIA and, 20, 161, 199–202
Clinton and, 197–98, 200, 201
Daghestani and, 225–27
Egyptian exile of, 106, 157, 164
family defections from, 198, 199
G. H. W. Bush and, 167–68
Glaspie's meeting with, 166–70
Gulf War aftermath and, 180, 181, 183, 192–202
G. W. Bush and, 218, 219, 245
King Hussein and, 160, 161–63, 165, 171–72, 173, 174, 176, 177, 185–86, 199–202, 248
Kuwait invasion and, 155, 171–79
misjudgment of U.S. by, 169–70
Nasser's similarities to, 156
overthrow plot against, 199–202
Persian Gulf War and, 171–79
post-invasion insurgency and, 229–30
Rabin's attempt to meet with, 192–96
Reagan and, 156–61, 164
Richardson's meeting with, 196–98
Rumsfeld's meeting with, 158–59, 163, 177
ruthlessness of, 163, 164
U.S. diplomatic relations restored with, 156–60
U.S. overthrow of, 218, 219, 220–27
Hussein, Uday, 162

Ignatius, David, 182
Intelligence Oversight Board, U.S., 137
International Monetary Fund (IMF), 154
Intifada, First, 154
Iran:
Chalabi and, 224
Israel's threat from, 245
Mosaddeq overthrow in, 18–19, 21
nuclear program of, 242
Shah's overthrow in, 143
Iran-Iraq War, 156, 161, 162, 163, 164–65, 166
Iraq, xix–xx, 25, 88, 118, 156–70, 242
Abu Ghraib prison scandal in, 243
al Qaeda and, 219, 228
Ba'ath Party and, xix–xx, 25, 106, 157, 164, 194, 224
Chalabi and, 199, 221–27
chemical and biological weapons and, 199, 219
Communists in, 8
Faisal's overthrow and murder in, xv, 8–9, 20, 225
G. H. W. Bush administration and, 166–70, 183
Glaspie as ambassador to, 37, 166–70
Israel and, xx, 156, 159–60, 165–66, 172, 176, 177
Israeli bombing of reactor in, 166
Kurdistan region of, 226–27
Kuwait grievances of, 165, 166–68, 173, 174
Kuwait invaded by, 155, 168–70, 171–79
missile program of, 199
nuclear program of, 166, 199, 219
oil industry and, 159–60, 162, 194–95

Iraq (*continued*)
Persian Gulf War aftermath and, 180, 181, 183, 192–202
PLO-Jordan conflict and, 103, 106–7, 122
post-invasion insurgency in, 229–30
Republican Guard of, 200
sanctions against, 192
Six Day War and, 157
Sunni tribes in, 228
U.S. invasion and occupation of, 156, 200, 218, 219, 220–27, 228–30
U.S. relations restored with, 156–59
Iraqi National Accord (INA), 199–202
Iraqi National Congress (INC), 199, 222
Iraq Intelligence Service, 225, 226, 229
Iraq-Jordan oil pipeline, 159–60
Islam, Muslims, 164–65, 228, 242–43
Obama's Cairo speech and, 238–40
Islamic law, xi, xii
Ismael, Hafez, 116–21, 127
Israel, xv, 22, 116
Angleton and, 66, 86, 130
Arab peace initiative and, 236, 241, 245
Chalabi and, 224–25
Egyptian peace treaty with, xix, 127, 142–43, 163, 190, 246
Golan Heights and, xvii, xix, 46, 55, 60, 91, 121, 122, 125, 126, 246
G. W. Bush and, 233–36
illegality of Palestinian policy of, 237–38
Iran as main threat to, 245
Iraq and, xx, 156, 159–60, 165–66, 172, 176, 177, 192–96
Iraqi reactor bombed by, 166
Iraq-Jordan pipeline and, 159–60
Jerusalem and, 75, 88, 127, 188, 190, 192, 203, 206, 233, 236, 246
as Jewish state, 216
Jordanian arms purchases and, 134–35
Jordanian peace treaty with, xvii, 187–91, 203, 211
Jordanian relations decline with, 202–4
Jordanian secret peace talks and, 85–91, 150–51, 181
Jordan-PLO conflict and, 103–5, 107
Jordan Valley bombing by, 66–67, 78
Kennedy's trip to, 41–42
Lebanon invaded by, 108–9, 139–41, 145
Madrid Conference and, 183–85
nuclear weapons and, 242

Olympic Games of 1972 and, 100
Oslo Accords and, 186–87, 190, 203, 208
Palestine security wall and, 230–32, 240
Palestinian right of return issue and, 214–17, 220, 233, 236, 239, 241
PLO and, 39, 103–5, 109, 145, 186–87
Sabra and Shatila massacres and, 109, 145
Samu, Jordan attack by, 39–40, 41
settlements issue and, 75–76, 143, 185, 217–18, 230–31, 232–36, 240
Sinai and, xvii, 55, 60
in Six Day War, xvii, xix, 51–59, 109, 116, 246
in Six Day War aftermath, 60–67
in Six Day War run-up, 36, 37, 39–40, 41, 43–50
Syrian raids on, 39–40
UN Resolution 242 and, 68–76, 77, 88, 142–43, 150, 184, 185, 188, 214, 219, 230, 233–36, 238, 240
U.S. and, xvii–xviii, 77, 120, 151–53, 159–60, 165–66, 230–36, 237, 242–43, 246, 247
Washington Declaration and, 187–89
West Bank and, xvii, 39, 42, 46, 55–57, 60–61, 62, 75–76, 86, 89, 91, 95, 125, 126–29, 139, 141–43, 144–54, 181, 186, 187, 190, 192, 196, 203, 206, 208, 230–36, 239, 241, 245, 246
World Court and, 75–76, 217–18, 230, 231–32, 237, 238
Wye agreement and, 207–8
Yom Kippur War and, xvii, xix, 119–26
Israeli Defense Forces (IDF), 126, 139–41, 145, 165–66

Jadid, Salih, 105
Japan, 28
atomic bombing of, x, 29
Jebel Amman, 31, 35, 46
Jericho, Palestine, 186
Jerusalem, East, xvii, 46
al Aqsa Mosque in, 2, 203
Jerusalem, Israel and, 75, 88, 127, 188, 190, 192, 203, 206, 233, 236, 246
Jews, Judaism, 66, 72, 77, 134–35, 160, 165, 216, 239
Johnson, Lyndon B., xix, 110, 228
Jordanian-Israeli secret talks and, 86, 87, 88, 89, 91

King Hussein's meeting with, 63
Six Day War aftermath and, 61–62, 63
Six Day War run-up and, 37–38, 44,
    47–50
UN Resolution 242 and, 71, 72, 73, 74
Joint Chiefs of Staff, U.S., Mosaddeq
    overthrow and, 19
Jordan, xiv–xv
    Ajloun forest in, 108
    Arab peace initiative and, 206–7, 214, 241
    arms shipments to Iraq through, 175
    Britain and, 1–2, 4, 9, 103–4, 247
    Camp David Accords and, 142–43, 145,
        162
    Chalabi and, 221, 225
    Communist Party in, 32, 33
    Congressional supporters of, 134–36
    economic crisis and riots in, 154–55
    Egypt and, 33–34, 37, 43, 44–46, 47, 48,
        50, 62, 123, 153
    Egyptian command of armed forces of,
        45, 46, 53, 57
    Eisenhower Doctrine and, 4
    intelligence service of, 4, 5, 32–35, 67, 96,
        100, 106–7, 116, 137, 153, 201
    international airline of, 38–39, 134
    Iran-Iraq War and, 162
    Iraq and, 106–7, 155, 164, 171–79, 185–
        86, 193–202
    Iraq's Kuwait invasion and, 171–79
    Israeli attack on Samu in, 39–40, 41
    Israeli bombing of Jordan Valley in,
        66–67, 78
    Israeli peace treaty with, xvii, 187–91,
        203, 211
    Israeli relations decline with, 202–4
    Israeli secret peace talks with, 85–91,
        150–51, 181
    Israeli security wall issue and, 231
    Kennedy trip to, 40–41
    law as winning strategy for, 237–38
    Madrid Conference and, 183–85
    Military Intelligence of, 122–24, 164
    National Charter of, 155
    oil industry and, 159–60, 162
    Parliament of, 12, 154, 155, 229, 241
    Petra Bank in, 221
    PLO and, xv, xvii, 33, 36, 39, 43, 45–46,
        47, 65, 78, 95–109, 118, 122, 123, 149–
        50, 153–54, 214–17, 248

postwar rearmament of, 77–80
Six Day War and, xvii, xix, 51–59, 246,
    248
Six Day War aftermath and, 60–67
Six Day War run-up and, 31–50
Soviet Union and, 77–85, 143
UN Resolution 242 and, 68–76, 77, 88,
    143, 149, 150, 184, 188, 219, 234–36
USAID and, 38–39, 97, 136
U.S. arms sales to, 134–35
U.S. lobbyist for, 113
U.S. military and economic aid to, 37–39
Washington Declaration and, 187–89
Yom Kippur War and, 122–26
see also Hussein, King of Jordan; Palestine
Jordan Valley, 66–67, 78, 88–89
Juma'a, Saad, 46, 96
Justice Department, U.S., Chalabi and, 224

Kabariti, Karim, 200
Kahane, Meir, 196
Kamel, Hussein, 199, 201
Kamel, Saddam, 199, 201
Kassim, Abdul Karim, 8, 20, 225
Kassim, Marwan, Kuwait invasion and, 172,
    175
Katzenbach, Nicholas, 56, 74
Kennedy, Edward M.:
    Israel trip of, 41–42
    Jordanian trip of, 40–41
Kennedy, John F., 110, 228
Kennedy, Mrs. Edward M., 42
Kerry, John F., 183
KGB, 34, 82–85
Khammash, Amer, 78–80
Khartoum, Sudan, Arab League summit in,
    64–66, 245
Khomeini, Ruhollah, 165
Kidwah, Nasser, 217–18, 230–32
Kimche, David, 180–81
Kissinger, Henry, xix
    Egyptian secret peace talks with, 117–21,
        127
    Hussein and, 117–18, 119, 124, 126–29
    PLO-Jordanian conflict and, 100, 103,
        104, 107–8
    Yom Kippur War and, 125–26
Knesset, Israeli, 196
Korea, x
Korea, North, 193

Kurdi, Saleh El, 54
Kurdistan, 226–27
Kuwait, 64
   Iran-Iraq War and, 165, 166
   Iraqi invasion of, 155, 168–70, 171–79
   Iraqi tensions with, 165, 166–68

Labor Party, Israeli, 181, 185, 202
Lahore, Pakistan, ix, xii
Latrash, Frederick W., 3, 4, 13
Latrun salient, Palestine, 72
Law, John, 101–2
Lawrence, T. E., 2
Leap of Faith (Noor), 179
Lebanon, xi, xix, 5, 13, 15–27
   bombing of U.S. Marine barracks in,
      169
   Christan Phalangist militias in, 109, 145
   Israeli invasion of, 108–9, 139–41, 145
   Madrid Conference and, 184
   Maronites of, 108–9
   PLO and, 108–9, 139–41, 145
   Sabra and Shatila massacres in, 109, 145
   UN Resolution 242 and, 69
   U.S. Marines sent to, 9
Lewis, Samuel W., 140
Liberty, USS, 55
Likud Party, Israeli, 180, 185, 202
Lion of Jordan (Shlaim), xv
Lloyd, Selwyn, 14
lobbyists, 113
London Agreement (1987), 150–51
London School of Economics and Political
   Science, 161
Look Over My Shoulder, A (Helms), 17
Lott, Trent, 223
Lumumba, Patrice, 131

MacKiernan, Douglas, 3
Maclean, Donald, 26
Macomber, Bill "Butts," 27–30, 36, 144
Macomber, Bob, 28, 30
Madrid Conference (1991), 183–85
Maginnes, Nancy, 117
Majali, Abdul Hadi, 229
Malik, Charles, 13, 14, 18
Marines, U.S., bombing of Lebanon barracks
   of, 169
Maronite Christians, 108–9
Marriott Corporation, 110

Massachusetts Institute of Technology
   (MIT), 221
Mayo Clinic, 185, 205, 207, 209, 210, 212
McCarthy, Joseph R., 135
McCone, John A., 110
McGill University, 216
McKenzie, Syble, 115, 139, 155
McNamara, Robert S., 49, 80
Meir, Golda, 90, 123
Memorial Sloan-Kettering Cancer Center, 205
Meshal, Khaled, 203–4
Metropolitan Museum of Art, 144
MI6 (British Intelligence), xi, 25–26
Middle East:
   Arab nationalism and, xii, xiii, 5
   Eisenhower Doctrine and, 4
   family and tribal ties in, xii, xiii
   Rumsfeld's trip to, 157–60, 163, 177
   Soviet influence in, 33, 34, 37, 38, 48, 53,
      55, 77–85, 107–8, 116, 121, 143, 184
   wars in, dates of, 156
Mohammad Reza Pahlavi, Shah of Iran, 19,
   143, 163
Morocco, 219
Mosaddeq, Muhammad, 18–19, 21
Mossad, 22, 65, 85, 86, 180, 203–4, 211, 225
Muashir, Marwan, 219, 235–36
Mubarak, Hosni:
   Arab peace resolution and, 207
   Kuwait invasion and, 171–72
Muhammad (Prophet), xv, 2
Muhuiddin, Zakharia, 53
Mukhabarat, see Dairat al-Mukhabarat
   al-Ammah (Jordanian intelligence
   service)
Muna, Princess of Jordan, 113, 115, 139, 213
Murphy, Richard, 156–57, 158

Nagasaki, Japan, x, 29
Nasir, Sharif, 5–6, 7, 13, 84, 97, 101
Nasser, Gamal Abdel:
   Copeland and, 20
   death of, 116
   King Hussein and, 12, 53, 57–59, 64, 65,
      247
   PLO and, 45
   prewar messages to Syria from, 44–45, 57
   Saddam Hussein as similar to, 156
   Six Day War and, xvii, xix, 52, 53, 57–59,
      116

Six Day War aftermath and, 61, 64, 65, 68
Six Day War run-up and, 37, 43–50, 57
National Charter, Jordanian, 155
National Football League (NFL), 111
Nationalists, Chinese, 30
National Security Agency (NSA), U.S., 55
National Security Council (NSC), 116, 117, 216, 232, 233
NATO (North Atlantic Treaty Organization), 106, 108, 164
Navy, U.S.:
    Jordan-PLO conflict and, 107
    Persian Gulf War and, 178
    Six Day War and, 54, 55
neoconservatives, 177, 192, 220, 221, 223, 224–25, 245
Netanyahu, Binyamin, 202–4
    Hussein's funeral and, 210–11
    Weizman and, 211
    Wye agreement and, 207, 208
New York Times, 130, 219
Ngo Dinh Diem, 131
Ngo Dinh Nhu, 131
Nimble AM 266, USS, 28–30
Nixon, Richard M., 110
    CIA misuse by, 130
    Helms fired by, 112
    Jordanian-Israeli secret talks and, 89, 91
    Jordanian-PLO conflict and, 104, 107–8
    Watergate and, 112, 127, 128
    Yom Kippur War and, 127
Nkruma, Kwame, 20
Nobeef, Operation, 116
non-official cover officers (NOCs), 15
Noor, Queen of Jordan, 58, 115, 144, 179, 183, 209, 210, 212
Northwestern University, x
Notre Dame University, x, xv
nuclear energy and weapons, x, 3, 29, 166, 199, 219, 242

Obama, Barack H., xiv, 216, 241
    Arab peace initiative and, 241
    Cairo speech of, 238–40
O'Connell, Jack:
    Abdullah II and, 212–13
    Amman chief-of-station post taken up by, xvii, 31, 35, 137, 247
    Amman station posting left by, 137
    Arab peace initiative and, 206–7, 214–16, 219–20, 230–31
    Carter-Saddam meeting and, 193–96
    Chalabi and, 221–25
    CIA joined by, ix
    education of, ix–xii
    Egypt trips of, xiii–xiv, 3
    Evangeline Bruce and, 182–83
    Eveland and, 13–14, 131–32
    FDIC job of, ix, x
    Gridiron Dinner and, 181–82
    Iraq and, 156–58, 174–76, 178, 193–96, 200–202
    Israeli security wall issue and, 230–32
    Khammash and, 77–80
    King Hussein coup plot and, 1–14, 27, 28
    King Hussein's funeral and, 210–13
    King Hussein's relationship with, xv–xvii, 33, 35–36, 70, 71, 81, 112, 209–10, 212–13
    law practice of, xvii, 58, 74, 110–16, 217
    Macomber and, 27–30
    "Peter" (CIA interrogator) and, 10–13
    Petrovsky and, 82–84
    Philby and, xi, 25–26
    PLO targeting of, 96
    Rasul and, 32–35
    Riedel and, 233–34
    Sisco and, 69–70, 73–74, 91–94
    Six Day War and, 51–59, 109
    Symmes and, 77–80, 91–94
    Treasury agents' questioning of, 114
    UN Resolution 242 and, 70–76, 238
    West Bank settlements issue and, 217–18, 230, 231, 233–36, 240
    West Bank wall issue and, 230–32
    wiretapping and, 33–35, 80–82
    World War II service of, x, 28–30
O'Connell, Katherine, 15, 31, 96, 110
O'Connell, Kelly, 15, 31, 96, 109, 110, 155, 213
O'Connell, Quinn, 111–12
O'Connell, Sean, 15, 31, 96, 110, 155, 213
O'Connell, Syble McKenzie, 115, 139, 155, 213
O'Connell & Glock, xvii
October War, *see* Yom Kippur War (October War)
Odierno, Raymond T., 224
Office of Economic Planning, Jordanian, 112

Office of Strategic Services (OSS), U.S., xiv, 21, 183
  CIA PA staff and, 16
oil industry, 111, 159–60, 162, 166, 173, 194–95, 245
Okinawa, Battle of (1945), 28
Olympic Games, xii–xiii, 100
OPEC (Organization of Petroleum Exporting Countries), 166, 173
Osirak, Iraq, 166
Oslo Peace Accords (1993), 186–87, 190, 192, 203, 208
Ottoman Empire, 2
Oxford University, xi

Pakistan, ix
  constitution of, xii
  Northwest Provinces of, xii
  Olympics and, xii–xiii
Palestine, 36
  Ayalon Valley in, 72
  East Jerusalem and, xvii, 2, 46, 203
  first intifada in, 154
  Gaza Strip of, 55, 143, 186, 196, 203
  Israeli military assault in (2002), 220
  Israeli security wall in, 230–32, 240
  Israeli settlements in, 75–76, 143, 185, 217–18, 230–36, 240
  Latrun salient in, 72
  West Bank of, xvii, 39, 42, 46, 53, 54, 55–57, 60–63, 75–76, 86, 89, 91, 95, 125, 126–29, 139, 141–43, 144–54, 181, 186, 187, 190, 192, 196, 203, 206, 208, 230–36, 239, 241, 245, 246
Palestine Liberation Organization (PLO), 146
  establishment of, 33, 36, 245
  Fatah and, 39
  fedayeen fighters of, 92, 95, 97–99, 101, 103
  Israel and, 39, 103–5, 109, 145, 186–87
  Jordan and, xv, xvii, 33, 36, 39, 43, 45–46, 47, 65, 78, 95–109, 118, 122, 123, 149–50, 153–54, 181, 214–17, 241, 248
  Lebanon and, 108–9, 139–41, 145
  Madrid Conference and, 184
  Munich Olympics attack by, 100
  Nasir as target of, 97
  O'Connell targeted by, 96

Oslo Accords and, 186–87, 190, 203, 208
  Palestinian representation conferred upon, 126–27, 128, 129
  postwar Arab League summit and, 64, 65
  Shuqeri as head of, 45–46, 65
  Six Day War and growth of, 95
  Tunisian exile of, 109
  West Bank control given to, 153–54, 181, 241
  Wye agreement and, 207, 208
Palestinian Liberation Army, 104, 105
Palestinians, xvii, xx, 40–41, 46–47, 62, 63, 92, 108–9
  al Aqsa mosque and, 203
  Arab peace initiative and, 206–7, 214–16, 219–20, 230–31, 236, 241
  Carter's support of rights of, 141
  Hamas and, 141, 203
  Jordan-Israeli peace talks and, 180–81
  law as winning strategy for, 237–38
  Madrid Conference and, 183–85
  Oslo accords and, 186–87, 190, 203, 208
  PLO as representative of, 126–27, 128, 129, 215, 216–17
  right of return issue and, 214–17, 220, 233, 236, 239, 241
  Sabra and Shatila massacres of, 109, 145
  self-determination for, 141, 145–46, 149–50, 155
  UN and, 230–32
  Washington Declaration and, 188
  Wye agreement and, 207–9
Parker, Richard, 59
Passman, Otto, 135–36
Pedersen, Richard F., 69, 70, 71, 73
Pentagon, 218
  see also Defense Department, U.S.
Peres, Shimon, 150–51, 202, 210
Perle, Richard N., 177
Persian Gulf War, xvii, 25, 37, 156, 170, 171–79
  aftermath of, 180, 181, 183, 192–202
Petra Bank, 221
Petrovsky (KGB agent), 82–84
Petty, Clare Edward, 130–31
Philadelphia Naval Yard, 28
Philby, Kim, xi, 25–26
Pickering, Thomas:
  Arab peace resolution and, 206, 214

Iraq's Kuwait aggression and, 173–74, 177, 178
Israeli settlements issue and, 217
Political Action (PA) agents, 16–21
polygraphs, 22–23
Potomac, Md., 115, 155
Power, Tyrone, 63
principal agents, 22–23
Punjab University, ix, xii

Quigley, Carroll, x–xi
Quran, xii

Rabat, Morocco, Arab League summit at, 127–28, 129
Rabin, Yitzhak, xx, 150, 151, 185, 202
    assassination of, 196
    Iraq rapprochement sought by, 192–96
    Israel-Jordan peace treaty and, 189
    Washington Declaration and, 187, 188, 189
Raborn, William, Jr., 110
Radcliffe College, 183
Rasul, Mohammed, 5, 6, 7, 9–10, 13, 100
Reagan, Ronald W.:
    Camp David Accords and, 145
    Iraq and, 156–61
    King Hussein and, 144–45, 147–48, 149, 248
    Middle East peace initiative of, 145–46
    Saddam Hussein and, 156–61, 164
Republican Guard, Iraqi, 200
Resolution 242 (UN), 68–76, 77, 88, 127, 142–43, 148, 149, 150, 184, 185, 188, 214, 218, 219, 230, 233–36, 238, 240
Resolution 338 (UN), 127, 150, 184, 188, 238
Resolution 598 (UN), 164
"Response by the Government of the United States to the 'Talking Paper' Presented by the Hashemite Kingdom of Jordan" (State Department), 148
Riad, Abdul Munim, 45, 53
Riad, Mahmud, 69, 72
Rice, Condoleezza, 233
Riedel, Bruce, 233–34
Rifai, Samir, 7, 234–36
Rifai, Zaid, 87, 89–90, 97, 119, 126, 154, 234–35
Right of Self-Preservation Under International Law, The (O'Connell), x

Riyadh, Saudi Arabia, Arab League Summit in, 236
Rockne, Knute, xv
Rodman, Peter, 117
Rogers, Bill, 228
Roosevelt, Kermit, 5, 19–20
Roosevelt, Theodore, 5
Ropes of Sand (Eveland), 132
Ross, Dennis B., 214–16
Rostow, Eugene, 61–62
Rostow, Walter W., 49
Royal Jordanian Airline, 38–39, 134
Rumsfeld, Donald:
    Iraqi-Jordanian oil pipeline and, 159–60
    Middle East trip of, 157–60, 163, 177
    personality of, 160
    Saddam Hussein's meeting with, 158–59, 163, 177
Rusan, Mahmud, 1–2, 4, 6, 7, 12
Rusk, Dean, 49, 53, 56
    UN Resolution 242 and, 73–74

Sabra and Shatila massacres (1982), 109, 145
Sadat, Anwar:
    Camp David Accords and, 142–43
    Hussein and, 127, 128, 143
    U.S.-Egyptian peace talks and, 116–21
    Yom Kippur War and, 121–26
Salah, Abdullah, 173–74, 175
Salameh, Ali Hassan, 99, 100
Samu, Jordan, 39–40
    Kennedy's visit to, 41
Sasebo, Japan, 29
Saudi Arabia, 2, 88, 247
    Kuwait invasion and, 171, 173
    nuclear weapons and, 242
    Persian Gulf War and, 176
Saunders, Hal, 74–75, 117, 124
Schlesinger, James R., 112, 130
    CIA dossier compiled by, 133
Secret Service, U.S., 115, 116
Senate, U.S.:
    Chalabi and, 223
    Church Committee of, 131–33
    Foreign Relations Committee of, 134
    Jordan support in, 134–36
    see also Congress, U.S.; House of Representatives, U.S.
September 11, 2001, terrorist attacks, 141, 218, 219

Shamir, Yitzhak, 150–51, 180–81, 210
  Madrid Conference and, 184, 185
Shanghai, China, 29, 30
Sharon, Ariel:
  G. W. Bush letter to, 233–36
  King Hussein's funeral and, 210–11
  Lebanon invasion and, 108–9, 145
Shiites, 165, 242
Shlaim, Avi, xv
Shultz, George, xvi, 145, 147, 151–53, 248
Shuqeri, Ahmad, 45–46, 65
Shuqri, Ali, 175, 195, 206, 211
Sinai Peninsula, xvii, 43–44, 48, 55, 126
  Giddi Pass in, 125
  Mitla Pass in, 122, 125
Sinatra, Frank, 144
Sisco, Joseph J., 69–70, 73–74
  Symmes and, 91–94
Six Day War, xvii, xix, xx, 51–59, 95, 105,
  109, 116, 157, 171, 246, 248
  aftermath of, 60–68
  events leading up to, 31–50
  Helms-Amit meeting prior to, 47–50, 53,
  59
  Israeli airstrikes at opening of, 52
  Jordanian losses in, 53–54
  rumor of outside countries' involvement
  in, 54–55
Sixth Fleet, U.S., 107
Smith, Jeff, 228
Snyder, Daniel, 115
Snyder, Drucie, 134
Snyder, John W., 134
Soviet Union, 14, 22, 242
  Afghanistan invaded by, 143
  CIA surveillance of nuclear program of, 3
  Egypt and, 37, 48, 53, 55, 116, 121
  Jordan and, 77–85, 143
  Madrid Conference and, 184
  Middle East and, 33, 34, 37, 38, 48, 53,
  55, 77–85, 107–8, 116, 121, 143, 184
  Philby as spy for, xi, 25–26
State Department, U.S., xvi, 21, 27, 35, 113,
  228, 248
  Arab peace resolution and, 206–7,
  214–16
  Chalabi and, 222
  Foreign Service of, 36–37
  Iraq and, 156–59, 166–70
  Jordanian-Israeli peace treaty and, 187

Jordanian-PLO conflict and, 99, 100,
  103–4, 107–8
Jordanian rearmament and, 77–80
Jordanian USAID funding and, 136
King Hussein coup plot and, 11, 13
King Hussein's disillusionment with,
  151–53
King Hussein talking paper and, 146–48
Middle East Bureau of, 53, 61
Mosaddeq overthrow and, 19
Persian Gulf War and, 179
Rumsfeld and, 160
and security of King Hussein's family, 115
Six Day War and, 49, 53, 56
Six Day War aftermath and, 61–62
Symmes and, 77–80, 91–94
UN Resolution 242 and, 69–70, 73–75,
  148, 240
U.S.-Egyptian peace talks and, 116, 120
Stone, Rocky, 18, 19
Suez Canal, 122, 125
Suez Settlement Agreement (1956), 44
Suez War, 43
Sunnis, 164, 228, 242
Swannack, Charles H., Jr., 229–30
Symington, Stuart:
  Jordan supported by, 134–35
  Vietnam War and, 135
Symmes, Harrison M., 96
  Jordanian rearmament issue and, 77–80
  King Hussein's conflict with, 91–94
Syria, xv, 22, 25, 43, 118, 134, 157
  CIA coup attempt in, 18
  Golan Heights of, xvii, xix, 46, 55, 60, 91,
  121, 122, 125, 126, 246
  intelligence service of, 23–24, 27
  Israeli peace overtures to, 61, 190, 193,
  245
  Israel raids launched from, 39–40
  Jordanian diplomatic relations with, 123
  King Hussein coup plot and, 7, 247
  Lebanon and, 108–9
  Madrid Conference and, 184, 185
  Nasser prewar messages to, 44–45, 57
  nuclear weapons and, 242
  PLO-Jordanian conflict and, 103, 104–5
  in Six Day War, 52, 55, 57
  in Six Day War aftermath, 60, 62, 68
  in Six Day War run-up, 44–45, 46
  UAR and, 7

UN Resolution 242 and, 69
Yom Kippur War and, 121–26

Taiwan (Formosa), x, 29
Tal, Wasfi, 36, 38–39
Talal, King of Jordan, 2
Talbot, Phil, 37–38
Taliban, 218, 219
Tehran, Iran, 21
Tel Aviv, Israel:
    Rabin's assassination in, 196
    U.S. embassy in, 180
terrorism, xiii, 141, 169, 218, 219, 244
Tibet, 3
Time, 109
torture, 243
Treasury Department, U.S., 114
Trone, Eugene W., xix, 116–17, 120–21
Trujillo, Rafael, 131
Truman, Harry S., 134
Tunis, Tunisia, 109
Tunney, John, 40, 42
Tunney, Mrs. John, 42
Turkey, 242

United Arab Command, 37
United Arab Republic (UAR), 7, 9
United Nations (UN), 93
    Arab peace initiative and, 236
    draft resolution on Israeli settlements
        and, 217–18, 230–31
    Dulles speech before, 11–12, 14
    General Assembly of, 13, 14, 75, 230, 232
    Hussein's peace efforts at, 63, 68–76, 248
    Iraq's Kuwait invasion and, 173–74, 176
    Israeli security wall issue and, 230–32
    mutual defense agreements and, 45
    Palestinian representation in, 230–32
    Resolution 242 of, 68–76, 77, 88, 127,
        142–43, 148, 149, 150, 184, 185, 188,
        214, 218, 219, 230, 233–36, 238, 240
    Resolution 338 of, 127, 150, 184, 188, 238
    Resolution 598 of, 164
    Security Council of, 68–69, 75, 127, 232
    Sinai peacekeeping mission of, 43–44,
        48, 142
    Six Day War run-up and, 43–44
United States:
    Afghanistan and, 218–19
    al Qaeda and, 141, 218, 219

Arab peace initiative and, 206–7, 214–16,
    219, 236, 241, 245
Chalabi and, 199, 221–27
Egyptian secret peace talks with, 116–21,
    127
Faisal II's overthrow and, 9
Iran-Iraq War and, 165
Iraq and, xix–xx, 9, 20, 37, 156–70, 171–
    79, 192, 193–202, 218, 219, 220–27,
    228–30
Iraq's Kuwait invasion and, 168–70,
    171–79
Israel and, xvii–xviii, 77, 120, 151–53,
    159–60, 165–66, 230–36, 237, 242–43,
    246, 247
Israeli-Jordanian peace and, 185–89
Israeli security wall issue and, 232
Jewish community in, 66, 72, 77, 134–35,
    160, 165
Jordanian-PLO conflict and, 99, 100,
    103–4, 107–8
Lebanon and, 9, 169
Madrid Conference and, 183–84
Middle East peace and, xvii–xviii, 86, 87,
    88, 89–91, 242–43
neoconservatives and, 177, 192, 220, 221,
    223, 224–25, 245
Saddam Hussein's misjudgment of,
    169–70
Saddam overthrow plot and, 199–202
September 11, 2001, attacks and, 141, 218,
    219
Six Day War and, xvii, xix, 54
Six Day War aftermath and, 61–62
Six Day War run-up and, 37–39, 44,
    47–50
Taliban and, 218, 219
UN Resolution 242 and, 68–76, 77, 88,
    148, 149, 184, 218, 230, 233–36, 238,
    240
Yom Kippur War and, 125–26
U.S. News & World Report, 101–2
U Thant, 43

Vance, Charles, 116
Vietnam, North, 117
Vietnam, South, 131
Vietnam War, 110, 135, 169, 181
Viets, Richard N., 139–41, 182, 235
    Carter-Saddam meeting and, 193–95

Viets, Richard N.(*continued*)
  Chalabi and, 221–22, 223
  and Clinton's meeting with King
    Hussein, 186
  Gridiron Dinner and, 181
  Iraq's Kuwait aggression and, 174–77,
    178
  Kimche and, 180
  King Hussein's funeral and, 210–11
"Views of General Meir Amit" (Helms),
  49
Villanova College, x

Walters, Vernon, 124
*War of Necessity, War of Choice: A Memoir of Two
  Iraq Wars* (Haass), 169–70
Washington, D.C., ix, x
  author's life in, ix, x–xi, xiv, xvii, 58, 74,
    110–16, 181–83, 213, 237
  Blair House in, 113
  FBI wiretapping of foreign embassies in,
    8
  Helms's meeting with King Hussein in,
    xviii
  Israeli embassy in, 85
  Jordanian Information Office in, 113
  Philby as British station chief in, xi
Washington Declaration (1994), 187–89
Washington Post, xviii, 74, 136–39, 181, 182,
  201, 229
Washington Redskins, 115
water-boarding, 243
Watergate scandal, 112, 127, 128
Watts, Arthur, 217, 230–31
Weizman, Ezer, 189, 192, 194, 210–11
West Bank, xvii, 39, 42, 46, 53, 54, 55–57,
  60–63, 86, 89, 91, 95, 125, 126–29, 139,
  141–43, 144–54, 181, 187, 190, 192, 196,
  203, 206, 208, 239, 245, 246

Israeli settlements issue and, 75–76, 143,
  185, 217–18, 230–36, 240
PLO as controlling authority in, 153–54,
  181, 241
Westinghouse, 113
Winks, Robin W., 26
wiretapping, 8, 33–35, 80–82
Wolfowitz, Paul, 221, 223
Woodward, Bob, 136–39
World Court, 237, 238
  Israeli security wall issue and, 230,
    231–32
  Israeli settlements issue and, 75–76,
    217–18
World War I, 2
World War II, x, xi, 10, 28–30
  OSS and, xiv, 21, 183
Wye River Memorandum (1998), 207–9

Years of Upheaval (Kissinger), 117
Yellow River, 29
Yellow Sea, x
Yemen, 99
Yom Kippur War (October War), xvii, xix,
  119–26
  Abud Hassan's uncovering of plan for,
    122–25
  aftermath of, 126–29
  casualties and losses in, 126
  cease-fire in, 125–26
  Egyptian planning for, 119–21
  Egyptian versus Syrian aims in, 121–22

Zahedi, Fazlollah, 19
Zeid bin Raad, Prince, 217, 231
Zein, Princess of Jordan, 113
Zein al-Sharaf, Queen of Jordan, 54
Zerka, Jordan, 106
Zia al Haq, Muhammad, 104